A Queerly Joyful Noise

A Queerly Joyful Noise

Choral Musicking for Social Justice

JULIA "JULES" BALÉN

RUTGERS UNIVERSITY PRESS

NEW BRUNSWICK, CAMDEN, AND NEWARK, NEW JERSEY, AND LONDON

Library of Congress Cataloging-in-Publication Data

Names: Balen, Julia, 1955– author.

Title: A queerly joyful noise: choral musicking for social justice / Julia "Jules" Balen.

Description: New Brunswick: Rutgers University Press, [2017] | Includes bibliographical references. | Description based on print version record and CIP data provided by publisher; resource not viewed.

Identifiers: LCCN 2017011525 (print) | LCCN 2017027500 (ebook) | ISBN 9780813588407 (Epub) | ISBN 9780813588414 (Web PDF) | ISBN 9780813588391 (cloth: alk. paper) | ISBN 9780813588384 (pbk.: alk. paper)

Subjects: LCSH: Choral singing—Social aspects—United States. | Choral singing—Political aspects—United States. | Gay choirs—United States.

Classification: LCC ML3917.U6 (ebook) | LCC ML3917.U6 B35 2017 (print) | DDC 782.5086/64-dc23

LC record available at https://lccn.loc.gov/201701152

A British Cataloging-in-Publication record for this book is available from the British Library.

∞ The paper used in this publication meets the requirements of the American National Standard for Information Sciences—Permanence of Paper for Printed Library Materials, ANSI Z39.48-1992.

www.rutgersuniversitypress.org

Manufactured in the United States of America

This book is dedicated to

Mary Lever, who first knew and nurtured my joyful noises

My son, Rain, who shaped who I am at least as much
as I had anything to do with shaping him

My beloved Heather, who sings to and with me daily

And those who raise their voices in joyful noise
in the interest of social justice for all

CONTENTS

A Queerly Joyful Noise

Introduction

Why Choruses?

"Listen up, people!" Our director is clearly irritated. The chorus has been missing cues, off time, and even occasionally out of tune. My lower back is speaking to me, causing my attention to wander. I came in early on that last entrance, jumping the director's cue and garnering his glare. He warns us, "We have to let our instrumentalists go at nine o'clock, but the chorus can stay till we get the rest of the show worked out. We can stay in this theater till midnight." I can feel the collective groan that no one dares express. Material realities focus us: the chorus pays the professionals (the director and instrumentalists) to be there out of singers' dues, ticket sales, and donations. He turns his attention to the musicians seated in front of us. It's eight o'clock in the evening.

We have been standing on metal risers for almost two hours, most of us after a full day at work. The risers are creaky and wobble more than any of us like. We are packed tightly—more than eighty of us—and have to place ourselves at slight angles so that we all fit. Each step is only about eighteen inches deep. Those standing on the front row must keep their feet to the front of the riser. Those in the middle row must keep centered. And those in the back row must stand toward the back of the riser step—a rather precarious position at best, but especially without a safety bar behind them. I am glad this time not to be on the top row, though I am cramped. Half a step one way or another affects someone else. There is much negotiation for space: "I can't see the director. Can you move a bit that way?" "Don't lock your knees—it can make you pass out," we remind ourselves. Breathe and bend, but not so that anyone can notice. Singers whisper needs and complaints:

"Your folder is hitting me on the side of the head!"

"I don't know why we don't just memorize this. Then we wouldn't have to hold these bulky folders."

"I'm glad he didn't make us memorize this one. I get nervous when we don't have our music in front of us."

The tenor next to me leans in to snark, "So what's her excuse now?" I could answer that she rarely solidly knows her part, but at least she's pretty reliable at just mouthing the words during concerts when she doesn't, unlike some people we know. Or I could counter that his pitch on the high notes is often slightly flat. I just raise my eyebrows and smile.

Why would anyone subject themselves to this? The baton goes up and we breathe, mostly together this time. The desire to sing well begins to overcome the distractions of discomfort. We breathe into the music, breathing together in time and space. Our months of practice finally evident, we exhale an exhilaration of song into moments of beauty that none of us could have without the others. Experiencing the choral is not the wild Dionysiac dancing and cavorting together or the carnival that turns the tables of power for which Barbara Ehrenreich grieves in *Dancing in the Streets: A History of Collective Joy*. But choral musicking[1] is a form of collective joy that queer[2] choruses engage to particular effect.

This opening story is likely to be recognizable to anyone who has sung in choruses—straight[3] or queer. Dress and tech rehearsals are times that most try our abilities to come together for our shared purpose. Like many of the stories in this book, it is a composite of experiences: mine directly, those I have witnessed, and those I have heard through formal interviews and many years of participating in and studying choral conferences and festivals. They are stories told in conference workshops and coffee shops, backstage and front of house in North America and Europe. Variations of many of the stories I tell in this book can be found in YouTube videos, films, promotional materials, programs, chorus websites, and listservs.[4] Much of my life I have sung, often in choruses. And as is true for many singers, my early experience was in church choirs. I have sung professionally in opera choruses as well as in coffeehouses and at weddings and funerals. I have even performed singing telegrams. But choral singing took a whole new turn for me when a queer chorus started up in my town. At the time, I joined to find respite while I was finishing my dissertation. Little did I know I was one of many thousands around the world doing the same thing.

About seven years later, in 1996, I attended my very first GALA (Gay and Lesbian Association of Choruses) Festival[5] in Tampa, Florida. Only a bit over five feet tall, I found myself standing in a crowd of almost five thousand choral concertgoers, probably about two-thirds of them gay men. The rest included lesbians, bisexuals, transgender people, and a few straight people, with a smattering of out and proud queers from around the world, all waiting to attend the opening ceremonies. That sweaty summer evening, as people were teasing, flirting, and calling out to each other, mostly over my head, it struck me just how big this movement is. Here I was standing with thousands of people from around the world who were eager to share their joy in and through queer choral performance.

This was the fifth of GALA's quadrennial festivals, and I attended everything I could. We stood packed in an enormous hall for opening ceremonies, enchanted by Dr. Maya Angelou's keynote address. And when she performed (as only she can) her poem "Still I Rise," we roared our pleasure at her taunting:

> Does my sexiness upset you?
> Does it come as a surprise
> That I dance like I've got diamonds
> At the meeting of my thighs?[6]

Her audacity had us daring to imagine the power of our own voices. Harvey Fierstein, Ann Hampton Callaway, BETTY, Romanovsky and Phillips, and Holly Near performed, making those opening ceremonies like none before. As the GALA Choruses website notes, there were "eighty-six choruses in attendance [out of the 155 registered member choruses at the time], 23 small ensembles, and more than 4,700 delegates" who participated. The festival "rank[ed] among the largest conventions ever hosted in Tampa." As is true for most choral festivals, participants had a choice of workshops on singing of all types, on organizing choruses, on fundraising, and on many other related topics. We could sing with the festival chorus that practiced and performed the festival anthem, "We Sing the Dream," commissioned for the occasion. There were eight full days of concerts put on by groups ranging in size from ten to more than two hundred, some performing commissioned works such as Robert Seeley's "Naked Man," Peter Winkler and Winston Clark's "Out," and Jay Kawarsky's "Prayers for Bobby."[7] It was possible—though truly overwhelming—to experience every single chorus performing. Unlike most choral festivals, there was no competition, only celebration of each other—all of us singing together.

The whole experience was exhilarating, though our performances were certainly a personal high point, as I am sure was true for most singers there. My chorus (almost thirty people out of a total chorus of more than fifty were able to make the trip) performed two consecutive concerts: first in a large hall seating more than 2,500 and the next in a hall about half that size—both nearly full. This remains the largest group in front of whom I have performed solo so far. (OK, it was just a series of "yeah, yeahs" on our commissioned "Hot" medley—but it was hot!) The audience roared their approval for every chorus's performance, large and small. Even with the catty remarks from a couple of diva queens I chanced to overhear during another chorus's performance, singers could not ask for a more enthusiastic audience.

Queer choral festivals around the world are noncompetitive. They celebrate the joy of singing in the company of those who recognize each other more fully—inevitably imperfectly, but definitely more clearly in some important ways—than the rest of the culture is generally willing or able to do. As one gay men's chorus leader, Ben,[8] noted, "We're working on creating something together that celebrates our lives, not just our sexuality, but, you know, ourselves as human beings, as artistic beings, and the uniqueness that we have, and present that to the public. Gay men are also this. We may be some of that other stuff too, but we are also this." And his cochorister, Geo, echoed, "For our gay audience we consistently affirm who we are, who they are, by doing what we do." The process of affirming a right to communal joy—internally and externally—rings throughout the stories of the social change work done by queer choral movement.[9]

As the GALA Festival progressed, you could almost tell who had already performed and who had yet to. The overall tensions of pre-show jitters steadily lowered. The exhilaration and joy mounted. The mutually empathic appreciation for singers daring to share their voices expanded with each performance. This seemed to me to be a social practice and cultural art form that held promise for healing the damage done by parents and schools, by the likes of Anita Bryant (whose antigay "Save Our Children" campaign fueled backlash against gay rights), by religious fundamentalism, and by the AIDS crisis—the damage done to nonconforming individuals but also to the larger society—in a way that I had not yet explored. How could I resist? Barely sleeping for nine days, I returned home fevered in more ways than one.[10] I have been studying the nature of this communal joy making and its value for social justice work ever since.

Chorus America, the largest umbrella choral organization in the United States, estimates that "42.6 million people in the U.S. sing in more than 270,000 choruses today." The organization goes on to claim in a 2011 article, "There are bigger spectator sports, but none with more participants than choral singing. Surprising but true: more Americans sing in choruses, chorales, choirs, glee clubs and other vocal groups—both professional and amateur—than engage in football, baseball, tennis, even Greco-Roman wrestling. (Fantasy Football has an impressive figure, with an estimated 27 million participants.)"[11] Although the solo artist receives the majority of the public spotlight (at least in more capitalist countries) both in terms of recording artists and through shows like *The Voice*, people around the world share their voices with each other and with their communities every day. We come together in groups large and small, religious and not, in community solidarity and across differences, for pleasure and possibly for social change. But queer choruses use this social form of communing in particularly interesting ways.

In a dressing room, a baritone fidgets with buttons on a shirt rarely worn and now tighter than is comfortable. Sweat already forming on his freshly scrubbed brow, he turns to the soprano dressing next to him. "Help, please?" Cooing, "Ohhh, baby! I'll get that for you," the soprano[12] finishes buckling zir belt. In a single gesture, ze fluffs the baritone's hair and wipes his brow, then tugs his shirt across his rounding form and fastens the buttons, patting his belly as ze finishes. "All good!" Decidedly masculine, with gray hair in a marine-issue cut and a muscled form, the soprano's actions are motherly. Zir attentions are queerly reassuring to this much younger baritone, whose family, the one he ran away from ten years ago, is waiting in the audience for the show to start.

By now his family must certainly know that the chorus is a queer one. He peeks into the audience again to see his father thumbing through the program and returns, rubbing his sweaty palms on the sides of his tuxedo pants. "They're still there!" The soprano has seen this story play out many times in twenty years with the chorus. It always amazes zir that people would choose this as a way to come out to their loved ones. "Not my style," ze tells me later. But it has always worked out well. In fact, it has worked out remarkably well.

The chorus gathers in the greenroom, forming their traditional pre-show circle, linking hands. They invite me to join. Some hands are hot, some sweaty, some clammy, some cold. All singers have varying degrees of butterflies in their bellies. One has already performed the preshow bow to the porcelain to settle his stomach. The circle is only vaguely round, snaking between chairs and instruments. We look at each other and breathe together. The chorus has grown and can barely fit in the room. In unison they take deep breaths evenly into the lungs to the count of eight, then slowly hiss the breath out to the count of eight. It's part of their ritual. Most every chorus, straight or queer, has a preshow ritual to calm the nerves, bring the group together, and focus on their shared purpose. The artistic director asks who has friends or family in the audience. The baritone blurts out his story, his amazement that his mother was still in her seat last he checked, and his nervousness. The group listens and breathes with him. Then an alto shares that her father is in the audience for the first time now that her mother, who refused to see her since she came out, has passed away. There are tears in her eyes and a sad smile on her face. The group breathes, some tearing up, with her. The basses holding her hands squeeze them a bit more attentively. Others name coworkers and special friends in the audience, the people they hope have shown up.

The artistic director waits for the stories to settle and then reminds the group,

> With every concert, your voices change hearts and minds. The joy you share in making beautiful music together melts away their doubts or fears. We heal ourselves and those who come to hear us of the damage from the hatred that some still preach. This is why you all spend the time and energy that you do pounding out timing,

memorizing music, refining your sound, listening to each other, so that we can create something beautiful together that even the haters have a hard time resisting. I am proud to be your artistic director. You have all worked very hard, and now is the moment to share your love of the music, of each other, and for our audience members. Have fun with it!

The group raises their hands together over their heads, intoning in a glissando from lowest note to highest, "Let's siiiiiiiiiiing!" With that, the group empties into the hallway leading to the stage, and it's a merriment of anxiousness as they find their places in the line to go on stage. "Were you in front of me?" "Wait, someone's missing here. Jena, you belong up here. Remember, we changed the order." When they all get on stage, the body memory of all their practice kicks in, and they sing their hearts out beautifully. I watch the baritone meet with his family after the show—all hugs and smiles.

This group is by no means alone in their stories, their practice, or their purpose. At last count (November 2016), nearly four hundred choruses from around the world were listed on the GALA website, ranging in size from about four to almost four hundred singers who perform an average of two to three concerts per year in a full range of venues from school auditoriums to Carnegie Hall and the steps of the Lincoln Memorial for U.S. presidential inaugurations. Groups also do community performances and singing workshops with kids and seniors. While the early majority of choruses developed in Australian, European, and North American contexts, there are a growing number in Asia, Africa, and Latin America. In addition, two other major umbrella organizations—Legato in Europe and Sister Singers Network in the United States—have additional member choruses. There are also a number of queer community choruses not affiliated with any of these larger network organizations.

The demographics of the choruses have changed somewhat over the years, with the most notable change being the increase in mixed choruses and the addition of trans and youth choruses. Unlike straight choruses, which are primarily mixed choruses, queer choruses remain primarily women's or men's. When I assessed the types of choruses listed on the GALA website in 2001, there were a little more than 200 groups: about

50 percent men's, 30 percent women's, and 20 percent mixed. Of the 393 choruses listed on the GALA website in late 2015, 173 were men's (44 percent), 130 mixed (33 percent), 76 women's (19 percent), 12 youth (3 percent), and 2 trans-identified (0.05 percent).[13] When we note that both youth and trans choruses are mixed, then the mixed category has grown to encompass 33 percent of queer choral musicking. This is a difference from straight choruses that we will explore in later chapters.

It's quite possible for singers and even board members of choruses to be only peripherally aware, if at all, that while we gather to practice each week, around the world there are hundreds of such choruses with thousands of singers also working to learn lyrics and notes, phrasing, and how to hold their parts in the sonic company of others. And while each choruses' board members might worry about how many tickets they will sell this year or how many ads in their programs they need to pay the bills, they may not know just how many others around the world worry with them. Nor are we necessarily aware of the scope of the movement, even as we sing for and with audiences that range in size from very few to several thousand. As a singer in (and at the time of my first GALA Festival, a board member of) a medium-sized, mostly white, mostly middle-class mixed chorus from a southwestern city, I had been only vaguely aware of the larger movement. Even now, when I tell people about this research project, no matter their gender identity or sexual orientation, the most common response is some variation of "Yeah, we have a chorus; do you know them?" This is followed by their surprise that so many people are engaged in the same enterprise of singing for queer social justice around the world. To experience the scope of it, to feel its international pulse as I did in 1996 and have repeatedly at subsequent festivals in Europe and North America, inspires me.[14] Mixing in the crowds at festivals, I have been not just personally rocked by the experience but intellectually curious. Why choruses? Considering all the ways that people might organize for greater sex/gender freedom, why are choruses one of the more compelling for so many people? Thus began my odyssey.

Getting at the link between music and social change is no easy task. Most of us intuitively assume there is a connection. As evidence, social institutions from the Catholic church to political parties to militaries throughout history have certainly made effective use of music to further their ends. Songs that may even go against our own strongly held values still have the power to stir deep feelings in us. We have only begun to scratch the surface of explaining how music, especially singing together, might work for social justice ends.

In *Playing for Change: Music and Musicians in the Service of Social Movements*, sociologists and active musickers Rob Rosenthal and Richard Flacks explain the challenges of nailing down how musicking for social justice works: "Researching the [music-movement] link runs into serious methodological problems."[15] Because musicking is always an embedded social practice, there is no clear way to tease out the specific role it plays. They argue that "vagueness, mystification, and confusion" characterize "much of what has been written about the music-movement link," because of music's social embeddedness. "The mere presence of music in a movement" does not "prove its effectiveness." Lyrics alone do not explain how they are received or used by listeners. Nor do they account for the effect of the musicking experience. The intent of a composer or performer "is not the same thing as audience reception." And audience reception is affected by a great many complex factors. Even the method Rosenthal and Flacks chose of getting "inside the head of each musicker" through extensive interviews has its problems. Noting the limitations of their own method, they write, "People may not realize how they use music or its effect on their thinking or behavior. They may romanticize it, or dismiss it, or in any number of ways distort its actual effect. . . . Further, they (and we) may easily conflate the effect of the music with other factors since music is typically experienced as one part of complex packages that may include romantic attractions, political allegiances, café discussions, and so on." Because "there is no scientific or consensual way to measure such matters," Rosenthal and Flacks adopted "investigative methods" that they hope offer some "ways to make useful conjectures."[16] In the process, they develop some very useful mappings of what they learned from their interviews, which I build on here.

Attempting to write about what exactly any musicking does for us makes clear that there is at least one reason we create music—it expresses so much that feels impossible to adequately express in words. Arguably because of this, many research pieces focus on quantifying what music does for us through brainwaves or testing for everything from serotonin to cortisol levels or through self-assessment surveys to get at perceptions of relaxation or stress. Those who do attempt description often turn to poetry, as I arguably do in places here, to fill in where more common word usage fails. My interviewees (as well as many more participants in workshops and conversations) got tongue-tied and teared up, often trying again and again, but always unsatisfactorily by their own accounts, to say exactly what queer choral musicking does for them. Even so, they gave me a great deal of material, which I both quote and synthesize here. Despite the challenge of articulating the effect that such musicking practices have, attempt it we do because it seems important to at least draw the outlines of how and why choral musicking affects so many of us so powerfully.

My intention with this book is not so much to tell individual stories, though I certainly do that. Rather, these stories help me sketch a larger picture of queer choral musicking as a social practice with a purpose. By comparing this form of choral musicking for social justice with musicking by labor and civil rights activists, as I do in Chapter 1, the relationship among the particular forms of musicking related to resisting particular types of oppression begins to emerge. And by comparing this form of cultural organizing for queer social justice with other related forms of such organizing, as I do in Chapter 3, the particularities that the practice of choral musicking offers to the larger movement become clearer. Though the individual stories shared here are definitely an important part of this picture, my goal is to assess our stories in the aggregate to explore what draws so many to this particular practice for the purpose of social change and thereby to offer some insights into both the role that such cultural practices play in social change work and the challenges to making change that lasts.

PART ONE

Finding Our Voices

1

Singing as Counterstorying Practice

[She] didn't want her name in the program when she first joined. And then the next year she was willing to put her first name in the program, but not her last name, and then by the third or fourth year she was actually willing to put her first and last name. And just the whole process, as a result of being in that chorus, she was able to come to accept herself but also be comfortable to be out. And if somebody did see her name in the program, she was willing to take that risk. –Ben

"Just call me 'Pete.'" Many singers would not use their real names. They just couldn't. It was too dangerous. Pete was not even a singer, but the partner of one. As a teacher, Pete could not risk being anywhere near as out as her partner was, at least not in the 1990s or even the early 2000s. It made her nervous that her partner was so out. The truth is, it remains dangerous in many parts of the United States today where it is still legal to deny housing or employment to those who variously identify as—or are perceived as being—LGBTIQ, even though marriage is now legal. Yet people still gather to sing even in parts of the world where admitting any queer identity can be punished by imprisonment or death. Nearly every chorus tells me a variation of this story—of not using real names (even among each other) at first, of using pseudonyms in concert programs, of members refusing to be photographed or to appear in any sort of publicity, of the fear and how it fades over time with the group. A romantic, Pete paid for love notes to Jess to appear in every chorus program. All the chorus members and their friends—all the important people in their lives—knew who "Pete" was. But the damage caused by the all-too-real dangers of losing housing, jobs, freedom, or even one's life fractures both the self and any sense of community. Such dangers coerce people into self-censorship and silencing in ways large and small, and these are the first hurdles that must be overcome on the way to developing and maintaining effective counter-stories[1] to the ones that enable the violence against those of us who do not fit the norms.

Silencing happens in ways that make it seem natural, not only to everyone who is not silenced, but even to those who are silenced, because survival requires internalizing the self-censorship. In such oppressive conditions, it is not unusual to hear straight people who freely display their sexuality on their desks at work with photos from their weddings and of their children wondering out loud why "those gays have to flaunt their sexuality." It is also possible to find a closeted gay politician calling for more punitive laws or a relatively out lesbian asking why those gay men have to dress in drag or leather at the local Pride event out of shame for what will no doubt be sensationalized in the media (one of many choral anthems, "The Gay Pride Parade," humorously comments on this media practice). We learn very early that others perceive certain people certain ways and that failure to recognize these differences and act accordingly can lead to varying levels of silencing (e.g., Don't Ask, Don't Tell), shaming, or even violence. Speaking up and out requires those who have been silenced to dare to make noise in ways that may go against their own personal sense of themselves as well as against the dominant cultural stories.

Doing so takes courage and happens in small steps—a process that almost every interviewee described. One chorus director, Gene, told me about his first TTBB (tenor 1 and 2, baritone, bass)[2] chorus's early years:

> Probably what's been most impactful for me is to watch the changes that have happened with others. And it's happened right from the beginning [1985] when I started the men's chorus, and we had 56 members our first rehearsal. And we had 80 the following fall and the . . . *Times* came to do a story on us. . . . And there were 80 people, and only 5 were willing to have their pictures taken. So they took just a picture of me. Then a year later, the *Herald* did a story on us, and there were about 40 that were willing to have their pictures taken, and so I watched that kind of change grow with people as they became more confident. And [at] our first pride concert, which happened only one year and three months after we were formed,

I had 102 men on stage with 20 members of the . . . Philharmonic, and Joy Davidson, who had just returned from doing the leading role in *Carmen* in both the Paris opera and Wolftrap as the soloist. It was amazing. So I have watched this change as people grew and were able to come out to themselves and their communities and their families.

In the early years, every chorus faced such varying levels of their members' willingness to be out.

Taking some of the first steps in this choral movement, many early lesbian feminist choruses, inspired by the women's music movement of the late 1960s and early 1970s, did not initially plan to sing anywhere except with and for each other. As Sage told me about one of the early SSAA (soprano 1 and 2, alto 1 and 2) groups, "In the first years, we were singing for fun, almost therapy singing. The woman we hired as director was herself a professional musician, a soprano. And she also had a real strong background in Gestalt therapy, so in a sense we were doing voice therapy." Every group of people who are denied full social recognition and value must begin the journey of social change by developing safe places where they can counter the social narratives that deny them dignity and affirm their stories of themselves and thereby experience being held in their full human dignity. If the larger culture denies us our dignity, we must find other humans who more or less accept us as we perceive ourselves. This predominantly white lesbian feminist SSAA choral group created, in their practice of singing together, a space to heal their damaged identities as women and lesbians. It was a place where they could begin to both literally and figuratively find their voices together.

Finding and maintaining voice—a socially empowered voice—becomes an almost primal piece of work that every movement for social justice must take on. And as the stories told by both my interviewees and the choruses as organizations make clear, it needs to take place on an individual as well as a group level. Such multilevel work complicates the challenges further because any such movement is always multivocal, even as those in the group are stereotyped into a single perspective and may themselves feel pressed to produce a common front. When we consider that gaining ground on social issues often seems to come down to who can make the most effective social noise,[3] if we are talking about changing people's hearts and minds (one of the slogans used in queer choral musicking),[4] it is no surprise that singing has played some role in many social justice movements, whether labor, civil rights, or queer movements.[5] The role played has varied and correlates in interesting ways with the oppressed groups' histories, each group's available resources (cultural capital), and the form of the oppression. Cultural stories that silence or denigrate the identities of whole groups of people must be challenged relentlessly until the stories change and silencing—denying the right to the full, polyvocal expression of any individual identities as socially valuable—is no longer the norm. The social form of singing together enacts this need for placing our voices together even as it allows space for exploring and nurturing the polyvocality inherent in all social justice movement.

In *Damaged Identities, Narrative Repair*, philosopher Hilde Lindemann offers a useful framework for understanding the role of counterstories in challenging unjust social narratives and norms as well as understanding what it takes for counterstorying to be successful in the face of dominant social narratives, or what are called "master narratives." Master narratives are made up of a pastiche of stories that offer the material from which all cultural identities are made possible. They define the limits and expectations and what roles different people are allowed to play in any social setting. These stories are renewed daily through repeated variations that affirm the rightness and "naturalness" of the social norms and are evident in everything from laws and legal practices to songs or advertising. In Lindemann's model, those of us working for social justice must first closely "read" these stories to find the places in them that do not accurately represent our lives or fail to represent us at all and thereby silence/negate part or all of our very existence. Then we must come together to strategically alter the master narratives by developing more accurate and persuasive counterstories. Finally, through repetition on many different fronts, effective counterstories take hold, gaining social traction and becoming part of the shared social narratives about what it means to be fully counted as socially valued.[6]

Much work for social justice tends to focus on changing laws. Laws are certainly some of our most potent "stories" about who we are (or are allowed to be) as a people. But master narratives must be changed at every level if laws are to serve their intended purposes. If the laws do not match the stories that tell us who we are, then we will not even know how to adequately implement them and are likely to actively thwart them. Reactions against the Supreme Court ruling on "gay marriage" offer some recent examples of people who are not willing to change their own sense of themselves and their perceptions of their rights and privileges just because a law has changed.[7] But we also see this resistance at work in arguments for keeping the Confederate flag, or in arguments of pharmacists who do not want to dispense birth control pills, or in inequitable practices of incarcerating people of color.

Changing hearts and minds requires changing the stories that make up who we are, or are able to be, individually and together in our society. People's feelings about themselves and others must change with every master narrative shift, because our senses of ourselves are woven from these and other more personal stories. Changing people's feelings about themselves and others takes time and many modes of expression. As Tyler, a singer, quite simply noted, "The minute you walk on stage, you are making a statement. You're making a statement saying these people are proud. They are not ashamed of who they are, and it is even more compounded by the fact that when they are out there on stage, they are good. And I think it does make a difference." Where changing feelings is concerned, communal singing, with its emotional mix of words and music, can play a powerful role.

Exploring in more depth why and how choral singing might play this role particularly well for people variously identifying as LGBTIQ calls for some comparative analysis of different kinds of musicking practices. Christopher Small offers new ways beyond the aesthetic to assess the power and meaning of music making for humans by analyzing and comparing different forms of music making as a human practice in his book *Musicking: The Meanings of Musical Performances*. Small's primary argument is that a culture's musicking practices express idealized relationships and that the types of relationships valued by the culture can be understood through the form the musicking takes. Small characterizes many musicking practices around the world, both historically and currently, as process, performance, and relationship-oriented communal practices. He includes in these descriptions musicking practices in Western culture up until about the eighteenth century. Such musicking is shared among people who know each other; it is not a practice commonly shared among strangers. The primary focus is on enjoying music making together. He contrasts these more communal practices with the highly abstracted form of musicking of the current Western symphonic tradition, where audience members are expected to sit as silently as possible rather than singing and dancing along. The Western symphonic form, he argues, values hierarchy and produces a sort alienation from each other and even from the music in a way that the composers whose compositions are thus made "sacred" might well disdain.[8] Musicking for social justice generally falls more on the communal end of the spectrum, but different versions have made particular and interesting use of the more abstract and formal precisely to counter specific forms of oppression.

Building on Small's work, sociologists Rob Rosenthal and Richard Flacks in *Playing for Change: Music and Musicians in the Service of Social Movements*, address some aspects of group singing throughout their study, but the primary model they focus on to develop their analysis of the uses of music in social movements is the more common practice of "minstrels" (a single musician or a small band of musicians dedicated to a cause) singing to, for, and sometimes with an audience. As they point out, there is no adequate way to measure the political effects of any given social movement's musicking practices, but from their extensive interviews, they are able to delineate four important social movement functions of musicking: (1) serving the committed, (2) education, (3) conversion/recruitment, and (4) mobilization. They map how these different functions have different effects in different times and places in order to help activists think more strategically about the resource that musicking might offer. They argue that serving the committed—what many might dismiss as preaching to the choir—can play some very important roles of "affirmation, reaffirmation, and sustenance," especially in maintaining commitment over long and difficult periods.[9] Because even those committed to a cause "aren't homogenous, but groupings of heterogeneous individuals who agree about some things but may be at odds about others," musicking plays the important role of "representing" the "shared beliefs that allow 'disparate strangers' to feel they are indeed a band of brothers and sisters, and reinforces those beliefs when much of the world is working to break them down."[10] Movements that weather rough times have strong rituals that include collective musicking. For example, "when union members end a meeting by singing 'Solidarity Forever,' they are linking themselves to a set of beliefs about their shared situation and tradition, and their potential collective power."[11]

Silencing happens in myriad ways and differently for different groups. In the case of laborers, for example, low wages and harsh working conditions limit speech because people need both time and money to speak out freely and make sure they are heard. The task of laborers fighting for fair pay and working conditions is to develop effective counterstories to the many variations of our dominant social myth that if you work hard, you will be rewarded with a good life—meaning a life of relative comfort. The majority of laborers throughout history have worked hard and have not been so rewarded. Anyone who spends time as a laborer knows that the work is grinding and is not generally experienced as rewarding. While one might manage to live a good life in spite of the social devaluing of the labor in which one might well and rightfully take pride, the actual number of people who make it out of what are usually family histories of low-wage and/or dangerous physical labor has not been as high as the myth suggests. In fact, in the United States, these numbers have been diminishing in recent years.[12] And yet in the United States, we are fed variations on the story of the "American dream" from birth. It is inescapable in any form of media, social institution, or social interaction. Anyone who makes use of social services is, in this story, failing the social mandate to "pull yourself up by your bootstraps." The ways in which this story plays out on every level of our lives make the task of changing such a narrative extremely daunting. Who, in the social context of this prevailing master narrative, is going to listen to people who are perceived as not doing well for themselves?

As Lindemann points out, master narratives such as the "American dream" retain the power to explain our lives—even against substantial evidence showing reality to be otherwise—in part because of their ubiquitousness and the assimilating and silencing qualities of such insistently repeated narratives. For example, in spite of the fact that we need farmworkers to pick and process our food and laborers to clean our buildings, haul our trash, make our clothes and electronic gadgets, or do any of the long list of tasks that support our freedom to do work like writing books, we are all encouraged to dismiss these necessary tasks as lowly, as beneath anyone of value. We are encouraged to assume that anyone who performs such work just doesn't "have what it takes" (usually understood as a good work ethic, or persistence, or intelligence, or diligence) to do better. Because of this devaluing of the work of laborers, those doing such jobs are rendered already morally questionable in their ability to argue for better wages or working conditions. Laborers are not on par with those who earn more and therefore do not deserve attention. Even potential allies for change, or labor activists themselves, are infected with this story. We may actively resist these thoughts and still find ourselves assuming that if low-wage laborers just worked harder, or had paid better attention in school, then they wouldn't be facing such harsh conditions. Against the grain of mythic narratives like the "American dream," one has to ask instead the questions that this set of stories, through their insistent repetition, effectively hide. In what kind of world is it OK to pay people doing jobs that we all need and want to have done wages that place them below the poverty line? Arguably, laborers and workers at almost every level today have lost a great deal of ground in this battle for the story since what might be considered the golden era of labor rights, when labor unions gained a living wage, safer working conditions, more reasonable limits on hours (a topic we might all be revisiting), and protections against child labor. During this heyday, they also made powerful use of music.

The study of the use of song in social movements has a patchwork history to date. For example, as Timothy Lynch notes in his introduction to *Strike Songs of the Depression*, "historians were initially cool toward these lyrical expressions of worker culture, reluctant . . . to accept them as legitimate historical sources"[13] or as important elements to consider in their cultural analyses. In the last two decades, scholars across a number of disciplines have increasingly begun to cross disciplinary boundaries and take cultural practices such as singing, which had previously been set aside as unimportant, more seriously. The use of song in labor movements in the United States has been documented as far back as the colonial period,[14] but most research has focused on saving historical tunes for posterity rather than analyzing their role in social change work. The early twentieth-century labor movement is one era of organizing that made very strategic use of music with which many of us are familiar and from which other movements learned and borrowed. For example, as Kerran Sanger notes in *"When the Spirit Says Sing!": The Role of Freedom Songs in the Civil Rights Movement*, the song "We Shall Not Be Moved" was "adopted from the labor movement in the United States and adapted for the cause of civil rights."[15]

Even as the labor movement, especially the Industrial Workers of the World (IWW), invested in music as integral to their organizing, producing hundreds of thousands of copies of what is known as "The Little Red Songbook," many labor movement songs of this era were composed or altered on the picket lines, in meetings, and during strikes. Building on songs that were familiar to most in genres ranging from the religious to the popular, strikers often composed together, making up lyrics to fit their present situation. After hard-won battles, the story of their win would be embellished in song to inspire more participation and further actions. Lynch notes that the use of song in this era of labor activism served pragmatic, social, and psychological purposes beyond the four basic functions laid out by Rosenthal and Flacks, though most of what Lynch describes fits best under "serving the committed." Pragmatically, concerts helped "raise much needed strike funds . . . [and] singing filled empty hours for striking workers, helping them escape boredom and restlessness and stay focused." Songs told their stories (articulating and maintaining shared identity), "described their oppression and articulated their claims for justice." Singing was sometimes even "employed as a strategic weapon, a diversionary tactic to distract company police." Psychologically, songs gave workers the opportunity to "vent frustrations and assert their strength"; singing together "instilled in them a sense of their own power." Socially, "song brought workers together physically and emotionally. . . . [Songs] communicated shared feelings, thoughts, and values [and] . . . helped build community and class consciousness among the workers,"[16] serving the committed as well as educating others. As we see from Lynch's portrayal, workers primarily had their workplace in common and sometimes housing—such as it was. But they may well not have shared racial, ethnic, religious, or other ties to hold them accountable to their shared cause.

Because of this challenge to their identities as workers, they had to develop a counterstory to emphasize what they shared as workers. They had to claim and continually hold each other in their shared identities as workers valuable to themselves and society. Even as the forces around them continually worked to devalue their personhood and their sense of community as workers, laborers had to practice holding themselves in their valued identities. Lindemann argues that the practice of holding each other in our identities is a moral act that can be done badly or well.[17] Using this framework, the laborers' singing together can be seen as an important practice of holding each other well—holding each other in healthier identities as valued human beings while actively letting go of the damaging identities that their workplaces imposed.

As we see in their songs, building momentum in the case of the labor movement called for several forms of counterstorying. An effective labor movement required counterstories that strengthened bonds among workers, perhaps most problematically across ethnic and racial differences, through a shared recognition of their power as a group. Their songs countered the prevailing story of valuing the individual over the group so that workers would understand their strength in standing—or sitting—together, and it substantiated their value to society. While there is some important identity formation at work in the songs, primarily in terms of workers valuing themselves as workers, a repeated emphasis of the songs in this era is the importance of standing together: union building. Union songs often serve all four functions of social movement musicking.

Emblematic of this is what became the anthem of labor, "Solidarity Forever." Sung to the tune of "The Battle Hymn of the Republic" (a.k.a. "Glory, Glory, Hallelujah"), its counterstorying power trades powerfully on the tune's deep cultural roots. "The Battle Hymn of the Republic" started out as a fairly simple camp revival song called "Canaan's Happy Shore"[18] and then became embellished as an abolitionist tune, "John Brown's Body."[19] Julia Ward Howe, who wrote the lyrics to "The Battle Hymn of the Republic," effectively intertwined these purposes to inspire Union soldiers to their cause in battle. Laborers traded on the moral, political, and militaristic feelings that the song's history inspired in those hearing and singing it. The lyrics of the labor revision offer a useful example of how making use of past tunes from varying contexts can play to a multilayered effect:

When the union's inspiration through the workers' blood shall run
There can be no power greater anywhere beneath the sun
Yet what force on earth is weaker than the feeble strength of one
For the Union makes us strong.

Chorus:
Solidarity forever, solidarity forever
Solidarity forever, for the Union makes us strong.

Is there aught we hold in common with the greedy parasite
Who would lash us into serfdom and would crush us with his might?
Is there anything left to us but to organize and fight?
For the union makes us strong.

Chorus

It is we who ploughed the prairies, built the cities where they trade
Dug the mines and built the workshops, endless miles of railroad laid.
Now we stand outcast and starving 'mid the wonders we have made
But the union makes us strong.

Chorus

All the world that's owned by idle drones is ours and ours alone.
We have laid the wide foundations, built it skyward stone by stone.
It is ours, not to slave in, but to master and to own
While the union makes us strong.

Chorus

They have taken untold millions that they never toiled to earn
But without our brain and muscle not a single wheel can turn.
We can break their haughty power, gain our freedom when we learn
That the Union makes us strong.

Chorus

In our hands is placed a power greater than their hoarded gold
Greater than the might of armies magnified a thousandfold.
We can bring to birth a new world from the ashes of the old
For the Union makes us strong.

Chorus[20]

These lyrics play directly on the emotional power of the song's biblical references. Howe's religious lyrics, which most every child would have known at the time, praise the glory of divine salvation on "judgment day," which is described in military terms—a vision of when all that is wrong with the world shall be righted, when "the Lord . . . has sounded forth the trumpet that shall never call retreat" and sifted "out the hearts of men before His judgment-seat." It is a jubilant victory march in the voice of "we, the saved," because "we" trusted in "the Lord." Even nonbelievers may feel swept into the song's emotional orbit by its marching cadence.

In the labor union version, the victorious power comes from standing together as a union. Those who do will be enabled to "bring to birth a new world from the ashes of the old." Laborers claim a place of social value as the ones "who ploughed the prairies, built the cities where they trade / Dug the mines and built the workshops, endless miles of railroad laid." In this counterstory, the country owes what it has to its laborers' efforts. Indeed, the voice of laborers becomes the voice of the country as they turn the tables based on the revaluation of their own handiwork: "All the world that's owned by idle drones is ours and ours alone." In contrast, the master narrative of the business owner as the one who is of greater value to society than the laborer is utterly overturned, with the owners portrayed as "idle drones" who "have taken untold millions that they never toiled to earn." In this counterstory, workers trade on the power of a particular Christian narrative about wealth and corruption: "It is easier for a camel to go through the eye of a needle, than for a rich man to enter into the kingdom of God" (Matt. 19:24, KJV). By calling out the owners, who have "hoarded gold," the workers are structurally aligned with those in the previous version of the song for whom "the Lord . . . hath loosed the fateful lightning of His terrible swift sword." The owners are doomed—indeed, damned. The repetition of this shared vision through musicking practices in meetings and during actions both held the workers in their identities as valuable to society and to each other while challenging society's overvaluation of the owners.

If songs were used to build and strengthen the social value of the identities of workers and union members, they did so based—as all movements for change must be to some degree—on identities already socially sanctioned and legible. For example, according to Lynch, Depression-era strike songs were highly gendered: women primarily wrote and sang emphasizing their socially affirmed identities as mothers, sisters, and wives, whether they were striking themselves or serving as allies to male strikers; men did so primarily as comrades, emphasizing solidarity among men. Women "expressed their support for unionization in terms of familial concerns,"[21] while men fought "in the name of worker loyalty and brotherhood."[22] Lynch notes that even their articulations of "manhood" differed: "When in 'Which Side Are You On' Florence Reece asked, 'Gentlemen, can you stand it? / Oh tell me how you can? / Will you be a gun thug? / Or will you be a man?,' she understood to 'be a man' as defending against who would 'take away our bread.' On the other hand, when Maurice Sugar exclaimed, 'Be a Man,' he meant for striking workers to answer 'the fighting call of brother.'"[23] Such use of prevailing available identities (worker, soldier, brother, wife, mother) in order to form new identities, let go of damaging identities, or revalue a denigrated one is absolutely necessary to social change work, though doing so is often a double-edged sword in work for social justice more broadly. One has to ask how to best make use of the identity scripts available but tweak them in ways that don't continue to marginalize or devalue others fighting for justice as well. The song "A Union Man" is typical of the type of counterstory developed to change the image of the laborer as unworthy of respect, but it very much leaves in place the highly gendered norms of the time:

> A union man is a loyal man
> He's tried and true.
> No matter how tough the going gets
> He sees it through
> He's always ready to hear the call
> It's all for one and one for all.
> Anyone can see
> A loyal man is he.[24]

Such portrayals were largely successful in expanding union efforts and winning an era of better working conditions across many working-class jobs, but they often did so at the expense of people of color and white women. Working-class women too were forming unions and striking at their jobs, but songs like this erase their participation—not just as mothers, sisters, lovers, and wives but as workers in their own right.

As Bryan Carmen explains in his introduction to *A Race of Singers: Whitman's Working-Class Hero from Guthrie to Springsteen*, "Determined to secure the dignity of the white worker, these heroes largely represented solidarity in terms of male bonding and homoerotic attraction, a strategy that pulled their politics in two directions at once. On the one hand, they envisioned a mutualistic society that emphasized equality, undermined the competitive ethos of capitalism, and imagined a more just social order. On the other, their formulation of solidarity often excluded women and people of color, thereby safeguarding, sometimes inadvertently, the social advantages ascribed to manhood and whiteness."[25] While the predominant whiteness of labor movement's documented music history speaks to practices of racism within the movement, within music history, and within the larger society, the power of songs from this movement nevertheless offered useful material for civil rights activists.

The use of song in the 1950s- and 1960s-era civil rights movement parallels the early twentieth-century labor movement's use as outlined above in a number of ways: bringing activists together physically and emotionally; building community (though of a different order than for labor movement); and helping activists cope with tensions, boredom, restlessness, and focus while communicating shared thoughts, feeling, and values. Civil rights activists, building on the successes of labor movement work, strategically engaged all four functions of musicking delineated by Rosenthal and Flacks. But civil rights musicking differed from labor movement practices in some important features, particularly in terms of space, purpose, available resources, and audience. While concerts were held to raise funds for the Student Nonviolent Coordinating Committee (SNCC) and activities like voter registration drives, they were not a primary form of civil rights movement's use of song, as there was not quite the same focus on raising funds as there was for striking workers, who needed monetary support to replace the wages they were losing while on strike. For civil rights activists, most of the singing happened in meetings, marches, actions, and jail cells.

While most labor activists shared a workplace where they were banding together as workers and making demands of the owners in large industrial settings like auto plants or other manufacturing sites, civil rights activists were protesting social ideologies and practices of segregation and discrimination. Labor activists were focused on the workplace, while civil rights activists were addressing racist attitudes across the spectrum of daily life, whether on the bus, at the lunch counter, at work, or in schools. In both movements, activists placed their bodies on the line, but a large portion of this bodies-on-the-line work in labor activism took place (and still does) in the form of picket lines or "sit-down" strikes focused on temporarily closing the doors of industry in order to press for their demands to be met. In contrast, civil rights activists of this era were often pressing their way into spaces to which they had been denied access, such as segregated lunch counters or bus seats.

Workers might not share ethnic, racial, or religious backgrounds and therefore had a need to create and maintain their solidarity by strengthening their identity as workers. The challenge of doing so across these social differences is evident in the complex uses made of these differences on both sides of labor battles. For example, bosses strategically manipulated the racism of white workers to divide workers against each other.[26] "Solidarity Forever" is just one of many examples of lyrics that emphasize the importance of sticking together—one of the movement's greatest challenges.

In contrast, black civil rights activists' racialized bodies created a shared identity enforced by segregation. Black churches, schools, and communities, while formed by segregation, served as a form of cultural capital in terms of organizing. Both labor and civil rights activists had to overcome historical and ongoing social messages devaluing their humanity that required shifts in identity individually and collectively in order to begin to find their voices, but because of the differences in the forms of oppression, the nature of the community building as well as the wellspring from which to feed the production of songs differed in some important ways.

As Sanger documents, growing and maintaining the movement required a constant redefinition of self for African Americans. The choice—and it was a choice that required much initial struggle—to return to songs that had the taint of slavery and seemed old-fashioned to many of the activist/singers at the time was not easy.[27] In the end, this choice won the day because it validated African American history, strength, perseverance, and personhood. By reclaiming a history that the larger society worked, and still works, to forget and erase, activists gave depth and resonance to the movement. These songs not only reminded the larger society of what had been survived but connected that history with the injustices that African Americans continued to face. They created a more effective counterstory by reconnecting the historical dots between slavery and segregation that the larger culture repeatedly whitewashed (and sadly still does[28]).

Building on this musically rich and painful history, civil rights activists of this era added or altered words, as did labor activists, based on specific situations as needed. Those who found themselves together in frightening situations speaking truth to power with their bodies on the line found strength, courage, and solace in singing together. As T. V. Reed notes in *The Art of Protest*,

> Music had long been a part of American movements including the antislavery movement in the nineteenth century and the labor movement in the twentieth century, among others, but the civil rights movement brought a new level of intensity of singing and left a legacy of "freedom songs" now sung all around the world. Songs were everywhere in the movement—in meetings, on the picket lines, on marches, at the sit-ins, in jail, everywhere. Songs, especially as embedded in a rich church culture and later in black pop music, formed the communication network of the movement, linking its spirit to centuries of resistance to slavery and oppression.[29]

These songs were forged by bodies and minds under pressure. For example, as Sanger documents, police regularly raided the Highlander Folk School in Tennessee to intimidate the activists attending this social justice leadership training center where blacks and whites illegally gathered together to discuss the nascent civil rights movement. One night when high school students were present, police forced everyone to "sit in the dark" while officers rifled through their things. Out of the dark, a girl's voice rose, singing "We Shall Overcome." In direct challenge to the fear no doubt rising in her body and all those around her, she continued the tradition of developing new lyrics to fit the situation and created a new verse: "We are not afraid, we are not afraid today." Sanger writes, "It was, according to [Highlander music director Guy] Carawan, the introduction of a new, especially relevant verse to an old, beloved song that provided the impetus for change within the singers. As the song was changed, so did the singers change; insofar as they felt better equipped to face their fear and overcome it."[30] In this way, the singers challenged not only the authority that would oppress them but their own sense of themselves in the face of the oppression. Like the laborers holding each other as valuable in the face of social devaluation of their identities, civil rights singers used song to hold each other in valued identities.

This example of the use of song displays important elements from the physiological to the communal to the negotiation of space, identity, power, and meaning evident in every such use of song for social justice movements. Who gets to speak; when, where, why, and how they can speak; and who defines whose identities and how—all these matter to issues of social justice. In this case, the student's singing, especially this new verse, challenged the power of the raiding police on many levels. We know that physiologically the deep, measured breath required to sing calms singers, slowing their heart rates. Its calming effect would be one way to deny the invaders a bit of their power to intimidate. By keeping themselves calmer, the activists were likely better able to respond intelligently to the situation rather than out of fear. Singing together defines a space and creates an experience of identity within community. In this case, the singers defined themselves as a human community with a shared voice that stood in direct refutation of the police actions attempting to mark that space and its participants as somehow "illegal." Symbolically as well as physiologically, the song calls on a shared humanity. In so doing, it not only rendered the police as "outsiders" to this community, insofar as the officers were not willing or able to join in or appreciate the song, but also showed the police to be the violent invaders that they were. The earnestness of the song, the voices together, and the genre itself, like prayer, countered any sense of guilt or wrongness on the activists' part that the police action attempted to impose. And it did so in a manner that the police were not equipped to challenge. As Sanger notes, the singers, through their singing together, were able to serve as "living refutations of the white myths regarding blacks"—the myths that the police in their actions were working to impose.[31] No words alone would have as effectively countered the invasion. This was a powerful moment of finding voice that amplified the counterstorying effect and that has resounded through movements for social justice worldwide.

Getting the word out—whatever that word might be—has been and remains relatively easy for those who have the means to gain "air time," whether through time, money, or social or political influence. But for those who would challenge dominant and dominating stories, the wherewithal to create a comparably compelling counterstory—one strong enough to create change—has always been a challenge. Both the early twentieth-century labor movement and the civil rights movement of the mid-twentieth century made very purposeful and strategic use of song from which many movements for social justice around the world have borrowed. While their practices were often developed and formalized in meetings, and while each movement had its minstrels who nurtured this musicking practice, one of the more important of these functions in both movements was the use of song during actions serving all four purposes that Rosenthal and Flacks delineate, but in ways that spoke specifically to the form of the oppression and the cultural capital that each group was able to bring to bear in calling for greater social justice. As such, it proved to be an important counterstorying practice. We also see in these examples further development of the importance of what too often gets dismissed as preaching to the choir but really serves a purpose whose importance is made clearer as we develop a greater understanding of the healing and empowerment that happens with a practice of holding ourselves and each other in valued identities while letting go of damaged ones. Singing together can be such a practice of holding.

2

Choral Musicking for Change

Sixteen women from a small town step onto the stage of one of the largest of several performing spaces at GALA's Festival 2016; Denver's Buell Theatre seats almost three thousand. There are approximately two thousand in the audience, mostly singers from the other choruses. Roughly two-thirds of those seated are men, many of whom probably chose this block of performances to see one of the movement's biggest and most highly regarded TTBB (tenor 1 and 2, baritone, bass) choruses, which will be singing at the end of the block. The sixteen women stand in a single curved line on a stage that dwarfs them—on which every move and sound they make is obvious to everyone in the hall. They do not have the five rows of twenty-five voices each standing behind them as the front row of the men's chorus that follows them will have. Their voices in this sense are both individually naked and utterly dependent on each other as each change in tempo, pitch, or timbre affects every other voice and their sound as a whole.

Nearly everyone in the audience understands this feeling of vocal nakedness not just intellectually but in their bodies. The group's first number is going well, though their voices sound thin in the Denver air, especially following one of the more polished mixed choruses blessed with a preponderance of strong voices. It is a thinness every singer in the audience has no doubt experienced—not enough breath flowing. Fear—the sheer terror of being this exposed in front of so many people—can tighten the body, the vocal chords. It's our animal selves preparing for fight or flight. Countering fear, their daring voices tumble forward mostly on key.

When they finish, the crowd cheers them warmly. They are a bit more confident on their second number—maybe because they know it better, maybe
because they made it successfully through their first, maybe because this
one is humorous, or maybe all three. And again they are warmly cheered.
On the next tune, three soloists move forward to the mics. Each takes her
turn on lines followed and filled out by the chorus. Then one forgets
her words. A split second of fear and shame spreads across her face, ripples
through her chorus, and is felt through the hall. She closes her eyes as her
chorus fills in vocally behind her, and some in the audience who know
the song softly sing the words in encouragement. She recalls her place
in the music and finds her voice, and they finish the song to a standing
ovation. The audience cheers her and this small, intrepid group for moving through feelings of fear and shame while standing tall, not allowing
their fear to silence them. There are moist eyes and smiles everywhere I
look. This particular choral musicking practice offers participants a chance
to hold and be held in their identities in some powerfully healing ways.
Theoretically, this sort of supportive identity practice could happen at any
choral event, but in all of the many events I have participated in over the
years, only in this movement have I experienced such unmitigated support. Something about this particular form of musicking serves important
purposes for LGBTIQ people.

As I covered in more detail in Chapter 1, when laborers gathered
together in halls to sing "Solidarity Together," they may have had a visiting "minstrel" (like Woody Guthrie) with a guitar and microphone leading
them, but the beauty of the harmonies or the challenges of the music itself
were not likely to be the focus of their singing so much as the enactment
in song of their solidarity with each other and their support for a shared
cause. Whether sung in the union hall or on the picket line, this and other
labor songs are a direct form of counterstorying practice. The lyrics reframe
laborers, in their own eyes and in the eyes of others, as more valuable to
each other and to society than are the business owners. Such a practice
holds them in more socially empowered identities.[1] Singing these lyrics
together not only creates a sonic space of communing for a cause, but the
lyrics and the holding of each other as valued community members in a
sort of lyric and musical mutual embrace counter the dominant stories

about laborers as expendable and less valuable than company owners—a narrative that enables companies to engage in poor labor practices.

And similarly, when a high school student at the Highlander Folk School dared to start singing "We Shall Overcome" as the police were raiding this Tennessee training center for social justice leadership in one of their regular attempts to intimidate civil rights organizers, she was putting into practice a strategy activists at the school were learning for calming and collecting the group to create a sense of their own empowerment to counter just such intimidation. Her own sense of empowerment was further instantiated as she created a new lyric—"we are not afraid"—that directly called out and challenged the police officers' attempts to intimidate them. No doubt the voices that joined hers sounded thin, given how frightening the situation must have been, but by daring to sing and create new lyrics that spoke to the situation, the group effectively used singing to enact and hold each other in their full human dignity and exercise their right to be doing exactly what they were doing—organizing together for greater social justice.

In both cases, the practice of singing brought people together to challenge social injustices, creating a sense of community and strengthening their shared vision for a better world. But they are not examples of choral musicking in the formal sense that is prevalent in queer choral movement. While there have been and still are more formal labor choruses, many of the ones currently active are no more than thirty years old. The most recent worldwide listing of such choruses shows only thirty-three choruses worldwide, three of which are queer choruses aligned in solidarity with labor,[2] as compared with more than four hundred queer choruses. A search for choruses directly identified with civil rights movement brought up none, but there was a pre-civil-rights-era black use of choral musicking.

A precursor to the use of singing in the civil rights movement developed out of the Great Depression and the Works Progress Administration (WPA) funding that supported the arts. One well-documented example of this was Elmer Keeton's WPA chorus. Historian Michael Fried documents the role of Keeton and his chorus in challenging oppression. Building on the work of a number of historians, Fried notes that "Keeton and his choir were pioneers who made cultural, musical, and social history in California as they successfully challenged our country's long, painful legacy of 'separate and unequal.'"[3] Arguing for the enormity of Keeton's legacy, Fried claims,

> His impact in California and on the West Coast paralleled that of Marian Anderson, Roland Hayes, and Paul Robeson at the national level. They each used their people's unique cultural inheritance and their own artistic gifts to nudge American society closer to justice. They each embodied the deepest aspects of the African American aesthetic—continuity, professionalism, persistence, community participation, resiliency, moral fervor, and undaunted spirit. . . .
> Sixty years ago, when Keeton and his singers lifted their voices in soaring songs celebrating freedom, equality, and dignity, they were renewing American black music's centuries-old call to, in the words of Langston Hughes's 1938 poem, "let America be America again."[4]

Much like queer choruses today, "Keeton and the Chorus weren't just singing to the black community. They were also singing a message of freedom and justice to America. They were saying in the music, 'we are just as good as you are!'"[5]

Like current queer choruses, black WPA choruses created hybrid music. They forever transformed the larger choral tradition by infusing it with spirituals, gospel, and blues that now are far more commonplace for many choruses to sing. As Olly W. Wilson, the noted composer and musical scholar, told Fried,

> Keeton, like other great black composers of the time, continued the tradition of changing the character of the music within the arranged, four-part chorus style, while maintaining the essence of the spirituals. What was important about the Negro spiritual tradition, starting with the Fisk Jubilee Singers, who initially were singing a vernacular folk spiritual, was that they began to arrange, and in doing so, the moment they went on stage, they changed the paradigm and created a new one. The new paradigm was the concert

spiritual, which is the idea of taking a folk tradition and simply performing it on the stage and altering it to conform with the necessities of the stage.[6]

Lacking the rich history of musicking that African Americans brought to choral musicking and eventually to work for civil rights, one that was already richly imbued with African American experiences and identities, queer choral movement instead has worked to slowly infuse mainstream choral musicking with queer sensibilities, identities, and experiences. Whether singing love songs or even religious music as written (while obviously staging these within a queer context), changing pronouns to make queer identities and relationships explicit, revising lyrics to well-known songs to create space to normalize and celebrate queer identities, or commissioning everything from anthems to musicals to oratorios, queer choral musickers use this highly emotive form to make more tangible for their audiences the loves and pains and joys and sufferings of queers, thereby humanizing identities that are still systematically denied full humanity.

Queer choruses have at this point commissioned hundreds of pieces, both new arrangements and completely new works. These pieces address topics from love and marriage to birth, death, and every imaginable human experience in between and are making their way into larger mainstream venues. For example, in 2001, the Twin Cities Gay Men's Chorus (TCGMC) reworked Tomie dePaola's 1979 children's book *Oliver Button Is a Sissy* and expanded it into a mixed-media movie, *Oliver Button Is a Star*, based on the story of a boy who likes to sing and dance rather than play sports. As the Online Computer Library Center WorldCat description notes, "This video includes comments from author Tomie dePaola, Arctic explorer Ann Bancroft, dancer/choreographer Bill T. Jones, and makeup artist Kevyn Aucoin about what set them apart from 'normal' children as they were growing up, and interviews with first graders about how they view boys' and girls' roles." The film has been used in antibullying programs around the country. In 2013, the TCGMC reprised the original show as part of their *It Gets Amazing!* show, their response to the "It Gets Better" antibullying campaign, with Ann Bancroft as narrator.[7] And the chorus made some of their stories available as well.[8] This is only one example of the many ways choruses around the world continue to effectively counterstory through choral musicking.

The purposes of the WPA choruses like Keeton's also parallel those of current queer choral work. From his interview with Dr. Lawrence P. Crouchett, founding director of the Northern California Center for Afro-American History and Life, Fried notes that each WPA choral performance had at least two purposes. Crouchett told him,

> First, blacks needed a means of both protesting their experience and expressing their aspirations, hurts, and interpretations of the assumptions of the majority group. The Keeton choir, through the selections of its repertoire, spoke to the black experience and the suffering imposed upon black people by the larger society. The other purpose of the concerts was to display their musical talent as trained musicians, not just as black people. In the Thirties, questions still existed concerning whether blacks were singing from heart or by memory, and here Keeton's choir was displaying the formal training they had, reading notes and singing according to the musical standards.[9]

Given the widely accepted stereotypes about African Americans at the time (fed by, among other forms, more than a century of broadly popular blackface minstrel shows that lampooned blacks as lazy, stupid, childlike, and superstitious), presenting themselves as accomplished musical artists in this formal context enacted a powerful counterstory even as the choruses brought their own musical traditions to bear upon it. To raise their voices together in beauty in places and forms that had been previously segregated enacted new possibilities for all the identities present. They enacted a more integrated society.

In contrast, for the predominantly white members of most queer choruses, singing on or off book (with or without choral folders with their music in hand) is not likely to make any difference in assumptions about singers' intelligence, yet there is a parallel in the need for expressing shared experiences to challenge another set of stereotypes. Black and queer bodies are still marked as abject in some overlapping ways. While

African Americans today still struggle against dominant white standards of beauty coupled with the multitude of ways black bodies continue to be perceived as animalistic, hypersexual, and inherently dangerous to white privilege, LGBTIQ-identified bodies of all races are often reduced to their gender/sexuality, hypersexualized, and perceived as dangerous to hetero-sexual and cis-gender privilege. Queers are perceived as disgusting to what Monique Wittig refers to as the "straight mind"—any mind that assumes and naturalizes gender and heterosexuality no matter the person's actual gender/sexual practices.[10] Repeatedly and emphatically expressing one's full humanity in the face of such social abjection becomes both an act of healing and an act of resistance. And choral musicking has played a role in both cases.

One form of social capital that civil rights activists and their precur-sors could call on to deal with such abjection was and is black church cul-ture. In *The Black Church in the African American Experience*, C. Eric Lincoln claims, "Black Christianity preaches a gospel of deliverance, the reality of a vivid flesh and blood Jesus and the urgency of spiritual rebirth . . . [that] also insists [on] social and economic liberation [as] part of the gospel. The story of black singing is a story of how black people 'Africanized' Chris-tianity in America as they sought to find meaning in the turn of events that made them involuntary residents in a strange and hostile land."[11] Speaking about the material effects of this hostile landscape, Fried quotes from his interview with ethnomusicologist Jacqueline Cogdell Dje Dje:

Blacks had no access, either as audience member or performer, to the music hall, the symphony, nor to many of the things that were available to and for whites and others in the larger society. As a result, they developed their own institutions, events, and opportu-nities in which they could be actively involved. Because the church was one of the few institutions within black culture that did not have interference from other groups, it became a major focal point for not only social and political activities in the black community, but for artistic expression and events as well. The church was a place where blacks received training and performed within the arts. It also provided an environment for critiquing individuals within

artistic endeavors. The church became the primary focal point
for . . . things that were artistically inclined, primarily because of
the exclusion within the larger society.[12]

So while racism created a sort of forced community born of segregation
that offered the civil rights movement ready-made social institutions to
support such a movement and labor activists had their shared workplaces
and communities, LGBTIQ peoples have historically been not only outcast
from their own families and communities of birth but denied the right to
their identities and any socially sanctioned communing with each other
at all. While in the Western world the raiding of gay bars, public shaming, or losing the rights to one's children is no longer common practice,
the majority of homeless teens today are still from families that have shut
them out. And in spite of laws now allowing gay marriage, the practice
of gay-bashing continues, and a range of backlash against recent political
gains seems to be growing.

While in larger metropolitan areas in much of the Western world it is
now possible for LGBTIQ people to gather openly, in many places in the
world, such a right to openly gather, if not outright legally denied, remains
dangerous to varying degrees. In fact, in spite of an increased cultural presence, with LGBT characters showing up in movies and TV shows and topics such as gay marriage openly discussed in the news, it is not safe to be
out in many rural communities in the developed world and certainly not
in most U.S. schools.[13] To compound the problem of LGBTIQ individuals
coming together as activists, the historical connections between lesbian
and gay, or gay and bisexual, or any of these and transgender or intersex people have been marginal at best and often antagonistic. The only
real common ground has been the shared experience of related forms of
gender/sexual oppression and the often violent denial of the very right
to exist at all. Because of the foundational differences in the histories of
oppression, queer choruses are as much about finding productive ways
to come together for communing across profound social differences as
they are about creating a new kind of community and new practices of
communing. This is a community not based on kinship ties, workplace,
or religion, though there are obviously ethnic/racial forces at work in choruses' formations. It is joyful communing in the face of social denial of

queer rights to any socially sanctioned communing. It is also about creating a public voice that can be heard, one that makes our identities more
socially legible.

While many more churches have become what is known as "reconcil-
ing communities," intentionally working to accept openly LGBTIQ members, many LGBTIQ people remain alienated from religion, though arguably
the legalization of same-sex marriage has shifted this to some degree.[14] Historically, because the nature of the violence against LGBTIQ people has
often been in religious terms, choruses (especially the primarily white
choruses) in this movement have lost members when they have opted to
perform religious material. Not only has religion been the primary basis
for legal denials of basic rights, but many churches have rejected LGBTIQ
people from their fold, encouraging families to do the same.[15] And yet
the desire to come together with others—especially for people for whom
such open and celebratory coming together has been, if not illegal, often
dangerous—clearly has a draw. As one choral member, Sydney, put it, "And
then I saw this thing about a choir, and I was like, oh, cool! Choral singing is something I have done all my life. It's very much a part of my sort
of family background. And so being in a choir, not in a church, because I
was very much alienated from the church, but in a community choir with
gay people—it was just like this whole new thing for me. It was like a way
to express something that was just incredibly powerful and wonderful for
me." In this way, Sydney and others like her are able to make use of this
particular form of gathering to claim an honorable social space for themselves that serves multiple purposes.

Picking up on some of the reasons for such a draw, May, a singer who
also once worked in an international choral organization, claimed,

> I think one of the biggest challenges about being gay or lesbian is
> combating feelings of isolation. I think music is comfort to many
> people, just in general, and when you add this network of gay and
> lesbian singers, people find their families; they find their sense of
> security and belonging. And we know that that's happening on this
> huge scale around the world. I think that that really helps people's
> self-esteem; it gives people great ideas to implement in their own
> communities. And I think it just makes us stronger as a gay and

lesbian people, just in general. I mean, there is strength in numbers.
So we provide a pretty important function that way too.

The parallels between the role of churches in many people's lives and the
role that the choruses seem to play in their lives grows clearer after listening to the language used by my interviewees.

Every one of my interviewees expressed the importance of the space
their chorus produced in their lives, and many described it as filling a hole
within them. Some articulated it as a space for freedom of self-expression;
others experienced it as a space of safety or nurturing, often standing in
for family, or as a community-building space. Many expressed feelings best
described as sacred or holy, though mostly without the religious conno-
tations. The importance of the space to be oneself is described by one
singer, Tyler:

> I think a lot of people, . . . their parents don't accept them. They are
> looking for someplace to be accepted, [or] maybe they are not out
> at work. They can't talk at work, but for three hours on a Sunday
> night, they can come to rehearsal and they can be who they want to
> be. They can be themselves. They don't have to hide anymore, . . .
> you can be yourself, and [feel] like "Hey, these are other people that
> are like me," and you tend to bond with them.

Or as Rick, a director of a mixed chorus, said, "This is a safe environment where they can use their voice, where they can exercise their voice,
and where their voice matters! That's one of the cornerstones, I think, of
the movement, that every voice should matter." Having a safe place to
express themselves with others like them after spending most of their time
with people who might not understand or see them for who they are is one
of the more common reasons singers gave for choosing this type of chorus.

Singers also find the relationships they develop to be more enduring.
Tyler said,

> I did theater a lot. I still do theater a lot, like community theater.
> And you get close to those people for a little while, and then the
> show is over, and you may stay in contact with some of them. But

[in] the chorus, I have made some of the best friends in my life that I will ever make. Even the people that I am not real crazy about, it's kind of like that big-brother sibling type of thing. "OK, I can make fun of them, but you better not" type of thing. We'll defend each other. I mean, there are people that, I mean, at times I can be grating to people, but even the people that I am like that to, . . . later they will put me in my place. What are you talking about? It's just family; I don't know how to explain it.

The closer interviewees got to their deeper feelings about their chorus, the more tongue-tied they became—struggling for words or saying, as Tyler acknowledged, "I don't know how to explain it." The interviewees' many attempts to more precisely articulate why choruses and the practice of choral musicking were important to them brought not words but a mix of smiles and tears, suggesting that the choruses fill some deeply emotional needs.

The safe space produced by queer choral musicking has increasingly been a draw for straight parents looking for safe and supportive environments for their queer children. Even before youth choruses became a growing part of queer choral movement, back when many choruses were still trying to figure out best practices about age limits for their choruses to protect the organizations and their members from any hint of sexual misconduct, there were already some supportive parents who were looking for a safe place and positive role models for their LGBTIQ children. Ben, a singer with a large East Coast TTBB chorus, recounted his story of

a straight man, a father who went to a chorus concert and had a wonderful experience and so forth. And just a year or two later, his son actually came out to him, and he took his son to a chorus concert later after that because he wanted his son to experience a positive gay environment. I think that what we can hope we do is make people realize that being gay doesn't mean that we hang out at bars every night . . . As important as television series like *Queer as Folk* and stuff or *Cutting Edge* and stuff are, we're presenting a whole other issue of we're not going to the disco club every night of the week. We're not hanging out in back rooms. We're getting together as a group. We're working on collecting something together that celebrates our lives, not just our sexuality but, you know, ourselves as human beings, as artistic beings, and the uniqueness that we have, and present that to the public: "Gay men are also this. We may be some of that other stuff too, but we are also this."

Because LGBTIQ people are still in many places marked as degenerate and therefore not deserving of citizenship, or even personhood, finding effective ways to interrupt and counter this dominant narrative can be healing for those identities damaged by such narratives and can also open a space for those who do not identify as queer to practice holding such identities as valued.

The act of singing together organizes and claims social power through specific forms of embodied communal practices. Singing together in general creates and defines space and social relations, sometimes allowing singers the opportunity to reframe the space and the meaning of the space itself for themselves and for others. We see this clearly in the many stories of the use of song throughout the civil rights and labor movements. Similarly, in one of the early incidences in queer choral organizing, the San Francisco Gay Men's Chorus performed its first impromptu public act, after only four weeks in existence, following the murder of Harvey Milk and Mayor George Moscone: "They sang a hymn by Mendelssohn on the steps of City Hall following the spontaneous candlelight procession of thousands of mourners [who] gathered there."[16] In doing so, the singers refuted the message that the double murder both materially and symbolically attempted to impose on all of them—that as gay men they did not deserve to live. The singers actively claimed their right—and the rights of all those protesting the murders with them—not only to life but to beauty, grief, and joy. As the first chorus of the movement to include "gay" in their name, they honored Milk's memory by being out. In responding to violent acts and denial of human rights such as this one, queer choruses have often engaged in singing together as a form of protest, but the preponderance of queer choral musicking occurs in more formal settings. So while there is an element of protest in queering the formal space of choral musicking, just as there was for the black WPA choruses, staking a claim to the value that the formality of the space and the choral art form itself confers, queer choral musicking is more than protest.

For each of these movements, the form and uses of these practices vary in materially important ways that speak to both the form of oppression and the cultural capital each group had or has available for their use. Labor activists have built on centuries of folk and religious song appropriate to the communities in which they organized, with the purpose of addressing specific industries. Activists in the civil rights movement built upon a shared history of song—particularly gospel and blues—that developed out of two of the largest and arguably the strongest cultural institutions African Americans had developed to that point: churches and popular music. By expanding the reach of these institutions into the sociopolitical realm, they productively challenged institutionalized racism. For LGBTIQ peoples, simply finding and developing communities are challenges to this form of oppression, but to do so in a highly cultured form that makes one's fuller being known and more knowable to the larger communities changes who and how we are able to be in the world.

PART TWO

Queer Organizing for Social Change

3

Practices of Identity

Queering Social Institutions

You may say I'm a dreamer, but I'm not the only one. –John Lennon

Imagine for a moment a world in which children are not gendered or sexed at birth; one in which all the qualities of being human are open for every child; one in which little humans are held and nurtured in their capacities for the qualities that most of us cherish when we find them in each other: kindness, compassion, willingness to share, sense of humor, ability to listen and reflect, honesty, creativity, intelligence, and so on. Imagine that the first question asked is not, "Is 'it' a boy or a girl," as if the child were not human until so labeled, or as if gender/sex were the most important thing about an infant, or as if only two choices exist. Imagine that the full catalog of human qualities and possibilities is held open for all of us. Imagine that as we develop, our differences from others are respectfully acknowledged and integrated into the web of what is possible for humans in creating and maintaining this more mutually respectful world rather than erased, silenced, or denigrated. Imagine that our presumed reproductive capacities and desires play a role in our identities only to the degree and at the time we so desire. Imagine that as children, our paths to our emotional, physical, psychological, and sexual awakenings are inspired by a range of creative human possibilities represented in the stories of our families, communities, and all media. Imagine cultural stories that nurture us all to be healthy in our relationships with ourselves and with others. Imagine that whatever "plumbing" we are born with imposes no particular social role on our identity except as we wish to take it up. Imagine.

When I ask groups I work with in communities and classrooms to imagine in this way, some have a difficult time imagining outside of our standard cultural narratives at all. It rubs too much against the grain of their sense of themselves and the world. Such imagining can feel too threatening for some. In fact, even John Lennon, in spite of his call for us to imagine a world beyond many of the story lines that shape us, evidently had some problems imagining a world in which queerness would be OK.[1] Even those who can actively imagine a better world tend to falter or give up when it comes to answering what it would take to change the world or even just our local communities. The distance between our visions of what ought to be and the realities of our own lives can seem too far to span. And yet many of us spend our lives not only imagining but attempting in our own ways to create the better world we imagine in large ways and small. Certainly those who participate in queer choral musicking see their work this way.

When many people think of work for greater social justice, they think of political advocacy groups, organizations like (in the United States) the National Center for Transgender Equality (NCTE), the National Gay and Lesbian Task Force (NGLTF), or the Human Rights Campaign (HRC). While such organizations do substantial on-the-ground organizing, their actual contact with members consists of little more than (e)mailings to sign petitions, call legislators, and ask for money. Contact among members is fairly uncommon and is most often either to protest political losses or to celebrate victories. Such organizations are important to creating change at a political level, but that change would not happen nor, more importantly, could it be maintained without grassroots groups working to change attitudes and shared cultural values as well.

Backlash can all but sweep away or substantially undermine what seemed like solid social change. Legal judgments and legislation supporting affirmative action and reproductive rights, for example, have been substantially rolled back due to very effective backlash. When enough people are uneasy with or ambivalent about such changes, the political tides can shift to undermine any legal protections—even Supreme Court decisions. We need to work for change that holds up against pressure from those who disagree. Doing so requires that the majority of people feel comfortable enough with the changes—feel them to be morally right—such that arguments against them hold little or no sway. These new values must be integrated into the prevailing cultural narratives—the master narratives. The new stories of who and how people can be in the world must take the fabric of the old stories and weave in new elements such that the changes become the new "common sense," so that to question them seems crazy to a large majority of people. Any changes to what counts for common sense require much more than a 51 percent popular vote or a Supreme Court decision. Deep and abiding changes do not come quickly or easily. They require multilevel ongoing work to keep the value of such basic cultural changes to the larger culture in the public conversation until these values become the norm to which all identities hew. Such change requires multigenerational effort.

Master narratives, as Hilde Lindemann explains, consist of "organic ensembles" of "repeated themes that take on a life of their own. Fragments of history, biography, film, fables, jokes, [songs] and similar narrative forms ring changes on the theme, as do proverbs, advertising slogans and other cultural artifacts."[2] Master narratives are very difficult to disrupt because they are everywhere assumed and generally not questioned. They are thought of as common sense. They also morph to incorporate or assimilate any social changes that might challenge their validity. For example, Lindemann notes that the heteronormative "boy meets girl, boy overcomes obstacles, boy wins girl for his own" story has many variations but is strengthened and increasingly naturalized and normalized with each retelling. This story contains elements for who each of us is able to be in the world, especially in terms of gender and sexuality.[3] Such stories gain strength from their connection to other master narratives. This story is tied to everything from the many variations on what it means to be male or female, to what marriage is, to what roles people are allowed to play with each other, with children, or in society. Any challenge to any piece of this web of stories potentially requires a questioning and reframing of the whole ensemble. For example, if the story changes to girl meets girl or person meets person, then who wins whom? Or do we (hopefully) throw out the idea of "winning" another's life altogether? What does this mean for the nature of love? What does it mean for gender identities or

reproduction? Anxieties about proposed changes to any part of these stories are amply evident in, for example, the many arguments against gay
marriage: "Next thing you know, people will demand to be able to marry
their dogs!"

Because these cultural stories are mutually reinforcing, they work in
concert to create a worldview, a "web of belief" that makes up a culture's
understanding of what it means to be human.[4] This web of stories constitutes beliefs about who we are, who we have been, and who counts as part
of our "we." These stories also enable or disable the visions of who we are
able to be going forward. Without shared cultural stories, we would be left
without beliefs or reasons to act in any particular way with each other.
They are so fundamental to who we feel ourselves to be and who we are
able to be with each other that even when such stories oppress us, we tend
to resist challenging even portions of the them because each thread knots
into the fabric of who we understand ourselves to be in so many complex ways. Philosopher Diana Tietjen Meyers explains, "What is at stake in
the perpetuation of culturally entrenched figurations of socially excluded
groups is nothing less than a society's understanding of the human species
and its place in the universe."[5] The power of master narratives and their
roles in our lives are not so easily altered or dismissed.

Consider civil rights movement: the fight for dignity for people of African descent is most definitely still going on, most recently in the form of
Black Lives Matter in the United States. While laws have changed, racism's
forms have morphed in response. To think of it as "the" civil rights movement contains the challenges to the 1950s and 1960s as if the problems
have been solved. This serves the story that we are beyond racism when
that is, by a preponderance of evidence, patently false. And yet the number
of white people who to varying degrees still believe or are easily swayed by
this falsehood speaks to the power of dominant (and dominating) narratives even in the face of ample evidence otherwise.

The fight for full personhood for those of African descent grew out of
a long history of both cultural and political activism to change the stories
about who people of African descent are and are able to be from anti-
slavery work (we are not property), through the blossoming of the Harlem
Renaissance (we are fully intellectual and artistic beings who nurture our
own culture even after having our ancestral ones stolen from us), to the

battle against lynching (we have a right to due process), to the actions of the 1950s and 1960s that most people think of when they think of this movement (we will not be segregated), to present-day work to end racial profiling and the school-to-prison pipeline (we deserve the right to be valued as full human beings in every aspect of our lives). The work continues today because for too many white people the value of their own identities—consciously or not—depends on not being black or brown.

Men who are careful to distinguish themselves from women, straight or cis-gendered people who are nervous about being perceived as queer in any way, and people with money who believe themselves better than those with less all have identities built on "othering." Such identities are structured on the story "I am not *that*." Sadly, those who are othered in various identities, in manners subtle and not, inevitably internalize these messages in ways that can be debilitating, damaging identities for which counterstories offer potential repair both for the self and for society. Lindemann explains: "[Counterstories] redefine a past that has been, until now, characterized incorrectly. They take a story that has (for the moment at least) been determined, undo it and reconfigure it with new significance."[6] Effective counterstories revise our mutual storying practices to be both more accurate and more inclusive. They not only challenge the underlying assumptions of the oppressive stories but reframe them in ways that allow openings for new ways of being.

Because our mutually maintained web of cultural and personal stories works to enable or disable our abilities to express our full being in the world, Lindemann argues, our storying practices have moral consequences. We can "hold" and/or "let go of" identities well or badly. In every human interaction, we engage in the production and maintenance (or disruption) of the stories that make up who we and those around us are and can be; therefore we have a moral responsibility to "hold" and/or "let go" of our identities well.[7] Most such interactions are simple and based more or less on standard scripts, like a play. For example, I open the door into a store and acknowledge the person walking out by holding the door for him. He might say "thanks," or he might grab the door over my head and insist that I go through first, denying me the opportunity to hold the door for him. In the process, everything from the ease or tension of our bodies to our facial expressions are saying things about how and in what identity we "hold" each other. Some men are clearly uncomfortable when I hold the door for them because I am not playing by a gendered script that maintains their sense of who they are and who they think I should be in the world. But who they think I should be in the world is not who I am, nor is it who I am willing to be. Within a split second in each such encounter, I am left to decide whether and how to effectively reframe who and how both of us can be with each other in a manner that, ideally, denigrates neither of us. If I let it be and tacitly enact the identity of the "little woman" that his action suggests while internally holding myself as fully empowered and human, then I internally "refuse" the narrative but have left him upholding and reinforcing the dominating gender story. As such, I have arguably acted unethically toward myself and him—allowing my own identity to be disrespected while dismissing him as unimportant to my life. That said, such internal refusal is often a first stage necessary to more substantive action for change. Or I can "resist" the diminution of my identity by countering his action in some manner that might be verbal, physical, or both in tones ranging from anger to warmth to good humor. We can perform these practices well or badly, but challenging and changing such entrenched narratives that deny us our full personhood is obviously work.

The social practice of holding people in (or letting go of) their identities (well or badly) happens at every level, from the most minute interpersonal to the institutional and global. Oppressive social practices both hold and let go of personal and group identities badly and do so to the benefit of one group over another. Arguably, social justice work is not done until no identity is formed or maintained through stories that denigrate groups of others, or until it is socially unacceptable to denigrate another in order to prove the greater social power of one's own identity. But most of us would prefer to leave all sociopolitical struggles behind and just live our lives in relative peace. One of the biggest challenges of long-term social change is that people's appetite for continuing the work waxes based on very recent incidents that incite action and then rather quickly wanes. Those dedicated to working for social change need to deal with the present situation as well as think creatively long term across generations. For a movement that has only recently been openly engaged in reproduction in the (relatively) traditional sense and whose "community" members come from diverse groups who historically have little in common except shared forms of gender/sex oppression, finding ways to effectively organize in the present, much less think in the long term, is challenging. And a big piece of this work is coming up with effective counterstories.

Successful counterstories develop out of groups of people coming together in safe spaces to rethink, reframe, and restory themselves as valued, moral humans in ways that free up their ability to act in the world and that can be mobilized for change in the larger culture. It is important to note that all counterstories must, by definition, operate within the context of the master narratives they challenge and therefore inevitably face the paradox of reinscribing that narrative to some degree. For example, Lindemann discusses the challenges faced by the "we're here, we're queer, get used to it" counterstory. While it has allowed more people to "live less closeted lives, . . . it might be argued that it has also accepted the terms, laid down by the master narrative, that construe homosexuality as an identity at all." But such arguments "must work within the constraints of the preservative forces of [in this case] an abusive, heterosexist power arrangement that marks a firm boundary between a heterosexual 'us' and a homosexual 'them,' [and] the ['we're here, we're queer, get used to it' counterstory] doesn't ask why a particular erotic desire should generate an identity in the first place when other desires don't." Even so, she argues, the note of defiance in being present "as queer, in perhaps more ways than one," resists even this element of the master narrative to some degree by "displac[ing] the discussion." A counterstory cannot uproot a whole master narrative but is "good enough" if it manages to "dilute the poison and so free the group members' moral agency," thereby increasing their ability to act freely in the world without denying the moral agency of others.[8]

As queers, our ability to act freely in the world remains partial and more tenuous than we might like to admit. The freedoms we are able to exercise have come into being through centuries of work that historians have only begun to seriously uncover, and if feminist or civil rights history offers any lessons, these freedoms can all too easily be erased. Knowing and sharing our own histories are necessary forms of resistance. While the Stonewall rebellion is rightfully celebrated as the moment when organizing for greater sex/gender freedom for all most powerfully coalesced in the United States, people had been speaking out, taking action, and organizing on these issues long before 1969.[9] In fact, very similar rebellions had taken place earlier in Los Angeles, San Francisco, and other locations that no doubt played a role in the building resistance to such police raids. Civil rights, labor activism, antiwar work, and feminist activism all created the sociopolitical space for conversations that challenged traditions, including those about sexuality and gender expression, to become public, and the conditions for change became ripe. There was freedom in the air and a questioning of authority, including the authority of tradition, at every level that made imagining new ways to think about relationships, family, and identity possible. As one who came of age in this era, my own sexual development benefitted from the incredible freedom that I had in opening to my sexuality because of this public cultural questioning enhanced by its timely coupling with the availability of the pill and the fact that most sexually transmitted diseases were easily treatable and that AIDS had not yet darkened our doors. Neither any generation before—especially those of us with active ovaries—nor generations since have enjoyed the same level of relative cultural and physical freedom to explore their sexuality.

As a confluence of counternarratives developed and began changing what had counted as "common sense" about, among other things, sex, love, and marriage, people whose lives fit the norms increasingly found themselves in situations that encouraged them to reconsider their own sexuality and gender identities in ways that made many profoundly uncomfortable. Everything from men with long hair to interracial dating threatened the identities of those whose sense of themselves depended on people of color and white women "staying in their places." A sort of perfect storm of the building backlash against both civil and women's rights successes propelled Ronald Reagan to presidential victory in 1980. Coupled with the onset of the AIDS crisis, the backlash all but closed the door to organizing around sex/gender freedom. Political and social attitudes supporting new possibilities for identities and our ways of relating gave way to fearmongering, turning the political tides and shifting attitudes in the "movable middle" to the right.[10] The focus of queer activists shifted increasingly to survival and what gains could be made in an era of backlash and retrenchment. Only in this century have conversations about what real sex/gender freedom might look like resurfaced to challenge the more conservative political shift of the past couple of decades' focus on military service and gay marriage.[11] Throughout this ongoing process of creating more effective counterstories, queer organizing has taken a wide variety of forms, from the expressly political to those seeking to create more safety for queer identities to exist by changing cultural attitudes so that queers might thrive.

Many forms of queer cultural organizing, from bowling leagues and bands to yoga circles, serve to entertain and create connections. But some organize expressly to change the culture in particular ways that have matured into forms of social institution building and queering. They form an array of counterstorying practices in the cultural arena that create space for not only imagining but actually making space to practice holding each other in (and letting go of) our identities in healthier ways. For example, Pride events, community centers, the Gay Games, and the Metropolitan Community Church share some purposes and scope with queer choral musicking and offer useful historical and material points of comparison for analyzing queer cultural change work.[12] Each is a form of organizing that responds to specific institutional sites of oppression. Each offers counterstories—in words, actions, and their persistent physical presence—that creatively contest strategic points of dominating narratives and serve to normalize a whole range of queer identities. Collectively through comparison, they offer insights into the relationship between the nature of sex/gender oppression and the socioemotional needs of LGBTIQ people and their allies. And this comparative analysis suggests ways we might better organize for longer-lasting social change.

In all movements for social justice, we are likely to find ourselves betwixt and between some common tensions as we find ourselves paradoxically claiming an identity even as we are challenging what it means to be that identity. For example, in any moment, there are those who tend toward assimilation and those who resist the status quo (and this might be the same person at different moments under different circumstances); those who happened to be at a flashpoint such as Stonewall, those who step in later along the way, and those who had been organizing all along; those on the front lines willing to place their bodies on the line and those who hang back and might even criticize those on the front lines (even if they may eventually benefit from the work of those they criticize); and those who react in a particular moment to oppression and those who plan as best one can for the most effective moment and way to resist. What any one person does at any one moment in any movement for social justice work might land any number of places on the spectrum of these often contentious tendencies, but it is no surprise that the large majority of any oppressed group may choose rather to keep their heads down and suffer the indignities because the cost of creating change seems too high. Even an act of refusal, in which one does not accept the master narrative about oneself, instead developing an internal counterstory while allowing the rest of the world to believe what they will and just dealing with the daily assaults and their consequences, is an important first step. Standing up and out can end for some in imprisonment, assault, or even death. Because of this, I think it is important to honor and value the many types of work it takes to change hearts and minds by better understanding how they are all part of a larger counterstorying process.

Pride

The Stonewall rebellion that today's Pride events commemorate was, by all accounts, an unplanned uprising. In an era of regular raids on queer bars or gathering places, it was not the only such rebellion against police harassment and brutality. Similar incidents in Los Angeles and San Francisco, as well as more organized protests in Chicago, New York, and Philadelphia, had not managed to gain the same traction for expanding the movement. As David Carter, author of *Leading the Parade: Conversations with America's Most Influential Lesbians and Gay Men*, argues in his article "What Made Stonewall Different," "Stonewall was of a different order for four reasons: it was the only sustained uprising, lasting six days; it was the only one that involved thousands of people; it was the only one that got much media coverage; and it was unique in engendering a new kind of militant organization (first the Gay Liberation Front and later the Gay Activists Alliance) as well as a new political ideology known as 'gay liberation.'"[13]

Elizabeth Armstrong and Suzanna Crage expand on Carter's history in their article "Movements and Memory: The Making of the Stonewall Myth," noting that part of the reason this particular uprising was able to gain its historic momentum had to do with at least three factors related to Stonewall's location in Greenwich Village. Greenwich Village's small winding streets enabled protesters to strategically outwit police who were not expecting any pushback. Second, the high percentage of seasoned political activists who lived in or frequented the area meant there was a critical mass of people with years of experience doing social justice organizing who spread the word and brought more people out to protest. Third, the nearby *Village Voice* offices held reporters who lived in the midst of the uprising and made the news coverage more engaged, giving greater prominence to reporting on a topic that otherwise might have been relegated to back pages. Armstrong and Crage argue that the event's "commemorability" due to these factors gave it legs to become the mythical origin story for queer movement.[14]

In the same vein, Carter argues that the response of others to what happened at Stonewall inspired the movement to new levels. Frank Kameny, "an activist in Washington, D.C., for years before Stonewall happened," told Carter, "By the time of Stonewall, we had fifty to sixty gay groups in the country. A year later there were at least 1,500. By two years later, to the extent that a count could be made, it was 2,500. And that was the impact of Stonewall."[15] This willingness of more people to rise up and organize in exponentially greater numbers than had been the case before Stonewall—to organize on the heels of the drag queens, dykes, hookers, and trans people, many of them homeless youth, who fought back at Stonewall—gave substance and form to the impulses and resistance to injustice that instigated the Stonewall rebellion. With additional voices, there is additional power that rendered these impulses—counterstories in the flesh—into larger social and political actions.

Building on the critique of culture by the feminist movement and the overall sexual revolution of the 1960s and 1970s, the "Stonewall" or "Christopher Street" events in the years that followed the rebellion actively challenged sexual mores in general, calling for a more broad-based sexual freedom, challenging not only laws against sodomy but the state's right to have any say in consensual sex between any two adults. For example, the Gay Liberation Front, which formed immediately post-Stonewall and organized the first march, stated as their mission "the complete overthrow of all heterosexist institutions, including marriage," and defined themselves thus: "We are a revolutionary group of men and women formed with the realization that complete sexual liberation for all people cannot come about unless existing social institutions are abolished. We reject society's attempt to impose sexual roles and definitions of our nature."[16] It's important to note that for all the revolutionary fervor evident in this statement, the transgender people and homeless youth who were beaten in the streets and precincts perhaps most viciously during the uprising tend to disappear. While arguably their positions would be bettered by the abolishment of institutions that "impose sexual roles and definitions of our nature," their voices and gender-nonconforming identities seem lost or at least inadequately referenced by the identity of "a revolutionary group of men and women" proposed here.

Many today fighting for and celebrating gay marriage or singing along to "Born This Way" might find the arguments of the era that made all this possible counterintuitive. For example, Carl Wittman's argument in "A Gay Manifesto" is worth considering in some depth for its contrast with many of today's assumptions about "the movement" and what this suggests about the morphing of social movements in response to changing social pressures. Wittman wrote the manifesto in an era of manifestoes that built on and responded to each other, challenging society to reevaluate almost every aspect of life and related values that had been taken for granted for generations. Wittman's arguments, while campy in style, are based on an antipatriarchal value system. He dismisses the idea that "homosexuality" might be genetic, claiming, "Homosexuality is the capacity to love someone of the same sex," with *capacity* being the operative word.[17]

While today we might let the letters LGBTIQ trip off the tongue, many in "the community" still have serious problems with bisexuality. But in his 1970 manifesto, Wittman argues more radically for something that is in keeping with scientific studies of sexuality[18] framed through a sexual liberation lens:

> Bisexuality is good; it is the capacity to love people of either sex. The reason so few of us are bisexual is because society made such a big stink about homosexuality that we got forced into seeing ourselves as either straight or non-straight. Also, many gays got turned off to the ways men are supposed to act with women and vice-versa, which is pretty fucked-up. Gays will begin to turn on to women when 1) it's something that we do because we want to, and not because

we should, and 2) when women's liberation changes the nature of heterosexual relationships.[19]

The forced dichotomy—gay/straight—is his foundational point of attack based on its role in the maintenance of patriarchal values. He argues that gay men, who have suffered at the hands of straight men, share a sense of oppression with all women and therefore should find it somewhat easier to reject their own patriarchal training.[20]

Along this line, he argues vehemently against patterning gay relationships on what he describes as highly problematic straight practices of love and marriage: "Marriage is a contract which smothers both people, denies needs, and places impossible demands on both people. . . . To accept that happiness comes through finding a groovy spouse and settling down, showing the world that 'we're just the same as you' is avoiding the real issues, and is an expression of self-hatred." Instead, he suggests, "Liberation for gay people is defining for ourselves how and with whom we live, instead of measuring our relationship in comparison to straight ones, with straight values."[21] Wittman's dismissal of marriage altogether as an institution, his optimistic assumptions (e.g., that feminism would fundamentally change the nature of heterosexual relations), and the valuing of human capacities as opposed to traditions or norms are all marks of the hopeful and visionary inclinations of that era.

These heady counterstories fueled all kinds of actions and reactions. People formed new sorts of family units; challenged each other to find their way beyond sexism, racism, classism, and so on; and organized new ways of being together, some of which still exist today. But many more failed, and Lindemann gives us a framework for understanding why these more liberatory practices are up against rough odds and why more radical counterstories have not won the day in the larger cultural context. Master narratives work to effectively assimilate or annihilate any attempts to challenge them. In social movements in general, the greater gravitational pull to assimilate to the status quo tends to soften the message rather quickly, blunting the more liberatory energy that brought the issue to the fore in the first place. This is obvious in the shift in political focus from sexual liberation to gay marriage.

Pride events are important to local communities on many levels—not the least of which is increasingly economic. Most Pride organizing committees share missions similar to that of the Twin Cities Pride: "Twin Cities Pride brings the greater GLBT community together to commemorate our diverse heritage, foster inclusion, educate and create awareness of issues, and celebrate achievements in equality. We create events that are open and inviting to everyone in the community, providing a safe environment in which individuals feel free to celebrate their relationships."[22] Such Pride organizations partner with a wide range of other for-profit and nonprofit organizations to support their mission. Some larger Pride organizations, such as Los Angeles's and New York City's, have developed into substantial fundraising opportunities that support social services in their communities.

The very fact that these events are now most commonly referred to as "Pride" is part of their evolution (some argue devolution) from the Stonewall/Christopher Street anniversary march-parade-celebrations that became known as "Gay Pride" or "Lesbian and Gay Pride" or "LGBTIQ Pride" and eventually just "Pride."[23] That a preponderance of the people and groups marching in recent Pride celebrations across the country are either politicians or corporations and that a primary theme has become the right to marry make them a far cry from the foundations of what journalist Andrew Belonksy calls the "nearly religious foundations for the greatest of gay traditions: Gay Pride."[24] While there are vestiges of what used to be more open demands for a more broadly construed sexual freedom in recent parades (including groups promoting polyamory or naked men caressing themselves openly as part of a nudity booth at recent San Francisco festivities), they are marginalized in the face of more assimilationist calls for rights that mostly benefit those with money, such as marriage.

Parades today are likely to include everything from a Safeway float with LGBTIQA Safeway workers functionally attesting to the company's support of LGBTIQ issues to marching anti-male-infant-circumcision activists. But there are signs that the spirit of coming out is, in some ways, still relevant even in this increasingly corporatized environment. In 2013, just weeks after the U.S. Supreme Court's decisions against the Defense of Marriage Act (DOMA) and California's Proposition 8, one of the most warmly cheered groups walking in the San Francisco Pride parade was the

Mormons for Gay Marriage contingent. While only about thirty marched in this group, the crowd's response suggests some understanding that amid the largely safe and comfortable floats of politicians and corporations, the (presumably) Mormon marchers were risking ostracism within their Mormon communities. This is just one of the more recent groups that could be said to be performing a new "coming out" enabled by the parades. It serves as an example of the way that the annual commemoration of an event in which people took to the streets and fought police for the right to do what came to be called being "out and proud" offers affirming space for public comment that challenges other "closets"—in this case, an opportunity for Mormons to come out as pro–gay marriage.

Pride events serve a number of important purposes in sociopolitical terms and serve some purposes that are similar to queer choral musicking. As Armstrong and Crage argue, the parades "proved to be ideal for the affirmation of gay collective identity and for the production of feelings of pride central to the emotional culture of the movement.[25] The emotional impact

FIGURE 3.1. Mormons for Gay Marriage contingent, arguably outing themselves more than most others marching in the San Francisco Gay Pride Parade on June 30, 2013, receiving loud support from the crowd. Photo taken by author.

granted the parade lasting cultural power." They are also an "excellent way to advance other movement goals" by "inject[ing] gay presence into public urban space" and "forc[ing] cities to accommodate gay existence" by "requiring police protection and official permits." As "large, colorful, public celebrations," the parades are newsworthy. The form itself allows for "expansion and varied levels of participation, including watching from the sidelines. They are versatile: participants can design new floats each year, and bystanders never know exactly what they will see. Parades can also be adapted to different contexts." Depending on local contexts, they might be "restricted to gay neighborhoods or go through central business districts. Parades can be more or less sexual, or more or less political. The form allows contingents to stake out differing, even conflicting, political positions." Because they have been annualized and have grown in size, people organize vacations around them, bringing revenue to the parade

FIGURE 3.2. Ventura County's Pride events, like many in smaller communities across the United States, focus more on community building and less on politics than some of the larger commemorative celebrations. Most years, Ventura's Pride events consist of a collection of booths at the beach or a park on Main Street with a stage or occasionally two for speakers and entertainers. Pride 2004 was on the beach. Photo taken by author.

sites. Some plan their whole summers to attend one Pride event after the other across a region. The sheer size and annual repetition creates news and yearly cultural review of LGTBIQ issues in the news.[26]

While by themselves the parades do not create legal changes any more than choruses do, like choruses, they play an important role in creating the climate in which social attitudes can be challenged and political change can be more easily nurtured and sustained. Pride events, like choral concerts, offer a counterstory in the flesh to any number of current versions of master narratives that would deny LGBTIQ people full personhood. Pride events can certainly be large, bringing more than a million people together in many of the larger metropolitan areas around the world, though most events are much smaller. While some larger metropolitan Pride committees develop events throughout the year, in most areas they only happen once a year. In many smaller cities, a year here or there might be skipped altogether depending on local leadership and funding. In large metropolitan areas, events often include a march or parade and large all-day or even multiday festivities that literally take up substantial public space and time to celebrate being queer. Most events encourage a wide range of participation, but political and moneyed interests have taken the lion's share of the space in many parades and increasingly influence the nature of the overall events. While corporate interests certainly bring more funding to the events (and, to a lesser degree, to the LGBTIQ community) and politicians bring greater news coverage and imply greater social support for LGBTIQ issues, they tend to sideline the social justice and sexual freedom elements that initially inspired Pride events. This change is perhaps the most striking difference from the event that Pride commemorates.

While every movement for social change has its own unique dynamics, in very broad strokes, those at the bottom of the social strata—those who have reason to feel they have less to lose—are often the ones who place their bodies on the line first and pay the price with rare rewards. They too often go unnoticed by the news or even in later histories precisely because of their lack of social status. For example, drag queen and trans activist Sylvia Rivera's story has luckily not been completely swept into the dustbins of history like countless others about whom we may have only tidbits at best. But her story offers a prime example of how the minds, spirits, and bodies of the most oppressed are too often used and discarded by more privileged, more assimilationist leaders in movements for social justice who are willing and able to trade on the fury and fight of those at the bottom but then too often trade out the needs of those they use in later political calculations, arguing that these fighters are "asking too much." Serving their own more privileged purposes, such leaders often argue that it is more reasonable to start with their own more assimilationist demands, leaving behind the needs of those whose lives were on the front lines to begin with. In doing so, the more privileged leave those who arguably paid the highest price betrayed by the very movement they spent their lives supporting. As Michael Bronski writes in his review of Rivera's life, "It was also not unusual for Sylvia to be urged to 'front' possibly dangerous demonstrations, but when the press showed up, she would be pushed aside by the more middle-class, 'straight-appearing' leadership. In 1995, Sylvia was still hurt: 'When things started getting more mainstream, it was like, 'We don't need you no more' But, she added, 'Hell hath no fury like a drag queen scorned.'"[27] This is an example of how, as Lindemann says, a "counterstory can misfire." By oversimplifying the issues or overgeneralizing their own experience, they produce a "we are who I am" counterstory to their own advantage and at the expense of those who rumble. Lindemann's example is Betty Friedan, who arguably helped to hijack feminist movement away from the needs of women of color, the poor, and lesbians to benefit middle and upper-class white women by offering her story as *the* feminist story. People with greater relative social power too often trade on the rumblings in the streets that produce the energy for the movement while leaving out those whose lives were on the line.[28]

Those on the more radical end of the spectrum (usually those at the bottom of the social hierarchy), because of their greater urgency, are too often the ones to make the noise that can be heard through the cracks in the master narratives precisely because their very existence troubles the norms. Out gender nonconformists, transgender, or genderqueer people, for example, are by their very existences "contesting" the master narratives that would erase them, placing them at greater risk for all sorts of violence. The more radical break open a space for those with more social and political clout to strategically step in (in part both because those with means do have something to lose and because they have cultural capital with which to strategize). It's important to note that Caitlyn Jenner, for example, is able to have the spotlight in the way she does because of those who came before her, but also, as Emanuella Grinberg points out, "thanks to her wealth and celebrity status[, she] is isolated from those forms of discrimination and harassment," or the violence to which the large majority of genderqueer people are regularly subject.[29]

Those with cultural capital and organizing skills, if successful, are followed by the less politically inclined, those who are more likely to live their lives as "refusers" or even "resistors"—those who might not accept the cultural stories about them and might even stand up to them in some private ways, but have yet to organize with others to change their status as a group—to become "contesters." Refusers and resistors may slowly feel more emboldened (perhaps even morally called) by the general increase in cultural noise making on their behalf to take greater stands publicly and privately that slowly create more broad-based social acceptance. With each additional group of voices, the counterstories change, usually becoming more conservative. So often lost in the process are the visions and the voices of many who placed their lives on the line in the first place—in this case, homeless teens, queers of color, and transgender people. Better counterstories celebrate all our voices.

Queer Community Centers

The voices of youth, queers of color, and transgender people are somewhat more evident in what might be considered the service sector of queer organizing: local LGBTIQ community centers. According to CenterLink, "a member-based coalition to support the development of strong, sustainable LGBT community centers," the first "lesbian and gay community centers in the country opened their doors in 1971 in Los Angeles, CA and Albany, NY." Their mission at the time "was revolutionary: that lesbian and gay people deserve to live open, fulfilling and honest lives free of discrimination and bigotry, with access to culturally appropriate social services, as equal partners in the cultural and civic life of the community."[30] Since the first doors opened, activists across the world continue to develop and maintain a wide variety of centers—some with more community-building purposes, some with strong social service missions, and some with both.

The original focus shifted with the onset of the AIDS crisis. Centers increasingly took on the responsibility of organizing and advocating for care, educating the community, and supporting prevention. Many centers have maintained that effort for all people who are suffering from HIV/AIDS, even with the shift in the at-risk populations moving beyond primarily gay men. As CenterLink notes, "Many of these earliest centers are still the major urban provider of AIDS-related services and prevention efforts." Even with the shift in focus to HIV/AIDS, queer community centers continue to "[offer] everything from 'coming out' support groups, to health clinics and meeting space for community organizing, [and] centers [in many areas have become] the hub of community activity and the catalysts for progressive social change." While there have been some ups and downs for center development and growth, most recently the extreme economic downturn of the first decade of this century, new centers are still developing, many in areas without much other support for LGBTIQ people, and these are often "the first point of contact for people seeking information, coming out, accessing services or organizing for political change."[31]

As of July 2016, CenterLink reported "179 Member LGBT Community Centers listed around the world," though there are obviously centers that are not members, because the online survey for their 2016 report went out to 256 community centers.[32] The June 2016 "LGBT Community Center Survey Report: Assessing the Capacity and Programs of Lesbian, Gay, Bisexual, and Transgender Community Centers," produced by CenterLink and the Movement Advancement Project (MAP), which is "an independent, intellectual resource for the LGBT movement [whose] mission is to provide independent and rigorous research, insight and analysis that help speed full equality for LGBT people," is based on surveys from 143 centers (up from 111 in 2014) that participated in their survey from forty states and Puerto Rico (up from thirty-two in 2014).

The report offers the following summary:

- In total, the participating LGBT centers serve over 43,500 individuals in a typical week and refer over 6,000 individuals to other agencies for services and assistance.
- Center patrons are disproportionately male, people of color, transgender, and/or low income.

- In a typical week, LGBT community centers are open to the public for an average of 44 hours. Ninety-two percent of centers are open in the evenings and 61% of centers are open on weekends.
- The majority of centers offer accessible parking (83%) and accessible bathrooms and drinking fountains (71%).[33]

The centers seem to fairly consistently offer refuge and support to homeless youth, people of color, and transgender people, with 82 percent of centers offering programs "tailored to LGBT youth" and "88 percent offering transgender-specific programming," voices and identities that are only recently gaining more prominence through queer cultural movement supported by such centers. Most centers offer some level of direct health services, such as "counseling, peer-led programs, and support groups, as well as physical health and other mental health services," and provide "physical health services to more than 272,000 people, and mental health services to more than 22,600 people" with an emphasis on wellness programs "emphasizing healthy eating, active living, tobacco-free living, and cancer support." In addition, more than three quarters of centers offer computer services for "job searches, keeping in touch with family and friends, and entertainment."[34]

In parts of the United States and many parts of the world, it is still revolutionary to claim that LGBTIQ people "deserve to live open, fulfilling and honest lives free of discrimination and bigotry, with access to culturally appropriate social services, as equal partners in the cultural and civic life of the community." The original missions of such centers are still needed today. In Los Angeles, which has the oldest, largest, and best-supported center, with a budget that equals "51% of the cumulative budgets of all centers reporting budget data,"[35] the focus can afford to be much more diverse. But for the large majority of such centers, meeting that basic mission can be a challenge in their local contexts.

As a piece of the larger movement for queer social justice, centers extend the work that Pride events perform annually throughout the year by creating a social presence and often a safe public space as well as creating a sense of shared community. The importance of such a presence and space cannot be overstated in terms of climate for those living in an area. Like the choruses, they create a sense of recognizable community that is especially important for those who are still denied that among family and communities of origin. Along with the additional social services role that most such centers play, their ongoing presence not only offers a safe space and affirms LGBTIQ people's lives but keeps the larger community aware of their claim to the right to coexist as full citizens by offering a public community platform from which to speak. They create a consistent day-to-day material counterstory in terms of physical space but also in terms of the actions the centers perform in caring for others. Countering the master narrative that queers are outcasts, the centers, like the choruses, offer a physical, embodied, and verbal narrative of a social loving embrace in the face of rejection. They institutionalize a healthier holding and letting go of queer identities.

I write this as one whose local center had to close its doors for lack of funding in the wake of the 2008 financial crisis funding cuts and can attest to the fact that the community has pretty much lost the sense of a cohesive coming together. While the board managed in the process of closing to find other local piecemeal sites for the various support groups, having a place that was ours together is a loss many of us feel regularly. We have also lost our professional local voice; we no longer have a spokesperson readily available to publicly answer questions about the state of LGBTIQ affairs in the area, allowing master narratives freer rein with no official local counterstories. The role of centers in creating a caring, life-affirming presence as a piece of effective local counterstorying, as well as a reliable and professional local voice on queer issues, calls for more analysis in the larger picture of queer organizing for social justice.

Queering Sports

If centers are the local social service arms of the movement, in the international recreational arena, the Gay Games, and more recently OutGames, have been challenging master narratives about gender and sports. Promoting goals that more directly parallel those of queer choral musicking—to create social change through engaging publicly in activities (in this case, sports) that set goals for a personal or team best rather than competition against others—the Federation of Gay Games states its mission: "to promote equality through the organization of the premiere international

LGBTIQA and gay-friendly sports and cultural event known as the Gay Games." With about 125 partner organizations, of which about 40 are formal member organizations (several of which are LGBTIQA choral organizations), its primary work is to produce quadrennial international events, which have recently grown to more than twice the size of the GALA Choruses Festival, also held every four years. Their site notes, "The first Gay Games took place in 1982 in San Francisco, bringing together 1,350 athletes from a dozen countries. The Games have been held every four years since in world-class cities. Gay Games VIII in Cologne in 2010 attracted over 10,000 participants from some 70 countries."[36] This number doubled for the 2014 Gay Games in Cleveland and Akron, where "[more] than 35 sports and culture events were held, with more than 20,000 people from more than 60 countries participating and visiting."[37] Like the choruses, the activity is, in part, about placing one's body in relatively institutionalized venues with pride to physically offer counterstories to master narratives that devalue queer bodies and queer lives.

As with the queer choral world, in which a number of national and international organizations produce festivals at the regional, national, and international levels, the sports world has organizations that plan competitions at different levels. While national and international umbrella

FIGURE 3.3. Castro scene circa 1980. SFGMC Archive.

organizations developed to bring local choruses together for workshops and festivals, the choruses each originated within their own communities. A primary focus of most queer choruses is local community building, often with a declared mission of creating greater social justice through song. In the queer sports world, for many years, local teams or people have participated together in sports, but the focus of the local lesbian softball team, for example, has more often emphasized getting together to have fun. The larger mission of challenging master narratives in the sports arena seems to have only become a more prominent focus with the development of international events.

To better understand this form of organizing, Gordon Waitt's analysis of the 2002 Gay Games in Sydney, Australia, offers some insight into the challenges of organizing through sports to produce greater social justice. He explores whether the games "subverted the heteronormativity of [male] sporting bodies that are metaphors for Australian national space."[38] In the process, he offers varying perspectives of such endeavors that are useful for understanding the complexities of queer organizing more generally. Based on both "participant observation and . . . in-depth interviews with over forty self-identifying gay and queer males living in Sydney,"[39] Waitt articulates the way in which the event produced transgressive and transformative experiences for many participants through its camp performances of standard sports traditions such as opening ceremonies and through the celebration of the homoerotics of sports. For example, he notes, "For respondents who participated in the Gay Games the opening ceremony in Aussie Stadium was a piece of pure camp. As a camp appreciation of opening ceremonies of international sporting events, the ceremony productively worked to undermine the role of sports bodies in national mythmaking, specifically the hetero-sexual definition of national space. The opening ceremony facilitated the creation of nonheteronormative visibility and space in a venue that is often oppressive towards sexual difference. In this way, camp at the opening ceremony was political by revealing fissures within the nation."[40] Breaking the rules that insist on keeping the homo social and not sexual was an important element that Waitt's participant interviewees found transformative. They were able "to show sexual attraction by cruising and by sexual excitement." As one interviewee noted, "Some of the divers were very aware they were eye candy.

They paraded up and down in their speedos in front of the crowd. That was quite an obvious part of the event."[41]

My guess is that, in general, athletes in all such events have some idea that they might be "eye candy," but in the heteronormative nationalist narratives of masculinity and femininity that straight events promote, while a woman might freely express her appreciation of a male form, men doing so would not be so easily accepted. In doing so freely, openly, and playfully, participants are "unsettling the unwritten rules about sport conduct." Doing so reportedly felt liberating for many participants, but what becomes clear from other, mostly nonparticipant, interviewees is the ways in which the story being told—the narrative of the Gay Games as they played out in Sydney—did not live up to the inclusive ideal it purports to offer. By Waitt's analysis, while successful in several ways, the counterstory failed on several counts.

Even more so than the shift in Pride events, which currently tend to sideline (though not deny access to) the more radical or socially uncomfortable, nonnormative elements of queer "community," Waitt argues that the 2002 Gay Games in Sydney, by their very dependence on the values and traditional social forms of white Western sporting, queered or not, reinscribed a narrative of difference rather than one of inclusion. They do so on at least two levels: the heteronormative disciplining and ideals of white muscle-bound masculinity and the economic class status required to participate. For the predominantly white middle-class participants who came closer to fitting these ideals, the event was experienced as transformative, but for those who were never going to fit the narratives inherent in these ideals, the Gay Games, despite claiming to promote inclusivity, reinforced hegemonic social divisions. Waitt notes that there are many ways in which the Gay Games, for all its desire to "promote equality," has elements of entertainment in common with gay travel cruises (another interesting site calling for analysis).

Waitt's analysis underlines the challenge of all such cultural organizing for social change. It engages specific forms of social practices or institutions that are already in existence while at the same time making productive use of the inevitable opportunities for change within the forms. As Waitt notes, given the "muscular masculinity" promoted by many Western nations (especially Anglo) as ideal, by camping up the rituals of

Olympic engagement, focusing on personal best more than competition, and openly celebrating sexuality with sports, the Gay Games do offer a transformative space—at least for some participants and certainly in the news world. According to Lindemann, counterstories are as much about healing the damage done as changing the master narratives. Clearly, for some participants, the counterstorying practices of the Gay Games serve at least that purpose. In a limited way, it also contests master narratives about sexuality and, according to Waitt's study, maleness, but it does so while leaving in place some narratives that continue to oppress others. We need to better understand both the possibilities and the limits of such organizing in each site. What makes one site of organizing more or less fruitful and in what ways than others? How might those working for greater social justice better make use of a variety of sites for organizing?

It is precisely because the normative narratives of masculinity, femininity, and sexuality are institutionally disciplined through sports at every level, from children's sports on up through the Olympics, that sports is a fruitful cultural site for creating counterstories. But there are other oppressive stories entwined in this web. If in its current form the Gay Games' counterstory fails in several ways, are there ways it might be made more effective? What are the limits and possibilities for changing master narratives that define sex/gender norms in different social and institutional settings? What kinds of identities does sporting lend to queering and to what degree? These are questions that organizers might consider in evaluating the degree to which they work to fulfill their mission "to promote equality."

Queering Religion

While for some spectators and athletes sports can serve as a religious experience that gives foundational, even transcendent, meaning and experiences to their existence, for others religion plays an important role in their sense of who they are in the world. Religious institutions in the United States continue to play substantial roles in everything from nation formation to sexual practices, making them another fruitful, if challenging, site for organizing both within and without. There are many ways activists have worked within faith traditions to create greater social acceptance for

LGBTIQ people—including support groups such as MASGD for Muslims; Eshel for Orthodox Jews; GALVA for Hindus; and for Christians, Dignity in the Catholic tradition, Integrity in the Episcopal tradition, and Axios for the "Eastern & Near Eastern Orthodox and Byzantine & Eastern-rite Catholic LGBT lay Christians." More broadly, the Gay Christian Network's mission is to "share that light and love [of Jesus] with one another and with the world" by placing in communion without judgment those who believe same-sex desire is a "call to abstinence" and those who believe in blessing "homosexual" relationships as much as "heterosexual" ones.[42] Some religious organizations primarily offer support to queer members within the faith, and many advocate for change and gaining greater acceptance within major faith traditions.

All play a role in changing social attitudes by offering what might be seen from the outside as counterstories that are too incremental or even problematic. But given both the strength of religious practice as a part of U.S. national and cultural traditions and its historical influence, as well as the comfort such religious practices offer many people (in ways that parallel what queer choral musicking does), the need to work with religious institutions in some form seems obvious. Indeed, contrary to popular assumptions about queers and religion, the Pew Foundation reports that LGBT people are staying active in churches and in their religious beliefs at higher rates than the general population.[43]

The development of the Metropolitan Community Church has a history that parallels the development of the Gay Games. Tom Waddell was a decathlete competitor in the 1968 Mexico Olympics who, because of his experiences there, went on to develop the Gay Games. Similarly, in 1968 Troy Perry, a recently defrocked minister of the evangelistic Church of God, felt "called" to create a new church for gays and lesbians. Both organizations are based on a similar logic: if they won't let us into their institution, we will create our own. And both forms of organizing were catching the waves of larger social shifts. Melissa Wilcox's "Of Markets and Missions: The Early History of the Universal Fellowship of Metropolitan Community Churches" lays out the nature of these currents, which are important to understand in terms of what inspired the development and success of such organizations. Based on analysis of related social movements, histories of the Universal Fellowship of Metropolitan Community Church (UFMCC), and her own interviews with members, her work contextualizes the place of the church in queer lives and the larger culture.

Wilcox's arguments extend from ones developed by Frances FitzGerald in *Cities on a Hill: A Journey through Contemporary American Cultures*. FitzGerald compares four seemingly very different communities that took shape during the same time period of the 1960s and 1970s—"San Francisco's Castro district, Jerry Falwell's Liberty Baptist Church, the Sun City retirement community, and Rajneeshpuram."[44] Each of these disparate groups shares several important foundational elements that influenced or enabled their development: (1) a strong U.S. tradition of creating "new communities, new movements of both secular and religious nature, intended for the betterment of themselves and their society" in conjunction with (2) "a new emphasis on pluralism rather than consensus"; (3) "an intensified focus on remaking the individual; and" (4) "a reorientation of identity and community." These foundational social changes were results of "economic and demographic shifts" that "were changing the family structures and living situations of many Americans, breaking up old neighborhoods and redistributing their inhabitants across the rapidly growing suburbs."[45] These changes inspired new versions of existing master narratives to shore up traditional identities that were challenged by these shifts as well as counterstories to allow new identities to flourish.

Extending FitzGerald's argument that "the Castro district was born, not simply from politics but from fundamental changes in the nature of identity and community in American culture," Wilcox argues similarly that the "UFMCC is a compelling example of a community founded on the basis of old American traditions and new American communities."[46] To support the weaving of old and new as it developed in the UFMCC, Wilcox references two earlier scholars' research on the success of the UFMCC. The first is Paul F. Bauer's study of Denver's MCC and is based on his fieldwork in the mid 1970s. The second is R. Stephen Warner's analysis "The Metropolitan Community Churches and the Gay Agenda."[47]

Bauer explains that Denver's MCC grew so rapidly "because it is a workable solution to the two major problems facing the homophile community: religious 'respectability' and social acceptance," a claim that Wilcox points out can be found in "many UFMCC publications."[48] Perhaps more important, Wilcox notes that Bauer argues that "the gays and lesbians attending MCC-Denver had been conditioned not to expect any social or political solution to their oppression" and that he "also makes the important observation that MCC congregations create strong social communities that assist members in dealing with their struggles."[49]

From a sociological perspective, R. Stephen Warner's article "The Metropolitan Community Churches and the Gay Agenda" sees MCC founder Perry as a "religious entrepreneur" whose success is due to a ripe "cultural market" not tapped by other religious institutions. Wilcox suggests that Warner's work does a better job of addressing the reason the Pentecostal tradition that underpins the UFMCC is an advantage. She summarizes Warner's arguments this way:

> [The] Pentecostal background of MCC is ideal for addressing the internalized oppression that plagues many members of the LGBT community. On the one hand, the conservative and essentialist assertion that homosexuality is innate and not chosen, combined "with the evangelical image of a benevolent and powerful God produces a surpassing affirmation of gay identity." On the other hand, the tradition of prophecy and divine inspiration within Pentecostalism supplies "a vision of grace" that can supersede both tradition and anti-LGBT interpretations of biblical law. Finally, Warner notes that, since religion has historically been a major source of LGBT oppression, it is a necessary factor in the struggle against and the healing from that oppression.[50]

In this excerpt, Warner offers a perfect example of how those working for social justice can effectively wedge a counterstory into the places that master narratives have inconsistencies, in this case making use of the stories that we are "born this way" and that "God doesn't make mistakes" and the Pentecostal promise of divine grace. Pulling these pieces of the picture together, Wilcox is able to take a larger view of the UFMCC and its growth.

Placing the UFMCC in the context of the larger queer social movement, Wilcox establishes the historical precedent in relationships between other social movements and their religious arms:

Granted, the Marxists in the movement would have been little interested in such an addition, but it is a fact of American history that, for every Marxist facet in movements of the 1960's and 1970's, there was a matching religious one. Marxists struggling for black civil rights had King's arm of the movement; the United Farm Workers often marched behind a banner portraying the Virgin of Guadalupe. The feminist movement sprouted many religious responses in the early seventies, from Mary Daly's radical philosophy to Rosemary Ruether's feminist theology to the feminist spirituality of *Woman-Spirit* magazine and the feminist witchcraft of Zsuzsanna Budapest. Moreover, liberation theology itself contains more than a dash of Marxism. If religion had joined Marxism in all of these other movements, the gay liberation movement was unlikely to be different.[51]

Noting the mutually hostile relationship between many religious institutions and LGBTIQ people, she makes clear from her interviews how difficult the negotiation can be for LGBTIQ people. Many who still hold dear part or all of their religious belief report that they find it more difficult to "come out as Christian" among other queer people than to come out as queer to straight people.[52] These are the people most in "the market" for their own church.

In her analysis, Wilcox points to five "external factors" that play a significant role in the success of the UFMCC: (1) Perry's use of the language and momentum of the "civil rights movement"; (2) "the evolving trends in theology" (most importantly, liberation theology and ecumenicism); (3) "the growth of evangelical churches in the late 1960's"; (4) "the responses of the mainline churches to homosexuality," many of which were taking up issues of sexuality anew and some of which were beginning to take a softer approach; and (5) "the gay liberation movement."[53] Just as Jerry Falwell's followers are drawn to his ideas by the mix of personal faith tied to political action, members of the UFMCC are called to action on behalf of social justice issues. Falwell's work to reinforce the very master narratives that were being questioned by the rise in movements for social justice had an easier task. Playing on people's fear of change is much easier than convincing people that change is good and right, especially if it feels as if such changes place one's own identity in question.

By creating a denomination that balances a variety of Protestant traditions modified to address issues of sexism and heterosexism within the
denomination's liturgical practices, Perry and his followers have created a
parallel social institution that challenges the heterosexist assumptions of
many mainstream denominations. Melinda Kane argues that the UFMCC
"is, by its very existence, a challenging [protest] organization because
of the strong, assumed contradiction between same-sex sexuality and
religiosity in the United States. The UFMCC has also directly challenged
existing religious norms through its petition to join the National Council
of Churches (NCC), essentially requesting full inclusion in U.S. religious
life."[54] The existence of the church, just as the existence of the Gay Games,
the community centers, and Pride events, enacts a sort of protest by making space for queer identities within and by slowly but insistently taking up
social space in the larger culture. Doing so increases integration of queer
identities into the larger social fabric while also, at least to some degree,
queering that social fabric. While the UFMCC still is denied membership
in the U.S. National Council of Churches and has only fairly recently gained
Official Observer status with the World Council of Churches, inroads made
in local communities and regions create an atmosphere of slow acceptance by the mere repetition of showing up as, in this case, Christian *and*
queer in social contexts that usually deny that possibility. This is especially
true in a media environment that insists on inaccurately representing the
relationship between queers and religion.[55] When we consider what it
takes to make change happen over the long term—changing people's attitudes at the core—such baby steps can add up. The question is, to what?
What kinds of identities are possible through incremental counterstories
in religious contexts? And what role does this play in the larger picture of
work for greater social justice for LGBTIQ people?

Janet Jakobsen and Ann Pelligrini's analysis of the role of religion in
sexual regulation in the United States, *Love the Sin: Sexual Regulation and the
Limits of Religious Tolerance*, offers some useful insights to consider when
attempting to answer these questions. Written as a "utopian dare of a
robust, contestatory, and radically inclusive America—one that lives up to
its promise of freedom and justice for all,"[56] the first half of the book argues,
"If (1) American national identity is dependent upon a sense of moral purpose, and (2) moral sensibilities are collapsed into religious belief, and

(3) sexual behavior is made out to be the last and best measure of the moral, then (4) religiously derived sexual regulation plays a formative role in our national life."[57] In a country based on religious freedom, this is not supposed to be true. Jakobsen and Pelligrini document the many ways that the United States fails to truly afford religious liberty and how particular religious views play a substantial formative role in our national life and thereby deny other religious views a right to define their own, especially as concerns sexuality and gender. They call out the Christian right's claim to "love the sinner, hate the sin" as foundationally antidemocratic in its promotion of a socially denigrating "tolerance" because it shuts out the possibility of any real pluralistic acceptance of religious difference. Their analysis of the basis for many of the arguments in Congress and in our courts in decisions surrounding the regulation of sex shows the degree to which religious freedom and sexual freedom are intimately intertwined such that we cannot truly have one without the other.

With this clearer picture of the degree to which sexual freedom and religious freedom are intertwined, they urge queer activists away from any "born that way" argument. Though this argument is in part based on the feelings many people have regarding their own sexual/gender identity, the authors argue that whether one is born that way or not should not matter at all in a pluralist democracy, as we should be free to express ourselves as consensual adults. Moreover, they argue that the born-that-way argument plays right into arguments for "treating" sexual "deviants" medically and can be used to look for "gay genes" with eugenic intentions just as easily as it can be used to argue for queer rights.

Instead, they argue for treating sexual difference as a social good, just as tastes in food generally are and religious differences should be. In the end, they argue, "[For] those who are in any way different from this dominant identity—whether in terms of race, ethnicity, gender, sexuality, class, physical ability, religion, citizenship, politics, or ethics (in other words, a lot of people)—to be included in the dream of America [should not require] setting aside, hiding, or bracketing what makes them different in the first place. Likeness can be a criterion for private organizations, but it can never be a requirement of belonging in a democracy. . . . Democracy has to be more than coercive homogeneity."[58] Variations on the idea that sexual freedom and religious freedom require each other have recently gained some airtime in relation to "gay marriage." In one case filed just months before the Supreme Court made "gay marriage" legal across the country, some progressive Christian churches in North Carolina brought a lawsuit against the state for denying the same rights to the LGBTQ marriages that their churches performed as it did to marriages performed by more traditional churches.[59] On the other side, a number of church groups and businesses are trying their best to claim their right to deny service or employment to LGBTIQ people.[60]

Jakobsen and Pelligrini's argument is compelling. Whether one is born that way or not should not matter in a pluralist democracy. That seems patently logical. And yet being born that way offers a counterstory against the master narratives that Jakobsen and Pelligrini document as having infected our legal system from the start. Particular religious master narratives have historically held such sway and continue to do so because they are the felt "common sense" of many citizens. Given the extent of such beliefs, how do we get to the place where a preponderance of people feel it is only common sense that consensual adults have a right to their own sexual pleasures and that the law has no business intervening? Is it possible that in some moments and places, within subsets of master narratives, one counterstory, an imperfect counterstory (as all counterstories inevitably are), can produce enough of a shift in the way people feel about LGBTIQ people that these people will come to believe that whether one is born that way or not should not matter?

While the work of the UFMCC actively reinscribes the politically dangerous essentialist "born this way" narratives, this story also importantly speaks to many people in a way that has arguably, at least for the moment, had a role in tipping the scales toward greater acceptance of LGBTIQ people in religious communities. Evidence of this is the increasing acceptance among people of various faith traditions of at least a conservative version of nonnormative sexuality. I do not find this particular gain very gratifying for many of the reasons Jakobsen and Pelligrini articulate, but it seems important to keep in mind the fact that the UFMCC uses a "born this way" argument within a context of evangelistic storytelling. In the context of evangelizing God's love, the claim that "God made me this way and God does not make mistakes" made within a community of people for whom belief in that love is an important part of their identity may be a place where that counterstory is good enough for the time being, even though it should not hold water in any courtroom or with any legislative body that purports to support freedom of religion. Such gains have potential if, through a greater understanding of the need for sexual freedom and religious freedom to go hand in hand, they can be put to use in the service of creating a more robust pluralism.

As LGBTIQ people of faith bridge the world of their faith traditions and the larger LGBTIQ "community," they create ongoing incremental opportunities for sociopolitical and cultural change. But how will these opportunities be used? Will they reinforce us/them values that leave the homeless youth homeless and transgender or more radically queer or atheist members of the "community" in the cold? Or will they create more inclusive communities with space for accepting real religious and sexual freedom? Understanding all these steps as part of a pluralistic movement seems important to more strategic action. In the realm of law, it is definitely important to leave aside the question of whether one is "born this way" or not. As Jakobsen and Pellegrini make clear, true freedom of religion requires sexual freedom and vice versa. But we need more analysis of how counterstories work within different contexts and how these stories are negotiated in the more pluralistic political sphere.

Imagining the world, and ourselves within it, differently can feel freeing, but creating the changes we imagine requires altering the stories that shape us at every level, from the personal to the social, institutional, and legal. Each form of organizing creates its own counterstorying practices within its own context and across contexts. Pride events most obviously counter stories that shame us around our gender and sexual identities. Community centers not only offer physical safe spaces and more consistently present public voices in LGBTIQ communities, but they counter the stories that queers, exiled from families and normative communities, will have no community at all. Queering sports counters that world's stories about queerness and athleticism, especially for athletic white gay men. And queering religion counters the stories that failing to live by sex/gender norms leads to hell, a narrative of damnation that serves as a primary source for many of the stories that attempt to shame us. Each site of organizing has its strengths and limitations. Each one enables healthier identity practices to varying degrees. The practice of queer choral musicking overlaps with and serves similar purposes to all these forms of organizing, though arguably in ways that are both potentially more diffuse and pluralistic. It is impossible to accurately measure to what degree one form of organizing by itself makes a difference because, as with all such work, it is a practice in the mix. But we can analyze the counterstorying practices at work within and across different forms of organizing to assess the purposes they serve and ask how we might leverage our resources for creating change to greater effect. With a better understanding of the processes by which change happens, we might more effectively counterstory, holding and letting go of our identities in healthier ways.

4

Queer Choral Musicking

Cultural Contexts

I've got a vision of a society where gay people have as much freedom as everybody else, and the vehicle that I find as effective as any
right now is the gay choral movement. 'Cause we can bring people
into the tent, and they enjoy it. They get used to us, they get to know
us, and we're not so scary. We also get to do it on our terms and not
theirs. . . . There is something about the universal language of music
that gives people a chance to get out of their own experience. And if
we can make music together, all of a sudden we've gone someplace
that I might not be able to go by myself. –Dan, a longtime singer and
chorus board member

We keep going on; we're relentless. AIDS didn't stop us, breast cancer's not stopping us, Jesse Helms isn't stopping us. He's stepping
down; we're still here, you know. We're still here; we're gonna be here.
–Rick, a director

Queer choral musicking began developing in the early 1970s around the
same time as civil rights and affirmative action were taking more serious
legal hold. Feminism was inspiring everything from the more mainstream
work for the Equal Rights Amendment, to developing local community rape
crisis centers and battered women's shelters, to lesbian feminist music festivals and separatist women's lands. And post-Stonewall gay liberation was
just beginning to get a foothold. Change was in the air. Starting in 1965,
the East Coast Homophile Organizations (ECHO) had been holding "Annual
Reminder" protests every July 4 at Liberty Hall in Philadelphia, proclaiming
the rights of homosexuals to "life, liberty, and the pursuit of happiness."

Stonewall ushered in a new era of more in-your-face protest for queers. People across the country were daring to be out and proud in ways that challenged every denial of people's rights to choose to be with whom they pleased. In Chicago, "Gay Liberation sponsored the first citywide dance at the South Side's Coliseum April 18, 1970, with 2,000 gays and lesbians in attendance. The ACLU worked with activists to make sure police knew that same-sex dancing was not illegal in Illinois. Even some gay bars believed this to be the case, and at least one was picketed until it allowed same-sex partners to dance there."[1] And while there were several events that summer commemorating Stonewall in New York (demonstration), Chicago (march), and San Francisco (gay-in), Los Angeles legally fought for and in the nick of time won the right to legally parade. The years that followed saw queer organizing blossom. Choruses are one of several forms of organizing that expanded to play important cultural roles.

Queer choral musicking shares with each of the four examples of cultural organizing examined in Chapter 3 (Pride, queer community centers, Gay Games, and the UFMCC) some interwoven histories, qualities, and purposes. While the choruses started forming around the same time as the Universal Fellowship of Metropolitan Community Churches (UFMCC in 1968), Pride (1969), and the early community centers (1969), they expanded substantially during the early 1980s, at the same time the Gay Games (1982) came into being. The choruses produce shows that commemorate much more than one particular uprising, as Pride does, and they do so at a full array of community events, from local festivals to rallies to presidential inaugurations. Pride comes once a year, and like other commemorative traditions, it has the potential to serve as a time of annual reflection on where we have come from, where we are, and where we still want to go. But as with other commemorative traditions, it is easily commercialized and loses its power to do much more than ensure a time and place for celebrating whatever Pride currently means to those organizing and participating. Choruses usually perform at their local Pride events, often reflecting and commenting on the current queer state of affairs through musical repertoire and expanding on the seriousness of the commemoration as well as the playfulness and joy of Pride. But beyond their similarities to and connections with annual Pride events, the choruses play a role not unlike the UFMCC insofar as singers meet weekly for a particular form of communing.

Singers meet to practice in sessions that generally run about twice to three times as long as the average weekly church service and often in a more focused and arguably more demanding form of communing. And like both the church and community centers, the choruses offer support to their members. As Ben summed up about his chorus,

> People are helpful. This is a family, and we treat it as such. The cards and flowers go out too [commenting on the birthday celebration at practice]; we have birthday cakes! That is especially amazing for an organization this size. I use this analogy from time to time, but it's been particularly poignant to me since taking on this job [artistic director]. My father is a minister, so I grew up in the church, and in many ways it's very comparable to the social aspect of a church family, where, in many cases, my father's church was a relatively blue-collar congregation. That's the only social group that these people are involved in, and so it is the potluck dinners, it is the, you know, when somebody's not feeling well. You know that you can call such-and-such and they'll give you a ride to the hospital or they'll come over and take care, babysit the kids while you're out doing something with your spouse. I mean, it's exactly that way.

In addition to playing these important social roles for their members, like athletes in the Gay Games, singers practice in order to share their performance with larger audiences, but what they have to present and the identities choral musicking enables are arguably more variable. In overlapping and in different ways than any of these other forms of organizing, queer choral musicking offers interesting opportunities to transform cultural understandings of what it means to be queer both for those who identify as LGBTIQ and for those who may not even recognize the alphabet-soup shorthand. While the UFMCC is expanding the identities possible for people of faith and the Gay Games is expanding the world of sports to be more inclusive, queer choruses are changing the choral world and the attitudes of audiences around the world.

Scope of Queer Choral Musicking

With a conservative estimate of five hundred choruses worldwide, ranging in size from four to around four hundred participants meeting weekly,
each producing on average two to three concerts a year for audiences large
and small, the sheer amount of time spent and number of people involved
in queer choral musicking mean that this form of organizing touches
many people's lives. Three major umbrella organizations in the United
States and Europe—the Gay and Lesbian Association of Choruses (GALA),
Legato, and Sister Singers Network (SSN)—each with international connections, support LGBTIQA choral group development by offering regional,
national, and international conferences and guidance materials on everything from musical techniques, CD production, and touring to political and
social activism through music. They each hold quadrennial choral festivals
(in alternating cycles), offer grants for everything from commissioning new
works to chorus development, and provide a variety of networking support.

The oldest of these organizations, the U.S.-based SSN, was born of feminist movement and is connected with the women's/lesbian music movement
of the 1970s, which saw the development of women's music festivals—a
few of which continue today. While lesbian feminist choruses had been
developing in local communities, SSN came into being in 1980 when, as
their website notes under "Herstory," "Echo (Linda Ray) of the Kansas City
Women's Chorus and Linda Small of the St. Louis Women's Choir started
the Sister Singers Network with a logo, letterhead, and a list of choruses.
It was their vision to create a feminist network of women's choruses
that could learn from each other and come together to share music. The
early SSN choral festivals were part of the Ozark Women's Festivals, until
the SSN outgrew them. The first separate choral festival that was hosted
by the SSN was in Kansas City in 1984."[2] While the network is primarily U.S.
based, as of July 2016 their website lists ninety-three affiliated choruses
(thirty-six of which are "member" choruses), including two from Australia,
five from Canada, one from Croatia, and two from the United Kingdom.
In the past, members have included groups from several other European
countries as well.

The Gay and Lesbian Association of Choruses (GALA) is the largest
of these organizations, with around 200 member choruses and a total of

FIGURE 4.1. Program cover from the first GALA Choral Festival in New York City in 1983, titled "Come Out and Sing Together" (C.O.A.S.T.). Twelve choruses from across the country—one SSAA, one SATB, and the rest TTBB choruses—performed for each other and opened a Festival Chorus performance to the public composed of all 1,200 singers.

393 choruses from around the world (220 from within the United States and the rest among thirty-two other countries from every continent but Africa) listed on their website in December 2015. GALA "was incorporated on July 26, 1983 and is now the leading association committed to serving the GLBT choral movement."[3] Speakers at the festival in summer 2008 announced that GALA at that point had produced some of the largest international choral festivals and was commissioning more original works than any other choral organization. Judging from the prominence of commissioned works throughout the July 2016 Festival in Denver, this changing of the choral repertoire through queer choral musicking continues.

Legato, based in Germany, last reported "104 choirs in 15 [mostly European] countries with more than 3,600 singers,"[4] many of which are not affiliated with either SSN or GALA. As of July 2016, this included a group from Moscow called Russian Secret, which has posted a very daring video on YouTube given the current climate in that country.[5] And at the Various Voices Festival in Dublin in 2014, a group formed of singers from various groups across Asia, Proud Voices Asia, performed after only a few live practice sessions together (as many of the festival choruses did). With live streaming of all the performances, family, friends, and allies from around the world were able to watch.

A number of smaller regional and national festivals have also been developing around the world, some more sporadically than others. For example, Canada has been holding its Unison Festival every four years since 1998 with fifteen to eighteen choruses from across the country participating each time.[6] Mallorca has held two small regional festivals in 2015 and 2016 with four choruses participating each time. And Italy's annual national choral festival, Cromatica, has recently been held twice. The 2016 announcement describes "a great Gala Night, on Saturday 21 [May], at the Auditorium of Milan, a most prestigious theatre for a joyous show with all the Italian LGBT Choirs: 9 choirs, more than 230 singers from Rome, Naples, Padua, Turin, Bologna, Perugia and, of course, Milan. Moreover, the night show will be opened by the most important choir of all, the Rainbow Children Chorus, where daughters and sons of same-sex couples will give voice to their right to be recognized as a whole family together with their parents."[7] Other regional festivals have come and gone and resurfaced over the years, as have the many choruses too underfunded to be consistently maintained but no less engaged in the work. Africa has seen groups surface and fall from the international scene. Latin America has as well, though groups there seem to be gaining staying power, as is true throughout Asia. Increasingly some of the better-funded choruses from wealthier countries and locales are partnering with more challenged groups around the world to develop their voices through choral musicking.

Choral Musicking as Cultural Formation

> I wouldn't probably get the same type of satisfaction singing in a straight chorus as I would singing in a gay and lesbian chorus. I wouldn't feel as welcome. I wouldn't feel a sense of camaraderie that I would in a gay and lesbian chorus, in a straight chorus. . . . I mean, even if they were very welcoming for gays and lesbians, it's different. –Bing, a singer

In 1996, as I stood in the Tampa heat among thousands of queer choral musickers at the doors of the convention center awaiting opening cere-monies for Festival V, I pondered the queer pleasure of choral musicking as a practice for social justice. Christopher Small coined the term *musick-ing*[6] to better express how music is experienced as a set of complex social

FIGURE 4.2. Anna Crusis Women's Choir, shown in this photo at a choral retreat in 1977, formed in Philadelphia in 1975 and is the longest-lived chorus in the movement.

practices. Music is produced within cultural contexts that both express and reproduce cultural values. In his comparative cultural analysis, Small considers every detail surrounding different musicking practices around the world, including space, time, rituals, expectations for performance on the parts of performers and audience members, and relationships among performers and their audiences. He shows how the types of relationships valued by a culture can be understood through the form that any given culture's musicking takes. If, as Small argues, musicking practices embody a culture's socially idealized relationships, then how are queers making use of this particular practice?

Consider, for example, the differences between a tribal drumming circle and a Western classical symphonic performance. Most simply, the former is likely to be communal, participatory, improvisational, and free, with a relatively high level of permeability in terms of performer and audience roles. Anyone might join in. Everyone is likely to know each other, and everyone's participation is encouraged. The point is to celebrate being together through sharing the musical experience. The idealized relationships expressed are communal. In contrast, Small explores the example of the practice of Western symphonic musicking, which tends to focus on dead composers and an obsession with the musical text as an art object. The director in this model functions as a kind of "divine interpreter" of the musical score made "sacred text" in a way that the composers themselves would have found strange. The audience does not actively participate. While there are times that directors decide to break with the formality for a bit, singing and dancing along would certainly not be acceptable in most symphonic performances. For those of us inclined to move or sing along to music, the concert hall seat, no matter how padded, can feel like a straightjacket. Audience members experience the concert very individually, though in the company of hundreds of (mostly) strangers. The faces of both audience members and musicians are often curiously nonresponsive even as the most passionate music is played. It would be hard to tell what any one person is feeling or thinking. Small argues that the idealized relations expressed in this form are abstracted and alienated. Such musicking, for Small, idealizes hierarchy, control, and technique over the human relationships that are core to most other musicking practices.

Choral musicking globally can span these extremes, but as it is prac-ticed in the predominantly white Western queer choral movement, it plays between them. Community choruses in general are almost always local and relatively communal, even when they sing "under" a paid director. The fact is that most community chorus members—straight or queer—must pay dues to be part of the chorus. Almost anyone can sing in a community cho-rus, and many gain pleasure from doing so. In fact, in 2011 Chorus America reported that in the United States, 13 percent of us sing in choruses of some kind,[9] up from the one in ten reported ten years earlier.[10] Because of this difference from generally more professionalized symphonic set-tings, community choral directors are more dependent, to varying degrees, on the singers for their salaries as well as for the quality of the singers' per-formance. The relationship between performer and director is generally somewhat less top-down and more service oriented than the symphonic model of Small's analysis, though there exists a full range of experiences, and some choruses operate in much the same formal way as symphonies.

As with symphonic musicking, community choruses usually perform the majority of their concerts in fairly standard formations, in rows on risers, and often dressed in a formal fashion similar to what symphonic instrumentalists wear—though usually with a little more color or flair. And they generally perform under the direction of a musical director. The audience is expected to remain quiet in the dark during the perfor-mance and to applaud at the proper times, except when invited to sing along or when the performance invites laughter or tears. Western choral musicking, while it can be quite formal in many of the ways that Small finds symphonic musicking to be, is not so neatly pegged. While some of those who go to see, for example, the NYC Gay Men's Chorus may well dress in fur, in general, choral musicking is more widely accessible in many ways than symphonic musicking. Tickets are often more reasonably priced, even when compared to community orchestra performances; the venues in which choruses regularly perform range from the neighborhood cof-feehouse, church, or school to the concert hall; and the repertoire is often more varied. These exceptions matter.

Most choral directors know that their audiences are not as likely to return if they have to listen to a full diet of, say, *liebeslieder*.[11] Repertoires range from opera to popular music, Broadway, and cabaret shows and are performed for a more mixed-class audience than symphonic music or opera generally serves. This requires working between and across standard genres, in some ways working to bridge differences. The extra color of choral costumes might erupt into playful variations with movement for a song or two, breaking the formal frame. Sing-along pieces connect the audience with performers and, in some cases, even the director or pianist will join in the song, thereby further breaking through the alienation upon which Small argues the formality of Western classical musicking practices depends for its abstraction and the illusion of purity and that writers like Alan Bloom find compelling.[12] The relationships among choral audience members, director, and performers are more porous on many levels. For example, those who come to hear a concert often are inspired to join the chorus so that audience members may become chorus members and chorus members may become audience members alternatively over time.

Perhaps the most important difference from symphonic musicking, aside from the fact that the songs have words, is that, even dressed in black on risers with matching black music folders held in front of them, each singer's body *is* the instrument he or she shares. It is an instrument that every audience member knows as well, intimately, in a way they are unlikely to share with any of the instrumentalists in an orchestra. Each voice, the fleshiest of instruments, when blended with others, creates communing in its very form as a soundscape that bathes both singers and audience. This is true for all choral singing, but it resonates in particularly important ways for people who have been denied community or communing and who are working to recognize and value their sense of themselves. Queer choruses use this easily accessible social form of choral musicking, which is structurally communal and potentially erotic, to produce beauty that serves as protest, healing, and community embodied all in the same moment. It lends itself well as a form to counterstorying in music that might be better heard and felt.

Work for social justice is a long-term process, so it is no surprise that, as with all movements for social justice, queer social movement in every form continues to struggle with issues of racism, sexism, classism, ableism, and ageism, as well as internalized homophobia or transphobia. The large majority of GALA choruses, like the participants in the Gay Games, are white and mostly middle class. This could also be said of most of the forms of queer social organizing covered in Chapter 3. White skin and social class privilege both create a greater sense of entitlement that empowers despite whatever else might be oppressive in any given individual's life. Having this privilege offers a relatively easier sense of a right to one's voice in the world and a greater freedom to stand up and claim it with fewer potential repercussions. Importantly, white privilege means one is not potentially torn between alliance to one's race and alliance with queers.

While scholars have yet to adequately study the many ways in which experiences of queerness might vary, a recent study on the difference between the coming out experience of white men and that of Latino men offers evidence that, as one example, the dominant verbal coming-out story serves white men in a way that it does not Latinos. The authors point out that much more research needs to be done, but while verbally coming out serves gay white men's sense of being "true" to themselves as fully autonomous beings, "the closet does not function in the same way for gay Latino men. Gay Latino men already are connected with a broader Latino community that understands and knows of the struggles Latino individuals experience due to their ethnic identity." Because of this, "gay Latino men utilize a different way of expressing their gay identity (and still feel authentic in their self-presentation) where verbal disclosure may not be a priority"[13] without suffering the sense of being closeted that white men tend to feel in comparison to what would be their otherwise privileged positions. While we can only speculate on this point here, the white Western choral form that dominates queer choral musicking practices may be both a symptom and a cause of this race/class self-selection within queer choral musicking. Some examples suggest this might be at least part of the case.

The most notable exceptions to the predominant whiteness of the choral movement in the United States include New York City's Lavender Light: The Black and People of All Colors Lesbian and Gay Gospel Choir and San Francisco's Transcendence Gospel Choir—the first transgender choir in the GALA network that, while small, is quite diverse. That these choruses identify specifically as gospel choirs suggests a correlation between the type of choral musicking practice that comforts and empowers both those who sing and their audiences and participants' related social histories. In terms of style, both choruses revel in the life-affirming nature of the gospel tradition. Contrary to the relative formality of much choral musicking, these choruses arguably build on the successes of earlier choruses, such as Elmer Keeton's WPA chorus, to use the more participatory call-and-response form of gospel as their primary focus (as opposed to simply adding the occasional gospel arrangement for some "ethnic flavor," as predominantly white choruses often do). In doing so, the gospel choruses claim the cultural space of the concert hall while breaking beyond the formality of the Western choral form. If you are not up and moving as much as you are able during one of their concerts, you are arguably not alive.

Further evidence of a correlation between choral musicking practices and ethnic self-selection is offered by the history of MUSE: Cincinnati's Women's Choir, perhaps the only chorus within queer choral movement that started out predominantly white but has successfully become a more racially integrated group. MUSE has worked strategically in a racially divided city to successfully reach out across racial divides through their musical practices. An important component of their strategy was to dare to sing outside the choral comfort zones of many of their white lesbian/feminist members. Many of the singers had rejected singing religious music at all based on predominantly white feminist principles that read traditional religious music as supporting patriarchal values. According to some of the long-term members, facing the cultural fact (as well as its potential emotional implications) that for African Americans the gospel choral traditions belong to a long history of fighting for social justice enabled white members to loosen the parameters of their own antipatriarchal practice in order to better enact their antiracist values. In the interest of fulfilling their mission, according to their history, "MUSE began her second decade by joining five other choirs nationwide in the New Spirituals Project, which featured new works by women composers in the African-American and Afro-Caribbean tradition. The New Spirituals Project concerts began a long-running collaboration with Linda Tillery, well known vocalist and African-American folklorist from the San Francisco Bay Area."[14] They are a much richer chorus for the effort.

Choral musicking is, after all, a cultural form, and queer choruses, as we shall see, arguably do as much work to heal and empower those who sing in them as they do to create change in the larger culture. A level of self-selected separatism seems somewhat inevitable in the process of initial movement development. We see this in every social movement for justice—a need for safe space for the people who are being denied full human rights. Such separatism may continue to be a necessary antidote to oppression for as long as any oppression exists. Just as with all trauma and healing, everyone heals in one's own time frame and manner. Nevertheless, it is important to regularly assess where privilege creates greater safety for the relatively privileged. Where do our counterstorying practices, like the counterstorying practices of the Gay Games (discussed in Chapter 3), keep in place or fail to adequately challenge related parts of the master narratives that leave others out of the new ways of being human we are constructing in our counterstories? If, for example, a group's mission includes creating greater social justice, then in order to serve that mission, it is necessary to assess relative privilege with oppression. When we understand oppressions to be related, then standing up for and with others means standing up for ourselves (a reality that choral singing arguably musically enacts). Choruses and other groups organizing for social justice do well to ask, How might we be better allies working to end a spectrum of injustices? How might we use whatever privileges we have to make the world a better place for everyone, especially those who are oppressed in ways that we are privileged? Where might our group be most effective? More choruses in this movement are asking these questions.

Choruses also struggle with a variety of access/inclusion issues. For example, over the course of the 1980s, many choruses followed in the footsteps of earlier women's/feminist music productions by including American Sign Language (ASL) interpreters as an integral part of their performances (some of whom occasionally delightfully upstage the choruses during performances). Most choruses make serious efforts to make both their practice spaces and their performance venues accessible, efforts perhaps hastened by the onslaught of HIV/AIDS. Many choruses offer scholarships for members who cannot afford dues, music, costumes, or travel. And many choruses offer free or discounted tickets for various groups. Most choruses struggle with being more inclusive or taking on broader issues of inequities in the substantive ways that would be necessary to render them more truly diverse, but they do take notes from each other's successes.

Unlike non-LGBTIQA choruses, which tend to be primarily "mixed"—soprano, alto, tenor, bass (SATB)—the queer choral movement in the United States started with mostly separate (in some cases, separatist) first SSAA and then TTBB choruses,[15] with SATB choruses generally developing later.[16] Each developed out of different, but related, social histories. Lesbians and gay men have strategically come together socially for centuries, either as hetero covers for each other or to fight back against heterosexism, but there is still antipathy among gay men for lesbians and vice versa. And identifying as lesbian or gay does not create an automatic sense of community with bisexuals, transgender people, transsexuals, intersex people, two-spirits, or those who identify as queer, nor vice versa among any of these identities. In fact, it can produce quite the opposite effect. As Alice, a bisexual singing with a mixed chorus, noted,

> I found that [for] bisexual people, there is some small community among the queer community that is still like, "You're weird. I am weird, but you're weirder." And it's kinda this sense that I got when I got there [with her chorus] at first. I had this one-off comment from this one girl who is not even there anymore about how weird bisexual people are, and I just shut off right away. OK, I had a boyfriend at that time and I [was] not going to tell anyone that I like girls, whatever. [Laughs] Yeah, so I just shut off, . . . and it took me three years to slowly dig back into it again and be OK, this is me!

Contrary to the common referencing today of "the LGBT community," that community, such as it exists, has been stitched together in the public imagination (including in the imaginations of those who identify as some part of it) as a way to strengthen the movement as a whole. But given the shared, if much differently experienced, oppression based on not fitting sex/gender norms, coming together across these differences has been essential to making movement happen. As Hsien Chew of the Pink Singers and Proud Voices noted of his queer choral musicking experience, "People always talk about LGBT community and, to me, I don't know if there is such a thing as LGBT community because it's so diverse. But if you talk about LGBT choral community, that definitely exists."[17]

SSAA Choruses

Women's/lesbian/feminist or SSAA[18] choruses began forming in the early 1970s as part of the larger women's music movement. The power of women's music movement and its form of musicking deserve much fuller study in their own right,[19] as the movement spawned festivals, recording companies, and tours for feminist musicians of all sorts, but with a distinctly lesbian flavor, some of which continues today. Choral groups like New York City's Women Like Me in 1971 were part of this cultural boom. As Catherine Roma notes in her article "Women's Choral Communities: Singing for Our Lives," "[Their] members were involved in reproductive health issues, abortion rights, equal pay and workplace issues, the ERA, the post-Stonewall movement for gay/lesbian civil rights, and/or the international peace movement. Thus, the choirs became the musical arm of the political activism of the singers, as symbolized in the Holly Near song, 'Singing for Our Lives.' Their multifaceted mission statements speak of musical excellence and social change as complementary goals and objectives."[20] SSAA choruses that participate actively in queer choral movement have generally had more complex identities as feminist as well as lesbian than the TTBB choruses; often SSAA choruses have missions that challenge both sexism and heterosexism, variously expressing the intention of challenging all forms of oppression. Because of this more broadly focused social justice mission, unlike the majority of the TTBB choruses, SSAA choruses have historically had straight as well as bisexual and lesbian members.

SSAA choruses, especially those that predate the TTBB choruses in their areas, are likely to be more democratic in their structures, less hierarchical, more consensus oriented, and less corporately oriented in terms of fundraising. They more often function on smaller scales, with smaller budgets, and depend on more volunteer labor. Most obviously, women still earn substantially less than men across the board and therefore have less to spend in general. The feminist ethic of "pay more if you can, less if you can't" also remains more common in terms of both membership dues and concert tickets. While there are SSAA groups as large as 250, the average is closer to thirty, and a chorus of ten to twelve is not uncommon. For these reasons, among others, many of the groups started small, and those that lasted have tended to stay substantially smaller than many of the TTBB choruses.

For example, one of the midwestern choruses came together in 1976 after some of the founding members were inspired by the Michigan Womyn's Music Festival, and word spread of the (now eldest GALA chorus), Anna Crusis. Sandy remembers that her chorus "started as a bunch of women who wanted to sing. We were not in school anymore; most of us were not church connected, so we didn't have those easy choirs to join. So we got together in living rooms, and this was a time when leadership was getting sort of a bad name; it was seen as synonymous with 'the patriarchy equals bad,' so nobody would take the lead even to say 'let's do this as a warm-up,' or 'let's sing that song,' or 'let's do it this way.'" It was not long before they hired a director, but they continued to sing together more as a community practice than as a performing group, only sharing their musicking in small doses and venues.

Slowly they started building their sense of their own voices and their importance to the larger community over time: "We would sing a song or two here or there, but not a lot in the first four years. We finally did our first self-produced concert in 1983 or 1984, where we actually hired the hall and set up the microphones, and did this all ourselves, and charged admission. Before that, we had performed at the women's coffeehouse a few times, and sometimes we were the full set of the performance there." This transformation from a safe space in which women sang with and for each other into a full chorus performing for their community did not always happen. There are still groups for which singing with and for each other is their primary purpose and many more that have gathered and dissolved over time, having more or less fulfilled this purpose.[21] Many women report how healing this space is or was for them in a world that remains largely misogynistic and heterosexist. Such groups have served as places for women, especially lesbians, to test out their voices, to develop trust among other women, and to come to know and trust some of their own strengths.

For those who might not know the history—and to frame the controversies, contentions, and struggles for SSAA choruses that developed through the 1970s—this was a time when, for example, it was completely legal across the United States for a husband to rape his wife. While the

Equal Employment Opportunity Commission (EEOC) had been estab-
lished for ten years, it had only recently been given any real teeth. While
cases were working their way through the courts (the tedious slowness of
which makes any activist groan), women were regularly denied opportunities for entry into all sorts of professions without proving exceptional
skills or abilities substantially beyond that required of any man to enter.
Beyond employment, women still had few rights and were barred from all
sorts of arenas of power or glory—even something as simple as the right
to run marathons was denied because women were considered incapable
of such strenuous activity and as requiring protection from it. Without
the Equal Rights Amendment (ERA), women have to battle for their rights
in each area of their lives (e.g., housing, banking, health care, child care)
separately on local, state, and national levels, much as gay rights activists have done and as feminist activists continue to do. And although
many states now have a fair amount of protection for women's full citizenship, the ERA, which would have barred discrimination in every arena
across the country, contrary to popular assumptions, never did get
ratified—another victim of backlash. In this context of contention, many
feminist choruses discussed everything the chorus did in terms of how it
supported or failed to support women.

Sandy recalls one way this questioning of every decision that the chorus made in feminist terms took shape. They commissioned one of their
first pieces in the late 1970s and considered hiring a man. Not only would
the chorus be giving money to a man rather than a woman, but their safe
space would not feel as safe for some members. The composer wanted to
come and listen to their voices to compose a piece specifically for them:

> He writes wonderful music, and this piece is no exception; it was
> just beautiful. Narration in songs, this piece is about persecution:
> persecution of witches, persecution of women as witches anytime
> they stepped out of line. Just beautiful poetry and beautiful music
> and controversy in the chorus about a guy writing it and him com-
> ing in to hear our voices so he could write the music appropriate to
> our vocal range and tone. Some people just had a bird about that.
> Well, you know, [it is a] perennial issue, and this was [in] the days
> of separatists and a time when women's chorus was women's space.

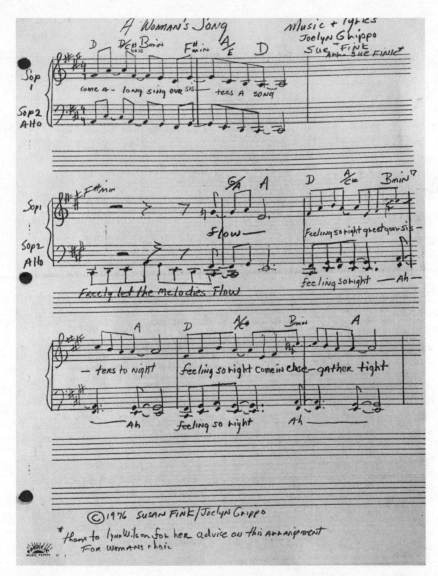

FIGURE 4.3. First page of a handwritten score from "A Woman's Song" (1973) by Joe-lyn Grippo and Sue Fink, composers of "Leaping Lesbians" made popular by, among others, Meg Christian.

It was a safe place for people who didn't have another safe place in their [lives]. And I look back now, and I say, "Oh, my gosh; we were fussing about that?" But at that time, that was a legitimate fuss.

While, as Sandy suggests, times and perceptions have changed, many of the women's choruses maintain a feminist and often even broader social justice analysis of their work.

Although musical needs and desires morph, because of the time period in which many of the SSAA choruses came into being, their roots are more in folk/women's music than any of the other types of choruses. They have historically been more likely to partner with Holly Near than Bette Midler in concert, for example, though through the experiences of musical exchanges at the quadrennial festivals, there is increasingly cultural exchange among all the different sorts of choruses. In fact, according to several TTBB chorus interviewees who have been part of the movement from the early years, some of the early SSAA choruses served as inspiration for the development of their own choruses, and the SSAA choruses have also often inspired greater social consciousness in some of the TTBB choruses. One might argue conversely that some of the TTBB choruses have inspired some of the SSAA choruses to greater performance flair.

TTBB Choruses

A few TTBB choruses developed in the late 1970s, but many more came into being at the time of the AIDS crisis and its aftermath. The first two were New York's Gotham Male Chorus in 1977, which became the Stonewall Chorale, a mixed chorus, in 1980, and the San Francisco Gay Men's Chorus (SFGMC), which came into being in 1978. In 1979, the Gay Men's Chorus of Los Angeles (GMCLA), the Seattle Men's Chorus (SMC), and the Windy City Gay Chorus (WCGC) were all founded. Many more across the country were inspired by the SFGMC's 1981 national tour. Given the developing AIDS crisis, these choruses soon served a pressing need for community in a time of profound loss and cultural backlash against civil rights, feminism, and gay liberation. It is impossible to say what role the choruses may have played had AIDS never happened, but that the TTBB choruses in particular played a

FIGURE 4.4. Members of the San Francisco Gay Men's Chorus at the Jefferson Memorial on their 1981 tour that inspired the beginnings of so many choruses around the United States.

very important role for gay men through that crisis and even today is amply evident throughout the archival materials and interviews.

Many of the TTBB choruses maintain memorial places on their websites and mark as part of their histories the number of members they have lost to AIDS—some having lost more members over the years than their substantial current chorus sizes of several hundred. Many interviewees discussed periods in which they feared the mourning would never end as well as the importance of the chorus in their own lives and the lives of the community both in commemorating the dead and in keeping the joy of living in the foreground. In his 2008 study of the San Francisco Gay Men's Chorus, Russell Hilliard documents the devastation:

> During this period (1980s), the chorus's membership decreased from over 200 members to a mere 60. Many members died during this time, and others were so devastated by the overwhelming grief, they left the San Francisco area. The chorus sang at memorial services and funerals and, at times, these services took place on a weekly basis. . . . In memory of the chorus members who died,

the chorus created a fifth section (choirs have only four musical sections), and the names of the deceased choral members are still printed in concert programs as the fifth section. There are over 200 names included in the fifth section of the chorus.[22]

Dennis Coleman, artistic director of the Seattle Men's Chorus, in his brief history of the choral movement in 1999, lists several goals of the choruses beyond the musical: "(1) to structure a musical community that provides emotional and spiritual support for its members, (2) to nurture positive self-esteem and pride within the chorus and the lesbian and gay community, (3) to care for member singers affected by HIV/AIDS and other traumatic life experiences, and (4) to build bridges of understanding, respect, and cooperation between the lesbian and gay community and society as a whole."[23] It is, of course, impossible to gauge the degree to which queer choral movement was fed by and grew in response to the convergence of backlash like Anita Bryant's "Save Our Children" campaign as well as the onslaught of AIDS, but there is certainly no question in the minds of those I interviewed that the choruses played an important role in responding to the hatred that the backlash produced. Geo simply affirmed, "There are members of the chorus who have just come out. The chorus is so affirming for them especially; it opens up a social world they've never known. Hello! It opened up a social world for me that I had never known. All of a sudden there was this huge family." He added, "I think for our gay audience, we consistently affirm who we are, they are, by doing what we do. And we do so much educating; it's all about educating the general society about who we are as gay men and women, bisexual, transgender."

As I began this study, an increasing number of HIV-positive people no longer had a death sentence hanging over their heads, and a number of members of TTBB choruses in particular discussed with me the changes happening in their groups as a result of this shift. In the aftermath of such great losses but also in the atmosphere of AIDS activism and increasingly robust (if more conservative) queer organizing, the sense of purpose shifted. Exploring this shift in more depth, Ben posited,

I think as a community, we as gays and lesbians, in the last two decades that the chorus was around, it was more about—yes, we are all in the same place; we're all together—a solidarity kind of thing, and it didn't really matter what we were singing. The fact that we were there, singing it together and singing to our own, was important enough; it was a statement. . . . And we've gotten past that, thank God, but now let's celebrate the fact that we've gotten past it. Let's celebrate that we celebrate our lives, celebrate our uniqueness and our differences. . . . [This] chorus is definitely in a mode of celebrating your lives, whether that means a very intimate moment as the cabaret reflected or the funniness or the outrageousness or the ridiculousness of some of our lives too. Still celebrating it nonetheless. We're as diverse and different as any other group, and probably more so.

SATB Choruses

The importance of men's choruses is evident; they have their own sound, [and] there's a feeling of brotherhood. Women's groups and feminist singers, there's a specific need for that and to have its own history, and then there's the mixed, and I think that is the one that is coming into its own now. –Rick, a mixed chorus director

There's other stuff that other choruses do to be a little bit more . . . activist, I suppose. Our chorus is not really that type of political activism as much, but I think there is something to be said about really pointing out the beautiful and the moving in that part of the gay and lesbian community. Bringing that out is probably something that a lot of people that are homophobic or very ignorant never even had that experience before. So I think that there is something to be said about giving people that. . . . So for me, it's like if you can change one heart or one mind by that, then it's worth it. –Shane, a singer

Mixed (SATB) choruses in the United States mostly have later and more various beginnings as well as generally more diversity of all kinds, though most are still predominately white. Smaller communities have been more likely to start with a mixed chorus, while larger metropolitan areas in the United States mostly started with separate SSAA and TTBB choruses. As

Gene, a director who had started with a TTBB chorus in the 1980s and then a SATB chorus in the 1990s, later reflected,

> Interestingly enough, I had my own preconceived idea that I would not see the closeness, the intimacy, the support between our individual members in a mixed chorus that I saw in the men's chorus. I think there are a couple of reasons for that. First, I didn't know the women's community. Second, when I started the mixed chorus in the early nineties, . . . AIDS was such a strong impact, was being so impactful on the men's choruses. In four and a half years, we'd already lost thirty-six members. . . . I thought, what will bring these people together? Because AIDS had certainly brought the men's choruses together. And I found that to be wrong. What brought them together was a love of the music and newfound friendship. In many ways, it was their differences that caused them to be closer as a group.

Members of mixed choruses speak passionately about the importance of coming together to bridge their differences, and Rick, another director of a mixed chorus, noted,

> I would say that the group [his chorus] seeks to change the way the GLBT community relates to itself first of all and that we are often facilitators for collaborations and working together, fundraising for groups outside of ourselves. In fact, mostly we do fundraisers for other people. For example, a recent one was when we had developed an arts consortium with the visual artists, with the Gay and Lesbian Band, and with the Men's chorus and ourselves. . . . And that arts consortium went and used all of its resources to provide a benefit day of wellness and health for a project for lesbians with cancer.

Evidence in my research suggests that bisexual, transgender, and gender-queer people have been more often found (or perhaps are more out) in mixed groups than in single-gender-identified choruses. In fact, several transsexuals interviewed were explicit in describing how the mix of gays and lesbians together balanced the harsher edges of gender norming that happens, especially in men's choruses, though as more people in the movement have become more educated about differences within "the community," increasing efforts have been made to reach out across our many differences. The newest additions to this movement are youth choruses and transgender choruses, all of which are at this time SATB and are far more likely to be comfortable with calling themselves "queer."

The fact that the mixed choruses category is a slowly growing segment of the GALA network (up to 33 percent of total choruses listed in 2016 from 20 percent in 2001) seems to me indicative of several slow shifts currently in process within queer cultural movements: a greater questioning of the categories of gender as well as sexuality, a slowly growing acceptance of a broader range of gender and sexual identities and practices, a growing understanding of the importance of women's issues to LGBTIQ issues, and a resultant willingness to ally more purposefully with each other. One small example of such shifts in thinking as they play out in choral practice is evidenced in a recent statement on the website of the Renaissance City Choir of Pittsburgh, Pennsylvania. Instead of referring to all tenors and basses as "men" and all sopranos and altos as "women," they have chosen to ungender these voicings: "In 2013, as an effort to be more welcoming to transgender individuals whose voices may not match their gender identity, we began referring to the two sections of our Renaissance City Choir as the Tenors/Basses and the Sopranos/Altos. In this way and in all ways, we hope to be welcoming to all who wish to find community with us and join in song."[24] While the SATB choruses are more likely to have moved more openly in this direction than the SSAA or TTBB, there is evidence of a growing acceptance of challenging gender categories across the movement. As Gene summarized,

> I saw [the choruses] be the family as people came out to themselves and their families and then became orphaned by families that turned them out. And their chorus truly became their family, and their support system, and the support system for men as they became more sick. People took care of them and took them into

FIGURE 4.5. A portion of Desert Voices: Arizona's Premiere Gay and Lesbian Chorus enjoying a moment after a community performance in Tucson, Arizona, 2003.

> their homes. . . . We sing not only for our lives but for the impact that we've had on each other, and the way we have built our own family and our own community has just been dynamic and dramatic.

Although most queer choruses perform a wide range of music (some do focus on specific forms such as madrigals, barbershop, or spirituals), the women's groups still tend toward performing music that is more feminist or social-justice-oriented with lyrics that are more overtly activist. They are more likely to perform works by women composers and often perform more folk-based repertoires. The men's groups tend toward more classically choral, pop, and/or Broadway-oriented repertoires. They are less likely to be overtly activist, except perhaps around gay rights or AIDS issues. The mixed groups show somewhat greater diversity in repertoire as well as gender, probably due to the need to address the desires of their broader constituencies. However, it is important to note that these generalized distinctions, truer in years past, are slowly fading as groups increasingly are inspired by each other's work.

Coming Together

I need this chorus in my life; they were brought into my life at a very
important time, and I recognize it and I cherish it, and I will always. I
hope it never ends, but you know, if it does, I will look back at this time
as one of the real cornerstones of my life that helped me find out who
I *truly* am and to be comfortable with it, to be able to articulate it and
to share it. —Rick

Festivals and leadership conferences where the various choruses come
together have offered rich opportunities for queer choral musickers and
allies to learn much more not only musically but also about the diversity
of sexualities, identities, social investments, and politics in their ranks.
It's important to note that unlike many choral festivals, queer festivals are
not competitive; they are profoundly celebratory. Every chorus is cheered,
from the smallest and least prepared to the grandest, the wildest, or the
most elegant. While musical excellence is certainly a goal, perhaps Mike,
the sound engineer whom I interviewed at one festival and who has
recorded everyone from Grammy winners to child prodigy performers, said
it best: "I wasn't a big fan of choir music until I came here. It's probably
the choir music I have been exposed to. It's unbelievable—I think I will be
listening to a lot of this in my car and on my iPod. . . . I think that people
can tell whether there is a real joy in the creation of the music, and I think
that in these [queer] choruses there is a tremendous joy in the creation
of this music." Expressing joy in who we are with each other in an atmosphere of acceptance of differences rather than discrimination against and
rejection of those differences remains an important and powerful act that
challenges both external and internal oppression. It is a physical counterstorying that, as Hilde Lindemann suggests, is necessary for change, effectively contesting the cultural shaming that persists.

These meetings have not always been easy. The clashes between values have occasionally interrupted the sharing of joy. When what one group
finds funny another finds offensive, there are bound to be some sparks.
One of the more contentious examples took place at the 1992 GALA Festival in Denver. An interviewee who was part of the group that registered
this protest reported on how their group came to stand together to make

their statement. Setting the context of her feminist chorus at the time, Sandy explains: "In the early nineties, we got very serious politically about antioppression work. There were some people in the group that were very vocal about this, and we started taking it very seriously and doing a lot of education of ourselves about it, challenging of each other." When one of the men's choruses performed "a song about Columbus and his men coming over, it was [a] very campy, very funny song, very well done," but the feminist chorus felt it denigrated Native Americans. Obliged by their own antiracist mission, they spoke up. She noted, "It's one thing for gay people to camp up gay stereotypes about ourselves, but it's another thing to stereotype the Indians that actually welcomed the new people." After much discussion and processing, the group drafted a statement that they read from the stage in the middle of their own performance: "We got hate mail. . . . We were hissed on the stage, and the audience started arguing amongst themselves, and we just froze for a minute ourselves and then went into our next song. We got support; we got crap." In retrospect, she felt that her chorus could have done a better job of confronting the issue by discussing it first with the chorus in question, perhaps developing some kind of statement together. Nevertheless, in the end she felt "that event caused a lot of GALA people to start thinking in terms of, 'Hey, gays are not the only oppressed people in the world, and it will not do for us to be singing about [how] the Indians looked threatening.'" Certainly a review of the shows, lyrics, and other choral materials over the years bears out a growing sensitivity to a wider range of differences, even if choruses have not always actively taken up antiracist or other more broadly social-justice-oriented attitudes and practices.

The choruses have come together and have grown in terms of their levels of acceptance and ability to bridge differences. I have documented changes in the tenor of audience comments since my first GALA Festival in 1996 as well as from reports of earlier festivals. At the 1996 festival in Tampa, Florida, for example, transgender issues were barely recognized at all, and more openly sexist remarks were not uncommon in the predominantly male world of the festivals. In spite of the fact that men still outnumber women and transgender folks by a large margin at more recent festivals, the tone has shifted to one of greater mutual support. At the 2004 GALA Festival in Montreal, the first transgender chorus performed to warm support from the audience. More recently, the Los Angeles Gay Men's Chorus has actively sponsored Trans Chorus LA as part of its outreach.[25] Moreover, an example of consciousness about the need for TTBB choruses to support women's issues is the commissioning of "Sing for the Cure: Proclamation of Hope," premiered and recorded by Turtle Creek Chorale with the Women's Chorus of Dallas in 2000 to raise awareness about

FIGURE 4.6. 1993 GALA Leadership conference cover.

breast cancer. "Sing for the Cure" has been performed by a number of the larger men's choruses in conjunction with their local sister choruses and was performed by participants from the U.S. choruses at the Various Voices Festival in London in May 2009.

When asked in surveys and interviews and in conversations and workshops, LGBTIQA chorus members in the United States and Europe report that their choruses serve as support groups, nonreligious spaces for spiritual experience and expression, and places for excelling both individually and as a team (this latter seemingly a stronger emphasis in the United States than in Europe). The choruses help develop pride in members and their communities. In the process of developing choral members' voices individually and as a group, as well as performing a variety of regular and repeated voicings of queer experiences as human experiences, the evidence shows that they not only support members to develop leadership skills that carry over into other work for social change but regularly create spaces for creative counterstorying.

Chorus missions articulate visions and goals that range from assimilationist to radical around sexual and gender norms. Finding the balance between art and activism in organizations that attempt to engage both to varying degrees creates ongoing tensions, with some choruses emphasizing one over the other. In order to deal with such differences among members or to incorporate versions of gender/sexuality that might not be as comfortably taken on by the whole group, choruses might split or develop ensembles to perform material that might be more musically and/ or ideologically challenging. Interestingly, the ways in which choruses tend to creatively deal with these tensions suggest richer possibilities in queering culture through the use of choral musicking than might be possible in the realms of religion or sports.

Clearly choral music production has been a compelling way for many to organize for social change. Almost all the mission statements of choruses and the umbrella organizations spell out variations on several important elements: building community, strengthening voices, and providing outreach for greater social justice. As with all the cultural organizing outlined here, building community plays an important role because that is one of the primary forms that the oppression of queer people has taken: first through the legal and sometimes violent denial of the right to gather (expressed again in the Pulse nightclub massacre in Orlando, Florida) and the concurrent cultural stories that deny the existence of any such community or right to community. The choruses use a social form, choral musicking, that is foundationally communal and produces beauty in the service of protest, healing, and community embodied all in the same moment. There is a reason tears mixed with smiles are a common response in the choral performances and festivals.

So many times in interviews, people choked up and struggled for words to express just how important their choruses were to them. One need only check out the YouTube video "GALA—Songs of Courage" for examples of how readily people are moved to tears when trying to articulate what their choruses mean to them.[26] A number of important themes are repeated throughout my interviews with chorus members, directors, and audience members about how participants view the power of queer choral musicking. Shane, a singer in a midwestern mixed chorus responded this way when asked what he thought was important about the work his chorus does:

> It's kind of like how many people have taken back the word *queer* or *faggot*, those type of words, and turned them around into something more positive. I think music can really do that—become a vehicle for that type of change. It's pretty hard to demonize a group of people when you had that group of people in an experience that has really moved you emotionally. It's hard to demonize people after that. . . . That's how I look at it, that's how I view it, to take something with a negative connotation and make it beautiful, and to make something beautiful.

Toward the end of this statement, where he repeats himself, he paused several times, thinking about how to say it, and he finally landed on making "something beautiful" out of "something with a negative connotation."

Bing offered a story of the power of music to stir emotion: "I mean, just in our last concert, there were a few songs where it was close to tears, you know. I mean, those are very powerful words and the music is so wonderful. I mean, that's the one thing with the music: even if there's no words, sometimes just music is very emotional and can bring those type of feelings out just from the music itself." The ability to open oneself and others to experiences, often transcendent places "that I might not be able to go by myself," recurs across the interviews and speaks to the way that choral musicking, especially queer choral musicking, does what Hilde Lindemann argues is a foundational moral act: the choruses "hold" well identities that otherwise are poorly "held" and/or "let go" by cultural narratives. Participants report being opened up to themselves and others in language that is generally reserved for love.

5

Choral Technologies for Queering

> Choose a box! Choose a box! . . .
> We're just doing what we're told.
> Now would you please step in the mold?
> Choose the F or choose the M![1]

Thirty singers stand spread across three levels of the five-level risers that easily hold two hundred. They are dressed mostly in black, some in dresses of varying lengths and styles and most in pants and shirts that range from tunic style to a variety of dress shirts. The majority are wearing a rainbow array of ties in various forms of knots, most around the neck, some worn as sashes. As their director motions to them, the singers raise their forearms into a caricature of a formal opera singing pose: elbows slightly lifted with the arms across the diaphragm, fingers cupped into each other with the right hand on top. In unison they primly sing, "Choose a box." And the hall bursts into laughter.

The setting could not be more formal. The Mormon Tabernacle Choir or the U.S. Army Chorus would happily perform in this hall. There are comfortably lush seats and room between the rows to move. The sound is excellent. The lighting is nuanced. The tech people are top-notch. In its regular lineup, the theater stages Broadway plays, musical theater, dance, and opera. The space, like all such performance spaces, is designed to focus the audience's attention in specific ways, to place a high value on what happens on stage. This architectural design encourages a quieting of the self to give full attention to the show. The structure itself "authorizes" whatever graces the stage.

Each type of show has its own genres, traditions, costumes, and expectations. In this context, variations on traditions signal new meanings.

Traditionally formal choral attire ("men" in tuxedos and "women" in matching, or at least similar, black dresses, nylons, and closed-toed shoes— and those are the only two gender choices) signals the high-art status of the music and suggests that the singers take their art seriously and expect the audience to do the same. In addition, a uniform look makes the individual blend into the group in a manner that mirrors the musical form of voices blending. Ideally, only in a solo should an individual voice be discernable from the ensemble sound. While many of the TTBB choruses in the festival perform in tuxes, most of the choruses have worked to develop some balance of variations between the traditional and something that signals "we're queer."

This chorus's variety in black with a touch or two of rainbow coloring is one of the most common variations of choral attire at the 2016 GALA Festival, especially for the SATB groups. It nods to the formality with primarily black but allows the form the black takes to vary. No two outfits are exactly the same, creating a sense of individuals who are acting intentionally together. And when they take their caricature opera-singer stance in unison, we know that they are about to poke fun in some way at the very tradition they are engaging in. Garden-variety choruses do this on occasion as well. The standard repertoire offers songs that make fun of every aspect of choral singing, some of which are performed at the festival. But this song calls into question a category that even lesbians, bisexuals, and gays still tend to naturalize in the binary form: gender. This concert block suggests that genderqueer is the new gay.

Because of its formal traditions, the practice of choral musicking offers a range of opportunities for queering and thereby for creating space for people to be otherwise, to imagine and enact being something other than the norm. From name choice to mission statements, advertising materials and arenas, organizational models, audition practices, repertoire choices, performance spaces, costuming, and staging, each chorus has opportunities for queering that might open and/or foreclose what identities they endorse. Each choice is an opportunity to counterstory.

How "out" the chorus will be and in what ways remain an ongoing matter of debate within and among choruses. Especially in earlier years, such matters were often hotly debated. More recently a question for older choruses has been whether and how to change their names to be more

inclusive. On just the level of names, for example, the Seattle Men's Chorus and their sister chorus, the Seattle Women's Chorus, while clearly gay
identified in their repertoire, in their mission statements, and on their
websites, are not as "out" in name as the San Francisco Gay Men's Chorus,
Portland Lesbian Choir, or Sing OUT! mixed chorus. Should a group out
itself on posters and take the chance of losing possible audience members before they get the chance to "prove" themselves (or perhaps more
accurately, seduce audience members) as well as taking a greater chance
on violence? Or is it better to wait to win the hearts (or at least the ears) of
potential audience members before outing the group? And how might that
play out differently in one place than another? At one point, the politics
were so hot that at an early GALA Festival, some report that the Turtle
Creek Chorale (TCC), the men's chorus from Dallas, was booed by some
audience members for failing to be adequately "out." While GALA's member choruses have grown less strident with each other over this issue, it
is also interesting to note some of the patterns and changes over time in
this regard.

Very few SSAA choruses that identify themselves with the larger queer
choral movement use "lesbian" in their names, though they include lesbian issues as part of their focus on feminism and greater social justice.
Anna Crusis, the chorus considered the grandmother of choruses in this
movement, speaks to this and their process of naming themselves on their
website: "The choir's unusual name has its origins in the Greek word 'ana-
crusis,' a word used in music to describe an 'upbeat' or 'feminine' entrance
to a phrase. Physically, it may be described as the precise moment of
anticipation and exhilaration, which occurs as a singer takes a quick, deep
breath before vocalizing. The choir finds the phrase fitting for the purpose
of defining ourselves in relation to music, a philosophy of feminism and
the joy of performing."[2] Those who experience heterosexism as another
form of sexism and understand it to be related to other "-isms" tend to
more carefully choose language in ways that will resist the gendered norms.

This speaks to one of the challenges in bringing lesbians together with
gay men, who do not often experience the connections between sexism
and heterosexism to the same degree. This difference in experiences is no
doubt part of why SATB choruses in the United States generally developed
later—most not until the late 1980s and early 1990s. It is important to note

FIGURE 5.1. Anna Crusis's 1978 concert flyer.

that this time period coincides with the period during which deaths from AIDS were mounting, as was the backlash against homosexuality, both of which brought lesbians out in greater numbers to organize around these issues. Given the support lesbians offered gay men during the height of the AIDS crisis[3] personally and politically, certainly lesbians and gay men were coming together to work against their shared oppression, and this included singing together in greater numbers. This most likely played a part in why SATB choruses developed later in many places in the United States and why they were more willing to negotiate their differences.

While many SATB choruses also see themselves as activist, they tend to focus more in their mission statements on community building within both the LGBTIQA "community"' and their larger community. In order to encompass the broader spectrum of their membership, they are more likely to add subtitles to their names, such a Desert Voices: Arizona's Premiere LGBT Chorus or One Voice Mixed Chorus: Minnesota's LGBT Mixed Chorus. TTBB choruses developed a bit later than the SSAA choruses did, and many report being inspired by the San Francisco Gay Men's Chorus's 1981 tour. Looking at the trends in naming for TTBB choruses, choruses that began in the 1980s are more than twice as likely to have names that are out in one way or another than those that came into being in the 1990s and 2000s. In contrast, the newest SATB choruses, youth and transgender choruses, tend toward being more obviously out, with names such as Sing OUT! or Youth Pride Chorus.

Beyond its name, a chorus might define itself in many other ways. Mission statements, websites, newsletters, programs, choice of music, and recordings all create a sense of the group. When comparing these variables across the spectrum and over several years, it is interesting to note on the more conservative end the ways in which, for example, the Turtle Creek Chorale of Dallas presents itself. To be clear, they obviously program gay-positive works and are active in their community, offering support

FIGURE 5.2. Three chorus logos that speak for themselves—Charis, One Voice, and Boston GMC.

and healing around AIDS, bullying, and most recently the Orlando massacre, but the emphasis in all their print materials is rather pronouncedly focused on their sound. There is no doubt that their sound is good and they clearly work for a blend that is elegant, but I use them here as a prominent example at one end of a spectrum in the movement that runs between an emphasis on musicianship and an emphasis on a social justice mission.

Reviewing the Turtle Creek Chorale website in July 2014 and then again in January 2016, it is not immediately obvious in either version that there is anything gay about the group, though the pictures that scroll so beautifully on the 2016 version hint at a gay influence for anyone who might be looking for that. Their 2014 mission stated simply, "Turtle Creek Chorale creates extraordinary musical experiences." One had to dig pretty deeply into their site before finding anything that might suggest gay men are involved. While the 2014 fact sheet's list of organizational memberships includes "GALA Choruses," one would have to know what that is in order to have any idea. In their 2014 press releases, the only mention of a gay men's chorus is when the directors of other choruses that use the word *gay* in their names are interviewed about the TCC—the term is never used

Volume VIII Number 3   Fall 1995

Providing leadership and inspiration to the Lesbian and Gay movement through excellence in the choral arts.

Turtle Creek's *After Goodbye: An AIDS Story* wins Emmy

After Goodbye: An AIDS Story, a one-hour documentary on the Turtle Creek Chorale and the grief recovery its members have experienced through music, won an Emmy Award for "Outstanding Informational or Cultural Program" from The National Academy of Television Arts and Sciences on September 12. The program has received nine other national awards including the prestigious New York Festival's Human Relations Gold Medal. Originally aired by PBS stations throughout the United States in 1993, the show's producer, local PBS affiliate KERA-TV in Dallas, Texas, estimates that more than 10,000,000 viewers have now seen *After Goodbye.*

Produced and directed by KERA's Ginny Martin and narrated by actress Ruby Dee, *After Goodbye* looks at the impact of AIDS on the Turtle Creek Chorale, which lost 60 of its 200 voices to the disease between 1983 and 1993. Rehearsals of *When We No Longer Touch: A Cycle of Songs for Survival,* a requiem composed by Chorale member Kris Anthony and

Turtle Creek Chorale Artistic Director Dr. Timothy Seelig with "After Goodbye" Producer Ginny Martin.

FIGURE 5.3. 1995 GALAGRAM headline about Turtle Creek Chorale winning Emmy for "After Goodbye: An AIDS Story."

about the TCC itself. Even the press release about their performance of "Alexander's House," which is described as "a gay mini-opera," does not out the chorus directly. The language in all the current press releases emphasizes the "uniqueness" of the TCC; only if one reads between the lines of such sections might one get the idea that this group is different in any way: "[The TCC's] power and sound hasn't been replicated anywhere, according to Harry Wooten, director of music at Royal Lane Baptist Church and artistic director of Irving Chorale. 'The chorale holds a completely unique position in the community in their choral sound and their larger philosophical reason for being,' he says. 'They have beautiful turns of phrases, and there's something visceral about their sound.'"[4] Interestingly, nowhere on their general website in either version could I find a clear statement of the "larger philosophical reason for being" to which Harry Wooten refers.

In 2014, one had to go to the liner notes of earlier recordings to find more forthcoming language. The most recent was a 2012 recording, "Family," that suggests the singing members of both the TCC and their sister chorus, the Women's Chorus of Dallas, with which they coproduced the CD, might be lesbian or gay with its use of "us" and "our." They state, "Dictionary definitions for 'family' fall miserably short of the reality of *our* daily experience. The gay and lesbian community has forged its own: a completely diverse group of people who choose to join together because of shared experiences and shared goals. Simply making beautiful music is the centerpiece of our shared goals as musicians. The struggle to overcome injustices perpetrated on us as individuals and as a group serves as a leitmotif throughout our shared life experiences."[5]

In 2016, their mission was updated to read, "Turtle Creek Chorale enrich lives through the common language of song. Our exhilarating talent captivates audiences with unforgettable moments. Every performance cultivates a shared experience of emotions, nourishing the soul with healing and energizing effects of choral music. We help unify communities by increasing support for the cultural arts."[6] The list of accomplishments that runs alongside the mission statement references nothing that would out the group, instead emphasizing the scope of their travels and the who's who of their connections, for example, Laura Bush (honorary chair), Queen Elizabeth II (audience), and Maya Angelou (shared stage). A site-wide search of the term *gay* turned up twelve results in July 2016, the majority from their blog and only three news stories: one announcing the group's performance at the Gay Softball World Series; another an obituary for one of their members, who was "recognized for his longtime service to the gay and lesbian community"; and the most recent and perhaps most out, their announcement of a concert to honor the victims of the Orlando massacre.[7] The newer site, while it offers even less historical or financial information than the 2014 site did, also offers more personal stories in which it becomes clearer that there is substantial gay participation in the chorus.

Over GALA's more than thirty years, a much wider range of strategies around self-representation and group identities has become more or less accepted, though some frustrations remain over the perception that the choruses with the largest budgets are TTBB choruses without the *g* word. The picture is actually a bit more complicated and would require more analysis than is appropriate here. Briefly, yes, the best-funded TTBB chorus is the Seattle Men's Chorus, but it is important to point out that they have strategically joined with their sister chorus, the Seattle Women's Chorus, as Flying House Productions. Their 2014 website (one of the most financially transparent of all the sites I studied) notes that with a joint singing membership of more than 670, they have a budget of $2,700,000+ (48 percent earned, 52 percent contributed) for 2013–14 with corporate sponsorship from companies including Wells Fargo Bank, Holland America, and Alaska Airlines. This is substantially more funding than any other similar choral organizations I could find. Though their names do not include any obvious reference to LGBTI or Q, in contrast to the TCC, both Seattle choruses leave no question about whom they are, whom they represent, or their purpose in making the world a better place for LGBTIQ people through song. Their now joint mission statement reads, "Seattle Men's Chorus and Seattle Women's Chorus entertain, enlighten, unify, and heal our audience and members using the power of words and music to recognize the value of gay and straight people and their relationships."[8] Of course, members of these choruses are not living in Texas.

The next chorus in the GALA network with a budget near to the Seattle Men's Chorus is the San Francisco Gay Men's Chorus, with a reported budget in 2012 of $1,356,333. And the Gay Men's Chorus of Los Angeles has a budget on par with the TCC's reported $724,613. While much more research would need to be done to assess the relationship of funding to a variety of factors, including a chorus's name, judging from the funding of choruses across the spectrum, areas that have larger, wealthier populations in general seem to have better-funded choruses and gender seems to be a greater factor than the degree to which the chorus is out in terms of funding.

Venues obviously affect whom a group can reach and in what contexts. A mark of greater social acceptance is the fact that queer choruses are increasingly being invited to sing at general community and even national events that include swearing-in ceremonies at every level. Perhaps one of the most widely viewed between television and YouTube is the January 2009 performance by the Gay Men's Chorus of Washington, DC (GMCW) as part of President Obama's inauguration ceremonies.[9] More commonly, queer choruses sing from two to four concerts per year in standard community choral music venues that can range from local church halls or community centers to concert halls. Many also do outreach by performing at local LGBTIQ events, such as Pride, or fundraising events that serve local LGBTIQ organizations. For many groups, these venues may be relatively safe and serve primarily to "sing to the choir." But it is important to note that this exercise serves more than one important social change purpose. First of all, just the act of singing together works to combat internalized heterosexism. Second, the most commonly shared type of story across choruses consists of some variation on a singer inviting family members, coworkers, or friends to concerts as the first step of coming out to them. The nearly[10] universal success of these stories speaks to the power of choral communing to overcome fears, stereotyping, and even religious prejudice. By changing hearts and minds, choral musicking may more effectively expand the network of allies. Finally, many of the choruses sing far outside the boundaries of comfort zones to do much more than sing to the choir.

Strategies for using choral musicking to queer culture include women singing parts written for men and vice versa; changing the words of songs to shift gender or to create more space for a variety of identities or even to shift the meaning of a song altogether; using costume and movement to camp up or politicize old standards; commissioning altogether new pieces from new arrangements of fairly traditional music, such as "How Can I Keep from Singing?"; developing works such as *Oliver Button Is a Star*, a twenty-minute musical production for children, which is based on Tomie dePaola's children's book *Oliver Button Is a Sissy*; or finally, commissioning full choral symphonic works such as *EOS* (2000) or the antiwar piece commissioned by the Portland Gay Men's Chorus, *BraveSouls and Dreamers* (2007), many of which might be performed by any chorus. Queer choral musicking has also produced a long list of historically based pieces that reanimate people from Joan of Arc to Harvey Milk. Whether unearthing erased histories, retelling known histories from a queer perspective, or keeping recent historical realities from being dismissed or erased, such commissioned works create, nurture, and maintain queer history and culture. In all, GALA choruses are producing enough new works that they are having a serious impact on the overall global production of choral works while counterstorying on a global scale.

I want to explore in more depth three examples of such queering at work: an early 1990s reworking of *West Side Story*; a composition commissioned in 2000 by a mixed chorus that challenges straight and gay people to appreciate transgender experiences; and GMCLA's singing of "*Canción de Todos*" during their South American tour. All these examples play on the power of popular forms to produce new meaning.

The queering of *West Side Story* was not difficult—indeed, some would argue that the gay lyricist, Stephen Sondheim, wrote with that latent intent. There is no denying that the song "Somewhere" is meant to stir the desire to have a place where one is accepted—a resounding theme in queer life. "Somewhere," "Tonight," and "Maria" have been performed widely outside of the musical and thereby work at deep and varied cultural levels to articulate a generalized passion and longing for something more than is culturally allowed. While the song "America" is considered offensive by many, the majority of the musical's songs are widely known and loved outside of the sexist, racist, classist, and nationalist context of the original story, which allows for a more freewheeling reworking of the story's themes. (It is important to note as well that this revision was an illegitimate performance not only in its queering of the material but in the ways it skirted the margins of copyright legality.)

The musical's story is a variation on the theme of Shakespeare's *Romeo and Juliet* placed in the context of gang warfare in the slums of 1950s New York that appropriates Shakespeare's critique of aristocratic practices for

FIGURE 5.4. Put together for the 2008 GALA Festival celebrating twenty-five years, the Songs of Courage: GALA Choruses Songbook cover.

capitalist purposes. *West Side Story* produces love in the context of the American dream, wherein women are mercenary and assimilationist, with the dream of becoming good little consumers, while their men are seen as backward such that the "liberation" of the women is dependent on the women being *vendidas*[11] (traitors) to their men and their culture (a theme that resonates with more recent U.S. narratives of "liberating" Islamic women).

This revision of *West Side Story* produced by a mixed LGBTIQA chorus misappropriated (although some might argue reappropriated) the story once again through a reorganization of the songs and some minimalist staging and lyrical revision by two of its wittier singing members. Performed as the finale of a show honoring the work of Stephen Sondheim, the order of the songs was shifted to fit the development of a different story of love disallowed. The sequence opened with "Tonight" sung fully as written and moved to completely new lyrics for "America," in which rather than memories of Puerto Rico being pitted against the dreams and realities of living in America, the local environment and politics were critiqued from varying angles. In the revision, lyrics about "population growing" refer to wealthy tourists and urban sprawl, the products of outside wealth negatively impacting the quality of life of local people, thereby transforming the original story's critique of female sexuality run amok into a critique of capitalist values (that underpin the original work) having run amok. Moreover, this critique of capitalist values is interwoven with a critique of the state of LGBTIQ rights in the area, implying a connection. This type of materialist feminist critique of politics performed via comedy in a Broadway musical style is one example of ways mixed LGBTIQA choruses bring together the "traditions" of the men's and women's LGBTIQA choral movements to produce hybrids that challenge the assumptions of both traditions and produce community and alliances among LGBTIQ people that might not otherwise flourish.

In this new context, the story's theme of socially unacceptable love/ desire shifts from love denied by gang boundaries to love denied by the state's restrictions on sexual freedom. The gang songs were transposed to articulate parodies of identities, making fun of stereotypes of lesbians and gay men while having fun with the stereotypes themselves. For example, the song "Gee, Officer Krupke" was easily transposed from a critique of the diagnostic tendencies of social services as they relate to "punks" to a critique of the equally problematic social diagnostics of gays. While the revision posits that "it's not a choice" to be gay, the men singing the song turn the tables on the diagnosticians, claiming that all they need to fix them is a man. In the original, the gang songs are entertaining dance numbers that work to solidify identities and conflicts. In both the original and this revision, the lyrics build on stereotypes, but in the original *West Side Story*, the use of stereotypes reinforces them because these stereotypes are produced by those with power about those who had no say in their representation. (Puerto Ricans protested both the musical and film versions.) In contrast, the mixed LGBTIQA chorus's selective use of the themes the songs suggest was on their own terms. They were using the stereotypes to reframe the conversations from their own perspectives. The switching of roles—tenors and basses singing "I Feel Pretty" and sopranos and altos singing "The Jets" song as the "The Dykes" song—offered comic relief to the rather heavy realities for the majority of both the singers and the audience members about the state of LGBTIQ rights in their state and their treatment at the hands of the law. A rabidly antigay governor was then in office, and the city police force's crackdowns on several common gay hangouts included harassment and assault of gay men. In this context, the revisions worked to allow LGBTIQ people to laugh at themselves while simultaneously claiming a right to the full range of identities (including the stereotypes) as well as sexual freedom.

While *West Side Story* maintains the tragic romantic form of *Romeo and Juliet*, wherein the stories variously critique the different social imperatives that create the impossibility of love and desire across socially constructed boundaries via the deaths that render the love more precious and the love that renders the deaths all the more tragic, the queered revision plays with the cultural capital developed over decades of popular use of the songs from *West Side Story*. The depth of the emotional and visceral responses that songs repeated over time both in and out of context carry offers rich opportunities for those who wish to shift cultural meanings. These songs have repeated themes of producing resistant identities in a social order that would erase them, of love and desire that refuse to accept social boundaries that would restrict them, and of "a place for us" in which such erasure would not exist and could no longer block those who don't fit the norms from living full lives—all themes that lend themselves well to the emotions and political demands of LGBTIQ people. In the queer politicized romantic version, the final numbers were not about death but rather about the hopefulness of love and desire overcoming social and political roadblocks. The duet between Anita and Maria, in which they conclude with the lyrics "When love comes so strong / There is no right or wrong / Your love is your life," is effectively queered and still left no dry eye in the house.

Rather than ending with the dirge of the original, the LGBTIQ version ended with a rousing finale of "Somewhere" that materially, if only for the moments of the show, produced that "place for us"—not just a dream of two lovers hoping to get away from the ghetto to a capitalist American dream where they would produce the standard American family but a dream in which the love, desire, and differences of LGBTIQ people are not othered. In all, the performance created a powerful counterstory that actively contested the state of affairs that the chorus members and their queer audience members faced at that time. And in the time and space of the concerts, it created a sort of place for us to imagine and even practice new ways of being.

An example of making new identities possible, ones that some gays and lesbians still have difficulty accepting, is a song commissioned by the Seattle Lesbian and Gay Chorus, "A Far Better Man."[12] This piece is an early example that articulates the experiences of a female-to-male (FTM) experience through a blend of pop, Broadway, and folk styles within the choral framework. This is not a high-art song, but it is earnest and presents itself as telling a transgender life story. Importantly, given the contexts in which this music is likely to be performed (i.e., queer choral concerts) and given the level of denial around such issues (especially in the context of the 1990s), it is quite possible to assume at the beginning of the song that the story is one of a gay boy "transitioning" into a different kind of man. Listeners, especially if gay, are already empathizing with the character who has faced rejection, thrown out normative images of manhood, and embraced the notion of becoming "a far better man" when, in the first chorus, it becomes clear that breast removal surgery was part of the transition.

The main character is presented as believable and, in taking the lead voice with choral backup, performs and produces transgender identity as a socially supported subject position in and through the structure of the choral form. Voices join together stronger on each repeat of "a better man, a far better man," indicating a positive social support for transgender people while at the same time opening up what it means to be a "better man." The telling of the story begins solo and continues as such until the line "and became a new man of my own," at which point the lower voices join in. They join with "ooos" on "I wondered how quickly the change'd be" and with words on the line "Who would I be in the end?" creating a sense of brotherhood around a questioning of the ways in which manhood is lived.

The full chorus joins on the theme and chorus of the song, "A better man, a far better man I've become," and on the last line, "I'm free from a life once confined." Voices split, with the higher voices (presumably lesbian identified) coming in on "my voice is much rougher" in contrast to the soloist's lower voice, and his voice then blends with the rest of the lower voices on "my hands are much tougher" in a way that confirms and supports the transition in the physicality of the voices themselves. The song and its performance celebrate and honor a transgender life story as important and related to those of gays and lesbians. In doing so, the performance of the song creates a musical "we" that instantiates a challenge to any insistence on sex/gender norms, even those evident in some LGB sections of "the community" through the shared joy of the song. By going for the heart, the song sidesteps the mind's trained insistence on gendering. The choral form's communal pleasuring, the deep joy and physical pleasure of communing through voices blending in song, can be productively used to resist such either/or constructions. In the sixteen years since this song came out, the trans repertoire has expanded into whole blockbuster sessions at the 2016 Festival dedicated to trans themes, with genderqueer artists' work, like Namoli Brennet's "Choose a Box," among them.

Another one of the many ways in which choruses queer the choral is to sing songs that already have a potent emotional impact for their audiences and to sing them as LGBTIQ peoples, both sharing and changing the meaning of the songs at the same time, thereby expanding opportunities for communing across identities, for being differently together. One example is a choral arrangement commissioned by the Gay Men's Chorus of Los Angeles (GMCLA) of a popular South American song of political resistance against U.S.-funded dictatorships for their 2006 trip to four countries in South America: Uruguay, Chile, Argentina, and Brazil. The singers' and audiences' responses to their rendition of "*Canción con Todos*" are documented in a video about the tour. The following is a translation of the song's chorus:

All the voices all,
All the hands all,

All the blood can be song in the wind

Sing with me, sing,
American brother

Set free your hope with a cry in your voice.[13]

By all accounts, the performance of this song, particularly in Santiago, was a transformative experience. "There wasn't a dry eye in the house," claimed one singer. Members reported that audience members repeatedly asked, "How did you know to sing that song?" followed by variations on attempts to express the power of the experience the largely straight audiences had in hearing their song from the chorus. As U.S. citizens proudly singing the South American song of resistance both for and with South Americans (in Santiago, the audience stood and sang along during the encore), the chorus validated South American resistance against U.S.-supported dictatorship. At the same time, the singers, and then audience members by singing with them, transformed it into a song of resistance to oppression of LGBTIQ people as well. In these musical exchanges, the chorus created spaces for mutual recognition of their different forms of oppressions. By singing this song as U.S. citizens, chorus members acknowledged the suffering that had been created in their names. But at the same time, their South American audiences, many of whom seemed at first to be attending more out of curiosity than out of support for LGBTIQ people, were brought face-to-face with another form of oppression that the chorus was asking them to address. Judging from the standing ovations and extended singing along on repeated verses, GMCLA managed to create—for those moments, at least—a bridge of understanding across these differences. In doing so, they were able to offer a moment of healing across the many differences and an opportunity for everyone in the room to be held in this new queered relationship as arguably better selves. It created a moment of powerful counterstorying.

A number of choruses travel regionally, nationally, and internationally in ways parallel to straight choruses. Most do this to attend choral festivals, but others travel with a range of intentions. One of the more common practices has been to travel to relatively friendly countries, perhaps where there are sister/brother choruses with whom the group can share the stage. For example, during the 2014 Various Voices Festival in Dublin, I spoke with members of both the New York City Gay Men's Chorus and the London Gay Men's Chorus, who had just finished performing together in London and were headed out for more joint performances. They repeatedly and excitedly made comments such as "We are the same chorus" and "We are brother choruses." The purposes in such cases are only slightly different from those of any choral group traveling to other countries: the opportunity to see, hear, and sing with other choruses, the challenge of new material and directors, and the chance to share artistic expression (and, for queer choruses, "community" pride) in an affirming environment of musical appreciation, as well as the occasion to visit other countries as tourists.

But some queer choruses do so with what might be considered evangelical intent. This version of international travel mixes activist/philanthropic work and pleasure by traveling to places that are potentially more dangerous, though often with tourist attractions, in order to support various LGBT services. Both types of travel usually develop through connections that leaders in the group have with people in the country who can help them gain entry to performance venues, local advocacy groups, and such. GMCLA's 2006 South American tour was one example. The chorus raised money to help fund the trip, including support for members who might not otherwise have been able to afford to go, and all the proceeds from the performances went to support local HIV/AIDS service providers and/or LGBTIQ organizations in the four countries they visited.

In the GMCLA documentary video about the trip, comprising individual members' stories and clips from practices, performances, community work, and news coverage, one story makes explicit the evangelistic mission as perceived by a young chorus member. He recounts sitting on a bus next to a young Mormon who was on his mission and striking up a conversation in which he explicitly finds common ground in their different forms of evangelism. As a result of finding this common ground, he evidently got an earful about the young Mormon's mission, but the singer effectively evangelized about the GMCLA mission by asking the young Mormon to sing with him a piece they were performing, an experience he describes in transformative terms, with the Mormon exclaiming, "Hey, you guys do good stuff!" Although I have no way to follow up to see what kind of influence this exchange actually had on the young Mormon's attitudes, the singer clearly felt that he had served his mission to "change hearts and minds through music."[14]

I have no doubt that some members of his own chorus might cringe at such a religious parallel in a way that many progressive activists might, but in my own struggle to find words to describe the sorts of emotional commitments that continue to sustain this movement, I find his explicit parallel useful. Queer choral musicking has a purposefulness that makes it strangely more like "having religion" than the average non-religious-based community chorus, but this "religion" is about neither any god nor politics. Many members would leave if that were the case. Instead, it is a sort of justice-seeking-through-shared-pleasure sort of evangelism. Queer choral musicking generally resists any overt connection to either religion or politics but reaches out to people with the earnestness of both through the creation of beauty in a form that instantiates community through musicking.

Such evangelizing through queer choral musicking—changing hearts and minds about LGBTIQ people—takes a number of forms. Many choruses create programming that moves beyond the queer community, reaching out to nursing homes, shopping malls, community organizations, and more recently and arguably daringly, schools. One Voice: Minnesota's LGBT Mixed Chorus has long made a mission out of partnering with local schools. Their January 2016 website notes,

> Now in its 16th year, OUT in Our Schools is a core program of One Voice Mixed Chorus, taking adult chorus members into St. Paul schools to engage students in learning and performing choral

music, exploring diversity to build understanding and awareness, and addressing gender and gender stereotypes.

OUT in Our Schools is curriculum driven, based on the diversity goals set by school districts. Through music and visual arts, One Voice has developed a curriculum to engage students in conversation about gender and gender stereotypes. This curriculum includes materials for teachers, three artist residencies in each school, and a performance combining middle-school youth with One Voice singers.[15]

Their artistic director, Jane Ramseyer Miller, speaking at the 2012 GALA Festival, challenged other choruses to reach out more to youth in their areas. Many choruses have done this through antibullying efforts and active collaboration with initiatives like "It Gets Better," such as GMCLA's tour of communities across the country, which partners with schools and local community choruses to create experiences that ask how to make it better now in each community.[16] By combining an opportunity for schools to offer extracurricular musical education along with the direct experience of singing with a group that identifies as LGBTIQA, many choruses are able to break into one of the most dangerous places for queer kids—schools—even as they functionally challenge one of the more hateful and inaccurate of the standard stereotypes: queers as pedophiles.

Queer choral musicking at its best effectively celebrates all the voices in the house. By making use of the formality of choral musicking with its residue of the sacred in Western traditions, queer choruses create strategic spaces for healing the damage done by oppressive master narratives. Queer choruses embody in their practice a compelling counterstory, one that challenges some of the most damaging stories used to oppress: that you are alone, that you have no right to commune with others, that all you think about is sex, that sex is not a social good (especially not yours), and that you have no right to life or joy. The practice of actively, publicly, and joyfully offering creative counterstorying that provides mutual pleasuring through sonic beauty is appropriate to the task because in its very form it creates that which such master narratives work to deny.

PART THREE

Communal Erotics and Social Justice

6

Emotions, Identities, and Choral Musicking

Never forget that justice is what love looks like in public.
–Cornell West

They may not remember what you sang, but they'll never forget how you made them feel.[1]

"My country 'tis of thee, sweet land of liberty, of thee I sing." This song of love to an idealized nation, to the unrealized ideals of a people, is the song that Marion Anderson chose to sing on the steps of the Lincoln Memorial on Easter Sunday 1939 after her humanity had been publically denied for the color of her skin. Because of her race, the Daughters of the American Revolution (DAR) had successfully denied her the right to sing in Constitution Hall, where she had been scheduled to perform. Anderson reclaimed her right to all that the DAR tried to deny her by drawing a crowd far larger than Constitution Hall could ever hold, as more than seventy-five thousand people came to see her that Easter day, and many more remember her for the history she made.

When Queen Latifah stood on the same steps to introduce the Gay Men's Chorus of Washington, DC (GMCW) at President Obama's 2009 inauguration, she drew a direct line between Anderson's claim to full citizenship and the rights of LGBTIQ people to the same. Echoing what Langston Hughes called "the journey of America to BE America,"[2] she retold the story of gaining full citizenship to include all the disenfranchised as *the* American story.[3] A clip from Marion Anderson's 1939 performance segued to soloists Josh Groban and Heather Headley, and the backdrop opened to the swelling voices of about a hundred GMCW singers. In the hope-filled atmosphere of the inauguration of the country's first African American president, their performance and its framing in the context of a long line of people who have struggled to gain full respect for their humanity, the predominantly white GMCW marked another part of the journey of America toward the realization of its highest ideals—freedom and justice for *all*.

While Anderson's performance probably changed few if any minds of the members of the DAR, her performance no doubt emboldened others to speak out and shifted the feelings of many in the country who were touched by her daring and the power and beauty of her performance. Similarly, when gay men gather to publically sing the refrain "let freedom ring," especially in such a high-level, ritualized context, not only do the singers make a physical and artistic claim to the song, the space, full citizenship, and national (if not international) attention, but feelings about the meanings of citizenship and liberty are given the opportunity to expand for many others.

We have ample evidence that feelings matter in some ways more than laws when it comes to social justice, though laws obviously matter as well. For example, the murder and incarceration of men of color in the United States in ways that replicate this country's racialized history of lynching and slavery offer material manifestations that civil rights laws do not stop people from feeling and acting out on racist beliefs, consciously and unconsciously. Recent studies on unconscious bias even in people who expressly deny having any bias show how ingrained such stories can be in the fabric of our identities.[4] Strongly felt beliefs materially undermine the effectiveness of any legislation. Such feelings about ourselves and other's identities and relations are nurtured and maintained through master narratives repeated in everything from family stories of who "we" are to advertising, songs, videos, films, and nationalist narratives about who counts in the "we" of citizenship. Such stories are not easily changed. Another recent example of powerful feelings about identities resisting legal decisions that uphold basic constitutional rights is evident in the backlash against the U.S. Supreme Court's action to legalize "gay marriage" across the country in the purported name of religious freedom. Many people are swayed by this argument about "religious freedom" because it upholds their own sense of themselves in the world even as it illogically denies that same religious freedom to people whose faiths or belief systems support gay marriage. Stories about who "we" are structure our feelings and therefore affect the practice and maintenance of such laws.

Culturally dominant paradigms that value reason over feelings encourage us to believe that we have free choice and make decisions rationally. Emotions should play no role in our decision making, they argue. But fields as far ranging as neuroscience and economics are taking emotions more seriously. Findings increasingly suggest that we should question our cultural and scholarly privileging of reason over emotions. The field of advertising alone offers ample evidence that our decisions are more emotionally based than not.[5] Repeated studies have shown how people who think they are not affected by advertising at all in fact are. It turns out that memories, the material from which even rational models gather evidence for decision making, are "state-dependent." In other words, memory mapping and recall are based on emotions at the time of the incident as well as the time of the recall.[6] There is increasing evidence that emotions inform all our decisions, and reason is at most a partner in the process and possibly only a rationalization after the fact.[7]

While I am not inclined toward the belief that the concept of free choice is an utter fallacy, a preponderance of evidence shows that emotions play important roles that clearly influence what we believe to be our reasoning processes. Past failures to recognize this in any number of arenas, from political science to philosophy, have left our understanding of human being, knowing, and acting impoverished. This dismissal of our emotions itself is based on ways of thinking that divide people against each other.

In the introduction to a germinal collection of social science essays that move in this direction, the editors of *Passionate Politics: Emotions and Social Movement* note how social scientists have been analyzing what they consider rational action while more or less dismissing, ignoring, or devaluing actions that seem emotionally motivated, as if thought and emotions are opposites rather than integrated and as if emotions are never really important. Offering a historical overview of how the scholarly "portrayal of emotions" in social movement research has been "flawed in many ways," they summarize as follows: "Emotions can be strategically used by activists *and* be the basis for strategic thought. . . . [Emotions] can be seen as an aspect of all actions and social relations. They accompany rational acts as fully as irrational ones. Like other aspects of culture, such as cognitive meanings or moral principles, emotions are shaped by social expectations as much as they are emanations of individual personalities."[8] Developing out of this and particularly of interest in relationship to queer choral musicking, they argue,

> If emotions are intimately involved in the processes by which people come to join social movements, they are even more obvious in the ongoing activities of the movements. The richer a movement's culture—with more rituals, songs, folktales, heroes, denunciation of enemies and so on—the greater those pleasures. Most discussions of the solidarity-building functions of movement culture have concentrated on shared rhetoric and beliefs rather than on the emotions that accompany them. Each of the [rational] components of movement culture that Lofland (1996) sees as embodying participants' beliefs—values, symbolic objects, stories, occasion, roles, and personae—also has an equally important emotional side, entailing joy, hope, enthusiasm, pride and affective attachment to the group. These are crucial to sustaining movements.[9]

By this measure, queer choruses perform important roles for the larger movement not only by creating a richer movement culture through ritual and song but by spreading "joy, hope, enthusiasm, pride and affective attachment to the group" from within and without.

In a related vein, Sara Warner's work *Acts of Gaiety: LGBT Performance and the Politics of Pleasure* resurrects the "play" of lesbian radical theater through case studies of lesbian-feminist aesthetic and political strategies that she calls "acts of gaiety."[10] And Benjamin Shepard's *Queer Political Performance and Protest* offers a cultural analysis of the role of play, or "ludic performance," in the political organizing of groups such as ACT UP. He writes, "Queers have always known pleasure is a resource. Play injects a high octane means with which to reimagine ways for people to connect, build public commons, and democratic vistas honoring notions of difference and possibility."[11] Shepard develops the importance of the joy and pleasure of play to sustained political action. He shows how such pleasure can be an end in itself for some participants and serves as a reason to stay involved over the longer term. But just as importantly, as both works develop in different veins, pleasure nurtures the creative thinking necessary to the work of organizing actions that effectively contest and reframe damaging master narratives. They both, as Shepard writes, develop an "alternate framework for an understanding of social movement activity and sustainability"[12] that foregrounds the interaction of emotions and action.

Both of these analyses of the importance of the pleasure in creating and sustaining queer social movement parallel some of my own findings in terms of queer choral musicking. Different kinds of pleasures feed different needs. For example, the work of groups such as ACT UP is intense and pressing and continues today.[13] They are working to save people's lives by creatively and persistently calling out inequities and demanding immediate action on everything from the development of pharmaceuticals to health care coverage for those with HIV/AIDS. The in-your-face kinds of pleasures and play that feed that form of activism serve their more radically immediate purposes. The sense of empowerment that comes from working with a group to plan and implement actions such as repeated "die-ins" at the Bush vacation home or at various pharmaceutical companies or interrupting presidential speeches can be intoxicating. One naked protest outside Penn Station on the eve of the Republican convention, according to their website, played a role in actions that "resulted in over $100 billion of debt cancelled in 29 countries—freeing up money to pay for the fight against AIDS and to pay health workers instead of paying back rich-countries' banks"[14] There is an emotional high that comes with such performances and the possibility of being arrested to bring attention to the cause.

Queer choral musicking's purpose is more diffuse and slower paced than ACT UP's work. The purpose of the choruses is expressly to change people's feelings about gender/sex differences—to "change hearts and minds," as one of the GALA Festival's themes succinctly stated. And the change of feelings is as important within "the community" as without. According to a number of my interviewees, queer choral musicking has saved people's lives as well: from suicide, from depression, from isolation, from desperation. Dan explains in some detail:

There is something about what happens in that room that is just—I don't wanna ever miss it again. . . . And it's true for the guys. Rehearsals are not just rehearsals. Yes, they are, but they also are opportunities for us to do an awful lot of support for people. I had one guy, a few years ago, come up to me in the bar and [he] just gave me this huge bear hug and he said, "You don't know what the chorus means to me." And I said, "Yeah, I think I do." And he said, "No, you don't: the chorus has kept me alive." And I said, "Well yeah, it's really important." He says, "No, no, no. I have been so close to killing myself as I've had to work through my issues of acceptance of my own gayness and as other men have been around me and talked openly about who they are and we've celebrated that in song." He says, "No matter how bad it gets for me, I've got that to hold on to." And you magnify that and it happens all over, maybe not quite as dramatic as that. And yet, yes it is! In many ways, it's always a life-and-death situation. And that's the energy that keeps me involved.

This singer's experience of the chorus suggests that the choruses are fulfilling for him what Hilde Lindemann argues is a moral obligation that the larger society fails to fulfill: holding him respectfully in his identity as a gay man. He is not alone.

Lindemann's simple yet powerful argument is that we have a moral obligation to hold and let go of each other's identities through our life changes as well as we can, because in most cases, this is a fairly simple thing to do and because we damage the other's humanity when we do not. Failing to hold others well in their identities "casts them out of social and moral life, and to live outside that is to have no kind of human life at all."[15] If we have a right to a human life, she argues, "then the requirement to hold other persons in personhood shares its justification with the requirement not to murder, and is equally stringent."[16] Our personhood is reciprocally dependent on each other's acknowledgement of it (though some have more power in this respect than others). Because our lives as human beings require that we enter the "practice of personhood," she makes the following case: "[Then] the rest of us in the practice have to commit to keeping you playing with us. After all, holding someone needn't take much effort: unless you stand in a special relationship to the person, eye contact, a smile, or a nod of recognition might be all that is required. Because the stakes for that person can be so huge and the claim on you is so small, it seems as if there is indeed an obligation to engage in this kind of holding."[17] These "improvised co-performances based on mutual narrative recognition"[18] often go badly, but she notes our general resilience with the daily interchanges: "Time can heal the lesser wounds to your identity, as most of us are fortunate enough to be able to forgive the small, often unintentional slights we constantly inflict on each other, but the people who have been powerfully present to us, in childhood in particular, can continue to damage our identities even though they died long ago."[19] There are at least two sites where failures of respectful "mutual narrative recognition" are potentially seriously damaging: in relationships with those who are "powerfully present to us," especially as children, and in relation to the larger cultural narratives that shape who and how anyone is understood to exist as human within our culture.

Noting how those close to us can hold or let go of our identities badly, even after death, she writes, "When someone you love treated you very badly during her lifetime—usually this would be a parent, spouse, stepparent, or grandparent—that person can be alive to you for years afterward, still 'telling' you how useless or selfish or stupid you are. The grandfather who molested you when you were in your early teens can keep on making you feel as if you're fair game for any man's sexual pleasure long after he's dead. The mother who continually criticized you can make you feel unworthy even as you visit her grave."[20] The identity-damaging stories that are part of both the family narratives and the master narratives can be particularly devastating.

Such damage to one's identity can often take years of therapeutic work to restory—to develop personal counterstories and relationships with others who will uptake and hold you well in a healthier story. It is important to note that such stories or counterstories must prove true through our actions over time or they will fail:

> [The] fit between my identity and my agency goes in both directions: if it's true that I act out of the tissue of stories that constitute my sense of who I am, it's just as true that I express who I am by

how I act. In fact, my actions are important criteria for assessing the accuracy of my self-conception. If, for instance, I see myself as a good driver but I've received four traffic citations in the last six months, others have reason to doubt, in this respect, at any rate, that my identity-constituting stories are credible ones.[21]

Practices of identity are cumulative based on actions over time. Of course, Lindemann also notes one way that "personal identities may be sites of contestation." Picking up from her work on damaged identities and narrative repair, she shows how this "is particularly true for members of minority groups who have been persistently misidentified by those in the dominant culture."[22] An obvious example here would be "driving while black," where bias, conscious or not, encourages people to read a person's identity through a prejudiced lens.

When cultural narratives deny even the possibility of an identity, they essentially create what she calls "impossible identities." For example, because transgender people are often perceived as misrepresenting a "natural" gender, they must deal with what she calls the "evil deceiver narrative":

When the identity-constituting stories circulating widely in your society allow you to be understood only as a liar or a deceiver, others are apt to treat you as if you have no right to exist. You are likely to be denied a job because your gender presentation doesn't match the M or F on your driver's license; you are subjected to beatings; you are raped "to teach you a lesson"; all too often, you are killed. There is no place for you anywhere, because there is no way for others to make sense of you. . . . You need counterstories that resist the evil deceiver narrative by offering concrete representations of the range of sexed and gendered possibilities—including the possibility of claiming for yourself one of the two genders with which most people identify.[23]

There is hidden labor in "managing others' responses" to any misreading of our identities that can lead to affronts or even violence. We normalize our identities or try to pass. There is a "loss to the person who is forced to engage in this labor,"[24] but for those dealing with prejudice, such "hidden labor can be necessary for survival."[25] Choruses offer a potential place for articulating and affirming many nonnormative identities, for lifting the burden of this labor more productively together.

Singers regularly refer to their choruses as *family* and often describe all the drama and dysfunction as well as the love and connection that term suggests. For those of us whose families often do not know how to fully include us, an important form of contesting the master narratives that leave us out is to create spaces that can more respectfully "hold" us in our identities. Because choral musicking is a structurally communal way of expressing the beauty and pain, the joy and grief of being human by mingling voices together in song, it has the potential to hold both performers and audience members in new identities.

Choral musicking as an activity allows a space for people who might not know each other on any other terms to come together to create something beautiful that they cannot create alone. These days, one can do it digitally,[26] yet choral musicking in the flesh, queer or not, in Western culture is one of the most common recreational group activities and, at least in the United States, beats out all other art forms in terms of participation. For example, "Chorus America . . . claims that 42.6 million people in the U.S. sing in more than 270,000 choruses today."[27] The practice is one that people generally find compelling, prompting the question, What *is* it that people are coming together to do? While there are choruses whose primary mission is artistic excellence and others that are religiously based, many are community choruses: people who come together for the pleasure produced by placing their voices in concert with others. What does it mean to place one's voice in concert with others? What kinds of identities and responsibilities does this art form create/allow and how?

For everyone who is able to vocalize and hear, imitating the sounds of those around us is one of the most important things we do as infants to enter the world of being human. If we are to be successful at being human in our culture, our families or caretakers must, as Lindemann explains, engage in "the process of identity formation, which, from the parents', siblings', and other caregivers' perspectives, is a complex procedure of holding and letting go of the various stories that depict and then no longer depict the child's rapidly changing self."[28] Our caretakers "hold" us in our personhood-to-be by helping us, among other things, gain language: sounds, gestures, and words, along with all their culturally circumscribed meanings and values.[29]

Watch any baby, and it's clear that our early vocalizations themselves are often pleasurable. Confident infants learn to self-soothe and express their emotions before words with the sound of their own voices.[30] This sound making before words produced in that utter vulnerability before we knew anything else constitutes our first music making, often in call-and-response form with our kin. In the very best of circumstances, these interactive vocalizations create a soundscape of loving regard that arguably seduces us into language, culture, and our understanding of our humanity. But our families, cultures, and languages inevitably limit who and how we are able to be based on their own all-too-human limitations and oppressive value systems.

Simply in terms of our voices, messages about where, when, and how our voices are proper, or not, are learned through this early musicking-into-language-and-identity process and continue refinement throughout our lives based on the ways in which others in our lives hold us in our sound-making practices. Depending on the messages we receive, we may learn to hate or love our own voices. Culturally our voices are valued and devalued along all the same lines of race, gender, sexuality, and other markers of social difference. We may retain, constrain, and/or repudiate the pleasure of our vocalization in response to these values. For most of us, it's a complex mix somewhere in between highly valued and completely silenced. Most of us do not feel comfortable burbling or humming just anywhere, though doing so might actually make us feel better. But singing within acceptable social contexts is one way in which many of us retain (and some exquisitely refine) this pleasure within our given social constraints.

Through most of human history, and still in much of the rest of the world, the intimacy of sharing the emotions aroused by musicking together has been and is done among intimates. Christopher Small notes that musicking most often has happened among tribal members, friends and family or in schools and churches, not among strangers.[31] However, in current Western culture, he writes, "we are prepared to laugh, to weep, to shudder, to be excited, or to be moved to the depth of our being, all in the company of people the majority of whom we have never seen before, to whom we shall probably not address a word or a gesture, and whom we shall in all probability never see again."[32] In contrast to these Western norms, "in the culture of villages, as well as of those quite small cities (by present-day standards), from ancient Athens to eighteenth-century Vienna, which up to the recent past formed the centers of urban culture, performers and audience members have known one another as members of the same community."[33] Through such communal musicking, "their mutual responsibilities and identity as a community was affirmed and celebrated."[34] The village smith might also be a violinist and the butcher might play trombone, and through the practice of musicking together, they would be acknowledged—or as Lindemann describes, held—in all their identities as valued parts of the larger community.

Some have argued that the "communal affirmation and celebration" of shared ideal relations that Small argues is evident in more communal forms of musicking is harder to come by in more metropolitan areas, thus placing people in a social experiment without precedent.[35] Anonymity is arguably both the gift and the bane of urban life the world over. It allows personal freedoms that more communal life does not, but it also creates a relatively new kind of labor in terms of developing relationships.[36] While through most of history, humans have been born into the relationships and communities that were likely to define them for the rest of their lives, for the first time in human history, this is not the case for many. The majority of households in many Western nations have been steadily tipping from being familial or shared to being a single person.[37] Because of our increasing alienation, while more likely to be on our own terms, our relationships with others require more thought and effort, as they are no longer merely given based on our birth and location.

Perhaps in more communal contexts, a wider range of human sound making as emotional expression might be acceptable, but in Western culture, perhaps because we are so often musicking among strangers in very defined spaces, what is considered proper in public or for audience members to do in any particular concert venue is likely to be circumscribed. For example, it might be considered acceptable to sing along at the top of one's lungs at a punk or heavy metal concert, where the soundscape is so loud that any audience member's vocalizations could not seriously intrude on the musical experience of anyone else. It certainly would not be acceptable to do so at an opera or symphonic performance, where even clearing one's throat or coughing may be frowned upon. And in everyday public spaces, singing a tune can prove uncomfortable. Having performed singing telegrams for a number of years in my youth, I generally had great fun breaking the frame of these conventions, as most people accepted it in good humor. But in a handful of instances, the gift was ill chosen and breaking this frame obviously crossed a line of propriety that the recipient could not accept.

Unlike in the majority of musicking contexts throughout history, Small notes that modern Western musicking is largely preplanned: "Very little here takes place spontaneously."[38] Whether for rock concerts, symphonies, or opera, we have extensive infrastructure and technologists behind the scenes to make the show go on. In fact, he argues that the composers whose work is now commonly ritually, if not religiously, performed to the score, would find the formality, lack of musical improvisation, or lack of community involvement strange: "No musician would give a whole concert on his [sic] own; local performers, amateur and professional, would be called in to collaborate."[39] Solo performances were not common until the late 1880s. In comparison, the expression of emotions through commonly musicking together, even for professional classical musicians, is now more socially circumscribed or contained. It is often strongly differentiated from the rest of life through dedicated spaces and musical forms. Whether the bacchanal of a rock concert or the more abstract, intellectualized experience of formal symphonic musicking, Western musicking practices enact our either/or values, values simplified into binaries.

Binary thinking is arguably foundational to our culture and, importantly for any social justice work, is at the heart of stereotyping and oppressive practices. For example, the belief that mind and matter operate in different realms is a master narrative that has fed both Western religious and scientific thought for centuries, if not millennia. Small writes of the scientific version that not only has shaped Western science but also has become "simple commonsensical reality" (despite substantial evidence to the contrary). Cartesian dualism is "the idea that the world is made up of two different and even incompatible kinds of substance:

matter which is divisible, has mass, dimensions and a location in space; and *mind*, which is indivisible, has no mass or dimensions, and is located nowhere and everywhere."[40] This either/or thinking supports the separation of groups of people from each other, as some are more associated with mind (the abstract and the pure) while others with matter (the mundane and the impure): for example, male/female, white/black, hetero/homo, and wealthy/poor, respectively.[41] Placing humans in either category arguably diminishes their opportunities for full personhood (e.g., boys should not be like girls because it degrades the qualities of boyness but leaves boys unable to cry without shame). But one category is always more socially empowered for not being in the other (othered) category.

In terms of musicking, emblematically, Plato worried over the socially degrading effects of song. St. Augustine self-flagellated over his orgasmic passion for chant. More recently, philosopher Allan Bloom expresses a version of the same anxiety by describing rock music as "masturbational fantasy" in contrast to classical music, which he claims as ennobling the soul in ways that encourage the listener to resist carnal pleasure—as if resisting carnal pleasure is necessarily ideal or healthy.[42] While Bloom's argument further validates Small's argument about the disembodied, alienated nature of Western classical musicking, it also makes clear that in a culture with long-standing master narratives that denigrate both embodiment and pleasure by allowing them only opposite and binarized forms (they are either pure or impure), the link between musicality and sexuality both frightens and thrills.

The desire to control such dangerous excitement in Western culture has historically created largely divided musical realms: proper formal (intellectual and abstracted) classical or art music, which maintains its social ranking by repeatedly differentiating itself from everything else. Classical musicking is seen by those like Bloom as purified of sexuality and embodiment through its emphasis on structure, its demanding virtuosity, and the discipline required to produce it, or sometimes even to listen to it. In contrast, the "everything else" from which this understanding of the classical distances itself includes aural/orally shared music and folk traditions that are meant to be easily participatory and are more about the shared experience than any virtuosity, though virtuosity of different sorts is widely valued. While musicians of all kinds often play with the spaces in between categories, certain identities evidently feel threatened whenever the boundaries that define their own are not kept clear.

As an example of these values in action, Liz Garnett offers a particularly close analysis of manuals for choral conductors in her article "Choral Singing as Bodily Regime." Despite the fact that the authors of these manuals argue that choral singing is a "universal" experience, Garnett shows how the proper choral practices described are implicitly, if not explicitly, related to social class, education, and often race. They assume a level of musical training that privileges the ability to read music (as we saw in the history of Elmer Keeton's WPA chorus) and "proper" pronunciation. Such practices are also gendered, through assumptions about appropriate vocal ranges, and sometimes nationalized as well. For example, Garnett describes how even in a more recent manual author's attempt to be inclusive, "repertoires that arise from oral traditions are seen as inherently outside the category of choral music, since their recent inclusion is seen as an 'influx' that is effected by their transformation into notated scores."[43] The classed and raced preference for "traditional notation," which requires Western musical education, over "rote procedures" that are perceived as "devoid of [musical] understanding" denigrates the musical practice and knowledge of many traditions. In this vein, she notes, "'world music' is also (as ever) a problematic term; its discussion here [in the manuals] solely in terms of non-notated idioms invites a connection with the term 'ethnic music,' which appears as either implicit or explicit euphemism for music from African American traditions."[44] We see in her analysis the lining up of binarized values that leave certain types of choral musicking outside of the category reserved for "proper" choral musicking.

Feminist and queer music scholars since the early 1990s have made clear the social meanings and political investments behind this web of interrelated social binaries: classical/popular, mind/body, sacred/profane, pure/impure, masculine/feminine, and hetero/homo.[45] They started queering the field by making explicit the connection between musicking practices and gender/sexuality. These authors describe and document some of the ways music is coded as both queer and feminine. In a culture that devalues both, they argue that in order to be socially proper, musicking practices require strong structure to adequately "masculinize" and "straighten" them. (Even so, the gender identity of male classical musicians is rendered suspect.) By purifying musicking practices of the devalued qualities associated with femininity, sexuality, and embodiment through cultural storying processes that repetitively distance proper musicality from sexuality in the ways that Bloom does, the power of musicking is contained in the interest of maintaining hierarchical and oppressive social values. Queer scholars show how such forms of musicking are culturally impoverishing and based on oppressive social constructions.

In her essay "Listening to the Sirens: Music as Queer Ethical Practice," Judith Peraino nicely synthesizes some important elements of the work of queer musicologists: "As a discursive practice, music is double-tongued, participating in both the normalizing and the abnormalizing of the subject, as Philip Brett's groundbreaking article 'Musicality, Essentialism, and the Closet' describes. Similarly, Suzanne Cusick, in another pioneering article, explores how music allows for a rethinking of sexual pleasure as nongenital and thus outside the phallic economy of power. As these and other scholars show, music demarcates a space and time wherein gender and sexuality lose clear definition."[46] Because of this loss of clear definition, new definitions are possible. Arguing for the ethics of self-definition as an aesthetic process, Peraino explains, "Music is notoriously resistant to legibility [the ability to easily read its meaning], . . . [and] it is this resistance to legibility that allows for the use of music as a strategy for configuring queer subjectivity. . . . In my opinion, that is part of music's enduring appeal and cultural work."[47] Her piece explores several different ways that music has demarcated "a space and time wherein gender and sexuality lose clear definition" to analyze how music has been employed at some key historical moments to challenge sex and gender norms and allow space for different identities. In the process, she shows "how music participates in both forming and questioning subjectivity,"[48] how it is an identity-forming practice. She goes on to claim that "music instigates exactly those ethical questions of individual conduct and self-definition in or against in-place social and symbolic structures in the individual's effort to *be otherwise*."[49] While it is clear that most musicking practices reinscribe social norms, music's "resistance to legibility," our inability to pin down its meaning, makes it a rich place to play with identity formations. Precisely because the stories that keep social norms limiting who we are able to be require constant repetitions and reinscriptions, they also present opportunities for queering.

Queer choruses make just such a use of choral musicking to question and form new subjectivities (who a person is able to be) in an "effort to be otherwise." Ironically, because of the centuries of choral music's "straightening" in the Western tradition and the intersection of musicality and sexuality in the space of the choral that master narratives continually work to hide, queer choruses are able to creatively counterstory the space of the choral into a relatively safe place for the ongoing social development and production of queer identities that challenge the binaries of male/female, homo/hetero and allow a place for everyone to be more fully human.

So what is choral musicking as a practice? Who joins? What are singers signing up for in such great numbers and why? If you are the average community chorus singer, according to a number of studies, you are likely to have had some singing experience, but often it's nothing more than expressing your joy in the shower or exercising your pipes along with a favorite singer in the relative privacy of your car. While some singers in community choruses have had previous experience singing in a chorus or even some formal voice training, most choral singers are amateurs. Because most singers only nominally "read" musical scores, if they do at all (which is arguably one reason singers are often left out of the Western category of "musician"), the "audition" required for entrance into most community choruses consists of a musical director checking your vocal range to see in which section your voice best fits. In some groups, if your singing voice or reading abilities are not up to their standards, you might be asked to take group lessons in reading music or vocal training before gaining singing membership. Or you might be invited to be a nonsinging member who helps with other elements of putting on the shows. In groups whose focus calls for a higher standard of musical excellence, the audition may include a sight-reading test and also require that you prepare a piece to perform for at least the director and accompanist, sometimes a committee, or possibly the whole group. In these cases, you might even be auditioning with people who are competing for the position with the chorus you want. But the majority of choruses are pretty broadly welcoming of anyone who can hold a note reasonably well. While there is definitely an element of self-selection, this still leaves a pretty wide variety of people coming together for some fairly intense communing through song.

The nature of choral communing can have much of the alienation that Small describes of symphonic musicians focused primarily on their piece of a much larger score, operating under the direction of the director as interpreter of the "sacred text." But given the embodied nature of the voice as instrument, the diversity of voices and abilities in community choruses, and the diversity of repertoire from folk tunes to classical and everything in between, choral communing is far less abstract in the experience than symphonic musicking might be.

The ways that different groups organize themselves can vary quite a bit. Group structures include the completely hierarchical, in which the musical director is sovereign and everyone serves that person's vision, to the completely consensual, in which everyone has a say and responsibility in the chorus's work, and every variation in between. Most choruses have a musical director who invites input to varying degrees because failing to do so at all can lead to disgruntled singers. Most directors must also work with and answer to a board that oversees the chorus's functions and may well include singers. In most choruses I have been in and/or studied, the majority of singers just come to sing their part and maybe help here and there. They are mostly content enough to follow the lead of their director and board to simply enjoy the pleasure of singing in their group. In most community choruses, there is some measure of balancing between the pleasure of singing together and the work for musical excellence. How these elements are balanced affects at least one level of who one is able to be or how and in what identities the group will hold its members.

Acceptance into most choruses requires attendance and active participation in a weekly rehearsal and a performance schedule, dedication to learning the music, and payment for the privilege of singing together through dues or fees to help defray the costs (the director and instrumental musician salaries, performance venue costs, the rent of a place to practice, etc.).[50] Community choruses often encourage or even require additional participation, sharing the load of all the tasks necessary to put on shows and keep the organization running. This might include planning the music repertoire (most commonly done by a director but sometimes in concert with a committee or occasionally through group consensus); creating rehearsal and performance schedules; managing the music collection; managing finances (budgeting, marketing, ticket sales, collecting income and paying the bills); managing performances (planning, preparing, executing and evaluating everything from space, lighting, and sound to costumes and staging); and managing people (choral community development, conflict resolution, etc.). Choral musicking is a community effort in more ways than just singing.

As with any group of people who work together to produce something they all care about, the level and type of caring, commitment, and ability to give can vary enormously. Most choruses have welcoming committees and/or section leaders to help acclimate a new member to the group's culture. In others, new members are expected to find their own way in the group or not. Different choruses allow for different levels of participation. For the more competitive, musically demanding groups, failure to participate musically at an acceptable level means you are likely to be let go. Some choruses cultivate a very particular sound and culture and only allow new members to join after a more rigorous testing period. Acceptance into some choruses might require consensus from the whole group, though that is fairly rare. Each element marks what the group, as a group, values: both the quality and scope of how they hold themselves in their practice of identity as choral singers and how they are likely to hold (or fail to hold) you. But for the average community chorus, unless you are actually disruptive to the group or the performances, you are not likely to be asked to leave. Once you are in, you are in. You are also likely to be welcomed back after any hiatus, even if you are not the best singer or the easiest personality to get along with. As long as you fulfill the majority of the requirements, the thinking usually is "the more voices, the better." In at least this sense, your voice matters.

As anyone who has done community organizing of any sort knows, such an open willingness to accommodate people with a wide variety of abilities, experiences, beliefs, needs, desires, and so on can be challenging. Without a strongly shared sense of group culture and/or effective leadership, the sort of pluralism inherent in the very structure of choral musicking, with many voices choosing to join together to produce a shared sound experience in spite of the inevitable differences, occasionally does lead to serious conflict. And yet so many choruses thrive.

As soon as we agree to join our voices with others, there is a way in which every voice must matter or it diminishes the experience for everyone. Experienced choral directors or leaders know and cultivate this value. As Corinne, a director, put it, "The challenge is to bring us all together into . . . into a circle of sound and of our individual voices. And so we . . . we don't try to find the same voice to match up, but we try to blend the voices that come to develop an individual voice so they find out who they are and their personal sound, but then to find the corporate and the ensemble sound. That's . . . that is one of my favorite things. And that's why I do this work." Effective directors inspire singers to listen and to value the blended sound. Many directors have a variety of mantras, such as "We have two ears and one mouth for a reason." They hold each singer as having something to share and hold them to account for doing so as well as they are able. While choruses more commonly manage to find their best sound together in fits and starts, effective groups intentionally nurture everyone's best expression on every level by offering or encouraging smaller group sessions or individual lessons and musical training or singer spotlights to celebrate individual skills/interests and even informal get-togethers, all in an effort to increase mutual respect. In so doing, the group holds each singer's voice as valuable.

The structure and process of (usually weekly) coming together creates and maintains identity practices for the group as well. Each chorus has its own culture, its sense of purpose, but there are several features that all choruses share and perform along a range of possibilities. All place their voices in concert with each other, but the nature of that singing can run the spectrum from singing primarily for each other to primarily for an audience; from extremely formal to very playful; from a focus on musical excellence to a focus on just being together in sound; from primarily relational to primarily artistic; and from only about a certain type of music to primarily about getting a message out—whether religious, social, or political. Each group's choice along these spectra can expand or limit the group's identity possibilities as well as its singers'.

Mission statements for the average secular community chorus are likely to include elements such as providing their community with opportunities for singers to sing together as well as opportunities for the larger community to hear choral music as an art form. There is often an educational component for singers and audience members. Sometimes a group focuses on a particular form, such as barbershop or madrigal—both a cappella singing styles. The following mission statement succinctly captures themes common to many community choruses: "The Lakeshore Community Chorus, an adult non-profit organization, is dedicated to the performance of varied choral music for the benefit, education, and enjoyment of its members and the surrounding lake shore communities."[51] Benefit, enrichment, education, and enjoyment or pleasure are the most common elements formally stated in choral mission statements.[52] While pleasure in one form or another is often acknowledged as valuable in this public way, it is framed and contained in the context of "benefit" and "education." In fact, the question of what type of pleasure one takes becomes more fraught in some religiously based choral groups. In this context, it can be considered sinful to take pleasure in anything more than evangelizing in song—"praising the Lord."[53] The only joy that singing should bring according to this way of thinking is in surrendering one's ego to God. The very fact that this becomes an issue for religious singers suggests that the nature of the pleasure that is possible through singing does not comfortably fit some religious narratives and norms.

What is it about the choral form itself that produces pleasure? A number of recent studies in a range of fields from neuroscience to public health to musicology have explored participation in choral groups, and their findings corroborate what my interviewees expressed. Musicking of all sorts can improve health, lower stress, release oxytocin (the bonding hormone), and increase other pleasure-related brain chemicals.[54] Singing has been shown to lower cortisol levels and have calming effects.[55] And choral singers of all sorts consistently report that their singing with a chorus is central to their feeling better about their lives. Without singing in a group, their lives would be less joyful.

Songs, in seconds, can move us to tears, plumbing the depths of joy and sorrow. When my eyes moisten at the sound of Mozart's "Lachrymosa" or when I find myself flushed with emotions at the sound of a song, especially those commonly played in my youth, I know that I am not alone. The ability of song to slip past our self-composure to stir deep emotion can even seem unnerving. The chaotic feelings stirred by music, especially when linked with the power of words and the sensuality of voice, make this contested terrain. Choral musicking negotiates these Western cultural tensions; queer choral musicking plays them to effect social change.

There is a nakedness to singing. As one choral director, Syl, put it,

> I often am really impressed by the singers. . . . I am really impressed by, like, that they put themselves out, really put themselves out in a really vulnerable, open kind of way. They show up at rehearsal, and I say here's what we're doing, you know? Go for it. I had a conductor, a conducting teacher, that told me . . . "Singers—they are about the most exposed creatures in the universe," you know? And . . . they are so far out on a limb, and they, I mean, those singers are just putting themselves way out there. So he told me, . . . he said, you know, "Your job is to love the singers and support them. You're standing there with your back to the audience; they're up on stage just full out, totally stripping themselves naked up on stage, and your job is to support them, really support them and love them." And I guess it's a very appealing relationship to me, you know? I love that feel; I love feeling that I am doing that with my singers. I am not interested in relating to them in a way where there is a satisfaction of doing what I want them to do. The satisfying thing is I'm facilitating their ability to create this beautiful sound.

While other musicians certainly make use of their bodies to produce music, they have a different focus—something outside of themselves to "play." For singers, their bodies *are* their instruments. As another singer/director, Corinne, put it, "There's just something about the immediacy of the human voice and how it's projected out and what it does for us personally as singers but also how it changes the air around us." It's very personal, the voice. Something as common as a stuffy nose changes the way the instrument itself works. Can it be that because of this nakedness, because of the opportunity it offers to be vulnerable to and with others, millions the world over join choruses?

Many of us have grown up with communal song in ritualized and/or institutional settings: religious services, school assemblies, around the campfire, or holiday celebrations. All these contexts serve to reinforce particular social values and identities (religious, national, group) by connecting the feelings of belonging produced through activities like singing together in ways that reinforce those values. The power of such practices is evident when, for example, the nationalist rhetoric of a country's anthem is able to emotionally move even those who do not support the nationalism such that they find themselves having to actively resist being moved by it.

This power is more than evident in the many negative uses of music, particularly song, to create a shared sense of identity among one group against another. As Bruce Johnson and Martin Cloonan note in *Dark Side of the Tune: Popular Music and Violence*, "That music is complicit in relations of power is a truism of popular music studies. Less often recognized is that musical transactions are therefore double-edged. Every time music is used to demarcate the territory of self or community, it is incipiently being used to invade, marginalize or obliterate that of other individuals or groups."[56] For example, songs to incite people to war historically construct an enemy as deserving to die. Of course, choral communing has been and can be manipulated to all sorts of ends, but this makes choral musicking even more important for us to understand. Insofar as music is an identity-producing and identity-maintaining practice, it is also a moral practice.

Keeping this in mind in a social justice frame requires that we consider the ways in which our own practices, including our choral musicking practices, are based on opening up to others as opposed to closing others out. As Lindemann notes in *Damaged Identities, Narrative Repair*, our counter-storying practices inevitably must be built out of the materials available, out of the culturally dominant storying elements and practices. Otherwise, they would not be legible at all. As such, the best we can hope for is counterstorying that is "good enough," counterstorying that effectively challenges the practices of oppression more broadly so as not to leave others out, counterstorying that calls to task the practice of leaving others out.

In its more benign or beneficent forms, whether queer or not, choral musicking offers a relatively safely structured way for people whose sense of themselves and others has been formed by the binarized value systems of Western culture to enact an expression of their ideal selves together, to hold and be held by each other in the mutual production of vocal sonic experiences that value every voice. But normative choral musicking practices tend to affirm and celebrate racialized, classed, cis, and hetero sex/gender norms. Queer choral musickers, while continuing to struggle with issues of race, class, gender, and other markers of social difference, make use of the form's formality and power to authorize otherwise oppressed identities not through laws but through emotional identification with and through the singers and the music. When the predominantly white GMCW stood on the steps of the Lincoln Memorial singing the words "sweet land of liberty, let freedom ring" to celebrate Obama's inauguration, their predominant whiteness stood celebrating our first mixed-race president, just as their place on the stage at his inauguration authorized them in their identities as gay, thus marking another part of the journey of "America to *be* America," to live up to its own ideals. Even if only for the moments of a performance, queer choral musickers have been able to successfully insert experiences and celebrations of new and changing identities, to affirm and celebrate a freedom of identity formation not so easily engaged outside the emotional embrace that the space of the choral enables. While there is still much counterstorying to do and there are improvements in our practices yet to be imagined, the practice of queer choral musicking shows potential to create spaces for counterstorying at its best and for holding people in identities that the rest of society immorally fails to hold.

7

Communal Erotics

Choral Musicking and Our Capacity for Joy

The conductor hit the downbeat and all this sound came out of me, but it wasn't just me, but it was all this sound around me. Just . . . it felt like it was just coming through my body, and I thought this, this . . . this is just beyond fun. This is real life. This is . . . this is the joy that we're living for. And you . . . you could just feel it in that sound. So I knew right then that this was my . . . this was my calling, why I . . . why I do this work. [Pause] I was very moved. I've never forgotten the physical and emotional feeling of that. –Corinne, singer and conductor

Did you know that whenever you sing full voice, your nipples get hard? –A chorus singer's lover

Erotics, ecstasy, communing. What do these have to do with social justice work? How do the quality, quantity, and nature of our communing matter? There are many ways that queer people have been and continue to be harmed by cultural narratives. As Hilde Lindemann outlines in *Damaged Identities, Narrative Repair*, oppressive master narratives harm people in at least two ways: (1) they keep members of the oppressed group from fully engaging their moral agency while concurrently (2) infiltrating their consciousness with self-denigrating stories.[1] Some of the damaging forms of social denial of full personhood for LGBTIQ people include specific denials of our erotics, ecstasy, and communing. The following are examples:

1. We are denied easy access in our formative years to affirming stories and role models that support full and healthy expression and exploration of our variously gendered and erotic natures (though arguably

this is a problem to varying degrees for all children in cultures that don't value sex as a social good[2]).

2. We are thereby denied an important potential link to the ecstatic in our lives and opportunities for exploring our capacities for joy.

3. Often growing up alone and shamed in our sense of ourselves, we are denied social access to affirming relations, ones that "hold" us in our identities in ways that acknowledge and respect who we feel ourselves to be until we are old enough to independently search out others like us. We are left to search for community that is fragmented and too often as youth are left to do so in dangerous circumstances.

Although in many parts of the world the state of affairs for queer adults is better than it has ever been, the reason so many homeless youth are queer is that many still grow up in families or communities that fail to hold them in their identities as they feel themselves to be. Effective counterstorying practices for people who have been harmed in these ways will engage all three elements—erotics, ecstasy, and communing—to change the stories surrounding this particular form of oppression and to heal individuals and communities from the damage. Our beliefs and feelings about ourselves and each other must change for any larger social change to take hold.

The importance of erotics and ecstasy to work for social justice may seem less obvious than the need for communing, especially given the long history in Western culture of denigrating emotions as feminine, irrational, and chaotic. Of course, such denigration supports webs of narratives that authorize some identities for full personhood and deny others. But denying full humanity to some people based on marking a human quality, such as emotions, or particular erotics as of lesser importance denies all of us a fuller understanding of ourselves. The erotic and ecstatic have been devalued in very specific ways that are core to the damaged identities of both women and queers. If one listens carefully to the experiences of queer choral movement participants, their experiences suggest that choral communing can be both ecstatic and erotic (in the fullest sense of that term) and is an important element in creating the sort of social change necessary for queer social justice. While these elements may have played a role, for example, in both the labor and civil rights movements as well, they play a particular role in healing the damage of both internalized and externalized heterosexism precisely because of the silencing and shaming about gender identities and sexual pleasure that function as a core element of this form of oppression.

Reclaiming the erotic under these circumstances becomes an important act of resistance, as Audre Lorde explains in her "Uses of the Erotic: The Erotic as Power." Lorde's erotic is both more capacious and emotionally integrated than the cultural narratives that work to contain it in ways that parallel attempts to contain the power of musicking.[3] She writes, "The erotic is a measure between our sense of self and the chaos of our strongest feelings. It is an internal sense of satisfaction to which, once we have experienced it, we know we can aspire. For having experienced the fullness of this depth of feeling and recognizing its power, in honor and self-respect we can require no less of ourselves."[4] Lorde argues that the erotic is a resource for personal and shared knowledge and power and that engaging the erotic in its fullest sense as a life practice produces a deeper self-knowledge that comes from experiencing and expressing profound joy that may (or may not) be experienced first or most profoundly through sexuality. It is this "resource within each of us" that can "give us the energy to pursue genuine change within our world."[5] We need this sort of energy to continue doing the work that social change requires over the long term.

Claiming our right to joy through full appreciation and experiences of the erotic becomes an important part of both self-care and social change work within a social context in which the erotic is "vilified, abused, and devalued," because "in order to perpetuate itself, every oppression must corrupt or distort those various sources of power within the culture of the oppressed that can find energy for change."[6] The erotic can be experienced in many forms: "[An] important way in which the erotic connection functions is the open and fearless underlining of my capacity for joy. In the way my body stretches to music and opens into response, hearkening to its deepest rhythms, so every level upon which I sense also opens to the erotically satisfying experience, whether it is dancing, building a bookcase, writing a poem, examining an idea."[7] Lorde insists that those of us who experience oppression must harness the power and responsibility to ourselves and others that comes from fully experiencing our "capacity for joy" in every aspect of our lives and sharing that capacity openly with others:

"Our erotic knowledge empowers us, becomes a lens through which we scrutinize all aspects of our existence, forcing us to evaluate those aspects honestly in terms of their relative meaning within our lives. And this is a grave responsibility, projected from within each of us, not to settle for the convenient, the shoddy, the conventionally expected, nor the merely safe."[8] Once we have that self-knowledge, it can permeate all that we do. If we allow ourselves to experience our full "capacity for joy," Lorde argues we are less willing to accept "being satisfied with suffering and self-negation. . . . Our acts against oppression become integral with self, motivated and empowered from within."[9] It takes people who are willing to refuse oppression because they have tasted something better to stand up against it effectively. Queer choral musicking offers musickers regular opportunities to explore their capacity for joy.

In the process, Lorde argues against our separation of the rational from the emotional, the logical from the spiritual. Presaging what neuroscientists are now claiming about knowledge being feeling based, though from a poet-philosopher's perspective, she argues that our deepest knowledge comes with our deepest feelings; it comes with the power of eros, not in its absence. Erotics, ecstasy, and the sacred come back together in Lorde's model rather than being opposed to each other. Extending our capacity for joy into all of our work counters the repression of that which is powerful in each of us. Additionally and importantly in relationship to the work queer choral musicking does, she argues that "the sharing of joy, whether physical, emotional, psychic, or intellectual, forms a bridge between the sharers which can be the basis for understanding much of what is not shared between them, and lessens the threat of their difference."[10] Given the disparate pieces of identity that often problematically huddle together in queer "community," LGBTIQ peoples need all the bridges we can build among ourselves as well as beyond. Queer choral musicking creates opportunities for just such a sharing of joy, and it does so in a form that encourages respect for every voice.

No doubt this sharing of joy has been part of the draw in the musicking practices of all social justice work, but there are some important differences. Musicking and social justice work might come together in any number of ways. For example, Rob Rosenthal and Richard Flacks focus on what they call the minstrel/audience model as a primary form that social movement musicking takes across the political spectrum. In this model, professional minstrels serve the movement by collecting, composing, arranging, rearranging, and performing in a wide array of venues. While the primary focus of their study is on the minstrel/audience model, Rosenthal and Flacks discuss the importance of singing along and singer participation in the process of movement building, though not choral singing. In terms of the production of songs, they note, "The democracy of song is exemplified by . . . folks songs," which are "disseminated orally," thereby promoting "modification of lyrics and melody." Following the development of that quintessential movement song "We Shall Overcome," for example, highlights the interplay of minstrels and organizers in movement work. They write,

> [The song] originated as a black church song in the nineteenth century, and was adapted by southern tobacco workers during a strike in the 1940s. That version of the song was adapted by Pete Seeger for public performance, then carried and taught to civil rights movement activists in the early 1960s by Guy Carawan. Once sung in the civil rights rallies, it continued to spread . . . around the planet to become a kind of universal protest anthem. . . . The popularization of "We Shall Overcome" and other civil rights anthems involved organizers, activists, and supporters of many kinds and from many social locations. Pete Seeger and Guy Carawan were both politically conscious minstrels whose interaction with local activists helped the process of song production and dissemination.[11]

They carefully show how the political use of songs in contestatory settings, while often "produced directly in struggle contexts," requires both the "creativity of local people reinventing songs drawn from their folk traditions" and "the deliberate efforts by organizers and minstrels to disseminate them."[12] While there might be labor choruses or concerts for pleasure, the purpose of the musicking in these cases is often more directly tied to movement work: to focus and structure meetings, at gatherings, on picket lines, or at protests.

Based on their extensive interviews, Rosenthal and Flacks delineate four primary functions of musicking for social change across the political spectrum: (1) serving the committed through "affirmation, reaffirmation, and sustenance,"[13] especially in maintaining commitment over long and difficult periods; (2) educating about the issues; (3) converting and recruiting people to the cause; and (4) mobilizing people into specific actions for social movements. Queer choral musicking does all these things, but in light of the work for social justice that it performs, I would bring Lindemann's work to bear on these to add two somewhat overlapping functions: (1) healing, developing, and maintaining healthier identities through counterstorying and (2) cultivating moral practices of holding and letting go of our own and each others' identities as we grow. In fulfilling these functions, choral musicking as a practice serves LGBTIQ people in particularly useful ways.

Queer choral musicking does not have minstrel leaders who are connected to or have become a voice of the larger movement in quite the same way that, say, Pete Seeger or Guy Carawan did. While the music of Bernice Johnson Reagon and Holly Near, for example, have certainly enjoyed wide play within the movement and both have filled various roles performing with and offering workshops for the choruses over the years, the choruses do not primarily look to them to be movement leaders or to teach and lead them in songs, though on specific occasions they have. Because choral musicking is based in more formal classical practices such as reading music rather than oral/aural learning, it demands a different level of commitment to learning the music. The choruses commission works more often than they look to "minstrels" as song leaders. And while the mission statements of the choruses express goals that to varying degrees articulate their intentions to change hearts and minds, the emphasis is at least as strongly, and often more so, on the pleasure and the quality of the musicking than on any direct connection to larger movement for social justice.

In terms of song production, for example, the choruses do change lyrics to fit specific political contexts and purposes as musickers in other movements do, and they appropriate any number of styles and genres to create desired counterstorying effects. While other movements have created their own songbooks for members to sing from, queer choruses have commissioned so many new compositions and new arrangements as to create substantial change to the body of all choral music available. The choruses themselves perform in ways that might parallel the work of the minstrel, but efforts to link choral musicking more directly to specific social justice work in the ways that labor and civil rights movement historically have, for example, has largely been local and dependent on connections between people in any given chorus and local leaders doing social justice work than on the scope of any larger queer movement. Though queer choruses have performed for everyone from presidents to royalty and on most every type of occasion—formal, informal, spontaneous (as in the case of the murder of Mayor Moscone and Harvey Milk, for example)— and they have performed in most every type of venue, large and small, including several times in Carnegie Hall, and though there are a number of festival anthems that have been rousing, the movement has not yet developed anthems to rival "We Shall Overcome" or "Solidarity Forever." Perhaps because of the emotional needs that queer choral musicking fills as well as the alphabet soup of the identities it holds, or perhaps because of its more pleasure-oriented emphasis, it might not. And it may not need to in quite the same way as other movements have.

These variations are related both to the difference in social form between folk musicking practices and choral musicking practices and to the particularities of the forms of oppression being addressed. While choral musicking definitely makes use of folk music and labor activist musickers might well form choruses to do their work, it's precisely the formality of choral musicking and its ties to religious and classical history that make this form particularly useful to queer movement for social justice. Laborers have their shared workplaces and connections through work, and those working for racial justice have families and communities that share their experience of oppression. LGBTIQ people have not historically claimed these shared spaces or relations as cultural capital for their cause, and many still cannot. In this way, the choruses serve as a foundational cultural building practice that other groups do not require in the same way. Although there is obviously an element of trading on the social class and predominantly white privilege of this form (excepting the queer gospel choirs) to create space for people to "be otherwise," the communal practice of choral musicking itself serves to hold identities in ways that the larger culture fails to do.

Having sung in choruses for most of my life and now after formally and informally interviewing participants, watching, listening, taking notes on, and researching the many reasons people sing in any chorus, but particularly queer choruses, it seems to me that activists tend to undervalue the power of artistic expression, certainly in this form, because we fail to adequately assess what we are up to in choral musicking. Yes, choral musickers love the music to varying degrees (though most choral singers have performed pieces they never learned to love) and we love to sing in harmony and dissonance with others. However, my research suggests that an important reason that people come together in this particular social form is to express and share in a potentially vulnerable and transcendent manner the full range of human emotions surrounded by others expressing and mirroring these emotions together in ways we do not commonly allow ourselves, especially in Western culture, and the formality of choral musicking makes this practice feel relatively safe for musickers—both singers and audience members.

The communing possible through choral singing is powerful. It begins with literal inspiration—to take in breath—the first requirement to singing. Doing this well, as a group, in time, together, is a challenge at first clumsily attempted. Slowly, through practice, it becomes a pleasurable rhythm, each body in tune with each other's breath. Not only does group song making require regular practice to make it beautiful, but it requires an intimate attention to each other simultaneously as individuals and as a group. At their best, singers listen to both themselves and each other's every breath, tone, and silence for cues with an attentiveness that few of us ever receive outside of the most intimate of relationships.

Choral singing requires the ability to hold one's own while constantly listening and tuning with others. Together singers are able to produce sound that no one singer alone is capable of producing, not only because we cannot sing two or more parts at once or because numbers increase vocal power, but because, even in unison, every voice is affected by the voices surrounding it, tempered in relation to the voices next to it. When the vocal sound produced is perfectly formed, the resonance materially thrills the singers, like a bell's clear ring through every cell of the body. It creates an experience of beauty and often deep emotion produced in relationship with bodies unmediated by instruments. It reaches us through language, as those of us with hearing knew it first: as vocal tones, rhythm, and sound, through oral/aural connections. It can be a space of the erotic in Lorde's sense because it is a mutually pleasuring experience and expansion of our capacity for joy. It is by no means always this way, but the practice of choral musicking offers this potential for any group of singers.

Along with Lorde's more full-bodied sense of the erotic comes acknowledgement of our moments of ecstasy—the places where, in the context of choral musicking, the embodied communal sharing of such joy can lead to what one singer at a workshop referred to as "the best group sex there is." This vein of expression runs throughout the interviews, suggesting that the erotic element is even more important in specific ways for those of us whose identities are damaged in precisely the expression of our erotic sensibilities. Queer choral musickers express moments of sharing profound joy, moments of ecstasy, with all the power usually associated with religious experience, but without the religion. These are experiences that make our hearts skip a beat, with a knowledge in our cells that we are part of something much larger than we comprehend, whose beauty makes us hold our breath, for which the exhale is the embodied expression of joy. Such qualities keep singers and audience members returning to this place of what I believe is, at its best, sacredly erotic communing.

If we understand the sacred as an experience of that which is greater than ourselves and are able to experience this not as an affirmation of some outside entity's power over us, as is the case in most religious contexts, but communally in resistance to anyone's power to oppress (including our own), then we lift the sacred out of the relatively closed realms of many current religious institutional practices to create a more open secular and polyphonic social practice for holding identities that are not well held otherwise. For those who have largely been left at the margins of both family and community life, such communing is not just compelling; it is necessary to enacting counterstories that allow us to know ourselves and for others to know us differently.

In my interviews with those in queer choruses, when singers attempted to express what exactly kept them coming back for more, words often failed them. Many said things like, "I just don't know how to explain it." Or they would make several different attempts and remain dissatisfied with their responses. For example, here is Syl's attempt to describe the power of queer choral musicking: "I love vocal sound. I think the whole thing about the fact that we have a voice at all, and the fact that our voices can make these beautiful sounds, is incomparable, and the fact that language can express the things it can express, the fact that poetry can do what it does, is also just miraculous. (Pause) . . . And then combining it with (Pause) . . . we get to have message and mission with GALA Choruses is like (Pause). . . ." Words failed her here, and physical expression—bringing her hand to her heart—had to suffice. For Syl and others, what keeps them coming back is something about the mix of the power of choral musicking generally along with the added mission of queer choral musicking to change hearts and minds.

David at first admitted that words failed him, but then he tried again and offered a description that suggests a state of euphoria: "[One] of my most memorable moments was [the] GALA [festival] in Miami in 2008. There was something about being able to sing for your peers, and just the feeling of euphoria when you come off the stage and you're welcomed with open arms from your peers. Not to criticize or judge or, you know, critique how your performance was, but just to embrace what each chorus does. And it was just in—incredible. (Pause) Words can't describe that. (Pause) I don't think I touched the ground for a half an hour after I came off the stage." He attempted to express what was important to him about queer choral musicking by describing a particular experience singing at one of the GALA Festivals, which, unlike most other choral festivals, are noncompetitive and celebratory. As he makes clear through his personal experience, the festivals create a large-scale space of mutual affirmation for, with, and across differences.

Expressing the ineffable more matter-of-factly, through a turn to the metaphysical, Dan explains, "Magic happens; lives are changed somehow, someway. If it weren't doing that, it would not have the drive that it does for me." Obviously the feelings about what queer choral musicking does for participants are powerful. They claim that it magically transforms lives, their own and others', in ways similar to what many religious organizations strive to do. They describe their choruses as family, and they even use parallel experiences with churches they grew up in and had to leave behind to describe the kind of family they mean. They claim choral musicking sustains them and offers them ways to see themselves and others anew, to practice new ways of being that go beyond merely contesting the master narratives to creating their own with a practice of a weekly embodied affirmation of their various selves as they understand them. In my own choruses, I have watched as people joined, unsure of their voices, and in the process of developing their singing voices with the group, they dared to gain a voice of leadership within the chorus and eventually working for social justice beyond the chorus. Variations of this story were repeated by more than half of my interviewees.

While we might place such work in the category of serving the committed, queer choral musicking complicates Rosenthal and Flacks's categories for musicking in the service of social movements. After interviewing queer choral musickers, I found that healing and healthy identity formation—individually and as a group—go beyond merely serving the committed in this case, and based on Lindemann's understanding of holding and letting go of our own and each other's identities as a moral practice, these functions need to be teased out as important to all musicking for social justice.[14] Given the challenges of growing up in families with varying abilities to understand queer identities and communities in which it is still often dangerous to grow up queer, experiencing such a strong affirmation by being held in sonic embrace with those who are willing to hold a space for each musicker to explore new ways of being can be an important antidote to identity-damaging stories that still shape peoples' lives as well as a way to embody counterstorying practice.

If we accept Hilde Lindemann's claim that holding each other in our identities is a moral practice, then arguably choral musicking in general is an ethical practice for holding identities that can be done well or badly. Because the choral form itself is structurally one that brings many voices together, requiring each voice to hold true to its own notes alongside others through dissonance and harmony, and because it invites singers to grow stronger of voice as well as to learn to listen well to others' voicings even as others' voicings challenge their own, every voice matters and every voice needs the others to create great choral sound. In this way, choral musicking arguably offers opportunities to practice some ways of being that serve a pluralist democracy.[15] While there are most often song leaders or directors whom singers agree to follow (or not), even within a very formally structured chorus, each voice matters and needs the others. Every voice has its own particular "grain"[16] that needs to accommodate, to greater or lesser degrees for different song genres, the grain of the surrounding voices. This agreement in moments of practice and performance to join voices in physically rather intimate ways—even when there might be great differences outside of these moments—offers a practice of holding each other in our differences as we come together to create something greater than our individual selves, sometimes even experiences of joy and ecstasy that often bring us to tears. While the form itself offers this potential, the practice, like all other human practices, can be done well or badly, musically and morally. What is interesting about the choral musicking form is that the most beautiful music generally comes from choruses whose members manage to listen well to and with each other, differences and all. In queer choral musicking we have a history of celebrating this particular practice, especially at festivals.

If we accept Christopher Small's claim that musicking practices express ideal social relations; that through musicking we are able to "explore," "affirm," and "celebrate" our values as people together; and that we effectively state through our musicking practices, "These are our values, these are our concepts of ideal relationships, and consequently, this is who we are,"[17] then straight choruses that do not recognize the ways in which their musicking practices erase or even denigrate LGBTIQ peoples, or primarily white choruses that do not recognize the ways in which their musicking practices erase or even denigrate people of color, or men's choruses that do not recognize the ways in which their musicking practices erase or even denigrate women, for example, are morally suspect by Lindemann's measure. I want to argue that we err when we try to simply "be inclusive," especially in cultural forms like choral musicking. Rather, we need to be more conscious on every level about the ways in which each of us is both oppressed and privileged. We do best to both respect our own and others' needs for relatively safe spaces to explore and express our identities with others while also remaining aware that the ways in which we do so might be at the expense of others. If we hope to live up to the inclusivity we espouse, of holding ourselves and others in our identities in healthy and supportive ways, then we will look for ways to change our own practices for greater social justice.

It is an inevitably imperfect process, but choral musicking offers practices for considering how to better embrace differences: acknowledging that there are many different voices in the room and making creative best use of each of those voices for greater shared purposes. So, for example, a primarily white gay men's chorus looking to create greater social justice might best regularly assess how well they balance the healing identity practices of their musickers (singers, artistic staff, and audience members) with using their privilege to more effectively address the social inequities of race and gender, among others. In what ways does the practice of holding themselves in their identities effectively denigrate others? Do they hold themselves and others in a form of masculinity that is based on heterosexist values that not only denigrate women but also denigrates themselves? The Portland Gay Men's Chorus stepped up to this task in an interesting way at Festival 2016 by singing "I Am Woman." In the context of social media's "#I am _____ (fill in the latest victim of violence)" to show support, their performance made an important statement.

These issues might be addressed on many levels, from the choice of music to the performance venues to kinds of community outreach. By allying with groups working on a range of social justice issues, not only do choruses expand their reach, but they more deeply serve their own social justice missions. Given the overall whiteness and relative class privilege of queer choral musickers, working with the homeless, those in prison, or local communities of color, for example, seems important. As Lindemann makes clear, there is no perfect way to create effective counternarratives, because they are inevitably to some degree tethered to current norms. Otherwise, no one would comprehend them. And creative social practices such as choral musicking are always creating narratives—counter and master—in both form and content. This places a moral responsibility on all of us to challenge ourselves to create increasingly inclusive counterstorying practices—ones that make space for respecting all our identities.

Queer choral musicking is an example of what Judith Peraino refers to as a "technology of the self that allows one not just to 'think differently' but to 'think queerly,' such that identity becomes undermined and entirely new ways of being suddenly and abruptly come into view," allowing "queer ethical subjects [to] emerge through musical self-practice." Such "queer ethical subjects" potentially undermine the subjectivity (the identities) authorized by the home, church, or state.[18] Such queer ethical subjects transform the either/or produced through binary logic and valuing systems (you belong or you don't) into a logic of both/and (you are different and you belong). Choral musicking practices enable the holding of different identities together in sonic embrace through dissonance, unison, and harmony, making the choral a particularly rich place to support the development of queer ethical subjects.

Queer choruses perform in the slippage between sociomusical dichotomies to resist them, producing instead popular and classical, activism and art, words and music, body and mind, trans and cis, female and male, and homo and hetero with an implied, if not stated, intent to transcend these binaries. To claim queerness in a place as ritually formal, proper, and normative as choral performances creates a place for us to imagine—and perhaps, for a time, practice—being new, ideal selves not based on othering, a place to produce queer presence/representations through embodied voice. Perhaps more than many other groups that come together to fight oppression, the very identities of those lumped together to form the alphabet soup of this "community" have been challenging to each other. In coming together to work our ways through these differences, the choruses offer some interesting models not just for queer movement for social justice but for all such movements.

ACKNOWLEDGMENTS

This work has been a twenty-year endeavor that never would have happened without the support of a great many people—far too many to name. There are, of course, all the members of the many choruses who inspire me by singing for social justice. This book could never have existed without them, especially the membership and leadership of the many choruses who invited me in, as well as the leadership of the larger international umbrella organizations: the Gay and Lesbian Association of Choruses (GALA), Sister Singers, and Legato. I am particularly grateful to Desert Voices: Arizona's Premiere Gay and Lesbian Chorus for supporting me through my dissertation years and for introducing me to the scope of queer choral musicking; to the short-lived but sweet little chorus Freedom Sings OUT!, cofounded with Susan Crespi in Ventura; as well as to the Lesbian and Gay Chorus of San Francisco, which certainly enriched the sabbatical year during which I finished this book.

The support of colleagues from the time I decided to take this project on has been priceless. In the early years of thinking through how to research queer choral musicking, colleagues at the University of Arizona helped me think through shaping research questions and processes. I am particularly grateful for the wisdom and support of Monique Wittig and Elizabeth Lapovsky Kennedy at this stage of the project's development.

California State University Channel Islands (CSUCI) has offered me substantial support from my initial research package to minigrants and sabbatical time. There is no way this book would have been possible without it. I am particularly grateful to Ted Lucas and Renny Christopher for their mentoring, guidance, and friendship, as well as the support of so many of my colleagues at CSUCI.

A number of scholars beyond my home universities have also offered their support for this project over the years. I am particularly grateful to Eric Rofes and Lillian Robinson, who both offered substantial moral support at rough points along the way.

Several people have played substantial roles in the grunt work of research and editing. Alison Reichle has offered moral support from the start as well as substantial research assistance. Heather Trumbower, John Bormanis, and several of my book group members—Marianne Slaughter, Jack Lindner, and Peter Chapas—have offered important feedback as the book took shape. And no one has been through more versions of this manuscript than Renny Christopher. Her incisive comments over the years have been invaluable and helped me find my way out of the weeds so many times I have lost count. I am forever indebted to her patience and keen eye. Of course, no book makes it to the home stretch without an editor, and mine has been phenomenal. From the time I met Kim Guinta, I knew I wanted to work with her, and she has proven my intuition correct at each turn. Her down-to-earth approach, honest appraisals, and sincere support for the project have made the process of getting this book done so much easier than it might have been.

The loving support of my family and friends who have listened ad nauseum as I worked my way through struggles and frustrations, who have attended decades of concerts, and who have cheered me on and off stage has sustained me. I am particularly grateful to have the best sister in the whole world, Rita Shilling. Finally, the unfailing loving support of my son, Rain Balén; of my daughter-in-law, Reiko Takahashi; and of the best spouse anyone could ask for, Heather Trumbower, is dear to me beyond measure.

APPENDIX

Methodology

Cultural studies research methods often include ethnography, historiography, and discourse analysis (in which everything is a text to be read within a cultural context). This interdisciplinary research usually takes place in relationship to a particular set of theoretical frameworks with a goal of getting at cultural meaning-making practices within particular contexts, especially as they relate to social power relations. As an exploration of the question of why so many people have turned to choruses to organize for queer social justice, this study documents the work of the choruses and their musicking practices, comparing them to other forms of musicking practices for social justice as well as historically placing them comparatively in relationship with other related queer cultural organizing for change. I make use of this comparative approach in order to highlight the particular meaning-making and identity-producing practices specific to queer choral musicking.

This book offers a cultural analysis of my own extensive participant observation—actively researching since 1999 but experientially beginning with my first lesbian-feminist choral experiences in the late 1970s. It includes information and materials from fifty-six formal interviews ranging from thirty minutes to more than three hours in length beginning in 2001; archival research at the Gay and Lesbian Association of Choruses (GALA) offices as well as the materials generously offered by a number of choruses; and materials I have gathered over all these years from my participation, including copious notes, e-mails, listservs, websites, and recordings. While my role in producing this research might be more like that of an artistic director, I place my own voice in this text as I have in practice and in concert, blending and balancing with the voices of many others. As is true for any piece of social analysis, I tell stories here. They are stories based as accurately as possible not just on my own perspective, nor primarily on the stories of others taken at face value, but on those stories cross-checked across sources primary and secondary wherever possible.

Methodological Challenges

As sociologists and active musickers Rob Rosenthal and Richard Flacks, point out in *Playing for Change: Music and Musicians in the Service of Social Movements*, "Researching the [music-movement] link runs into serious methodological problems."[1] Because musicking is always an embedded social practice, there is no clear way to tease out the specific role played. Wanting not to fall into the "vagueness, mystification, and confusion" that they argue characterizes "much of what has been written about the music-movement link," they map some of the challenges: "the mere presence of music in a movement" does not "prove its effectiveness"; lyrics alone do not explain how they are received or used by listeners and do not account for the effect of the musicking experience; the intent of a composer or performer "is not the same thing as audience reception"; and audience reception is affected by a great many complex factors. Even the method they chose of getting "inside the head of each musicker" through extensive interviews has its problems because "people may not realize how they use music or its effect on their thinking or behavior. They may romanticize it, or dismiss it, or in any number of ways distort its actual effect. . . . Further, they (and we) may easily conflate the effect of the music with other factors since music is typically experienced as one part of complex packages that may include romantic attractions, political allegiances, café discussions, and so on."[2] Because "there is no scientific or consensual way to measure such matters," they adopted "investigative methods" that they hope offer some "ways to make useful conjectures." In the process, they offer some very useful mappings of what they learned from their interviews that I build on here.

While their primary questions are "How can music affect human action?" and "How is music a *resource* for social movement?"[3] mine are "Why and how have LGBTIQA people been making strategic use of choral musicking for social justice?" While I also worked to get "inside the head(s) of [a range of queer choral] musicker(s)," I analyze this and all the other materials I have collected through a comparative cultural studies lens. This analysis makes use of a number of philosophical and social science frameworks.

Participant Observation

My participant observation began before I ever thought to study queer choral musicking. As a singer in a nascent mixed queer chorus who was also completing a dissertation on power, embodiment, and language, I found both my own desire and those of my choral companions particularly strange and deeply pleasurable. The practice of choral singing in Western culture is intimately tied to religion such that finding high-quality choral scores—ones that are musically gratifying and artistically challenging (within a Western-trained musical context) but are not religiously based—was difficult. I was not alone in my discomfort with singing religious music, especially Christian music, in the face of the Christian Right's backlash against queers and women. And what was it about this particular form of musicking that drew us together—what were its particular pleasures? As I stepped up to leadership in my chorus and began to better understand the scope of this highly embodied practice, I started by taking notes, gathering materials, and attending as many related events as possible. In all, I have almost thirty years of choral singing experience that includes several years in professional choruses—including opera—about fifteen in college/university choruses, and more than sixteen in queer choruses, as well as a smattering of smaller, less-defined group singing experiences. I have attended several queer regional and national choral leadership institutes, five GALA Festivals (Tampa in 1996, San Jose in 2000, Montréal in 2004, Miami in 2008, and Denver in 2012), and one Various Voices Festival (Europe's festival) in Dublin in 2014. At each of these events, I have participated in workshops and trainings on everything from singing techniques to choral organizing and its challenges. I have gathered all the evidence I could that might help me better understand and articulate the relationship between the practices of choral musicking and creating greater social justice. Evidence includes notes, workshop materials, and documentary photos of workshops in practice that captured diverse queer choral musicking experiences across twenty years and two continents.

Interviews

The fifty-five interviews took place between 2001 and 2014. My initial Institutional Review Board (IRB) required that I maintain anonymity for my interviewees in spite of the fact that many of those interviewed were irritated by that requirement. The sense of the IRB in 2001 was that I could be placing my interviewees in danger by outing them. In fact, because many states still do not have employment, housing, and other protections in place for LGBTIQ peoples, this is arguably still true. In later years, IRBs approved the option to use real names, but for the sake of consistency, I have chosen to anonymize all interviewees, except in a few rare cases in which I have permission and the stories and people are well known and/ or there is some value to making the details more specific. Interviewees included two trans people (one genderqueer and the other MTF), twenty-eight women, and twenty-five men.

The choice of interviewees was not randomized, as funding for this study was quite limited and doing so was beyond my means. That said, I did make every effort in my outreach to find as broad a spectrum of participants as possible. Many interviews took place at festivals or conferences and took place any time I was able to travel to strategic metropolitan areas where I would have access to a range of choruses. All interviewees are self-selected through my personal interactions with choruses, e-mail lists, and the support of GALA. I was able to gain interviews with singers, directors, organizers, composers, supporters, and audience members from the U.S. East Coast, West Coast, Midwest, South, and Southwest, as well as a few Canadian, Irish, British, Australian, and German singers, organizers, and directors.

I have tried to balance SSAA, TTBB, and SATB experiences as well and have interviewed singers and directors from all three almost equally. Given the predominance of TTBB choruses, this might skew the picture a bit, though the longest interviews in terms of time spent and lengths of transcripts were with those from TTBB choruses. Many of the people I interviewed have been involved with more than one chorus over a number of years and some at the same time. The movement is predominantly white, as are my interviewees, with only two people of color in the mix. To balance this part of the picture, I took part in a number of workshops and events whenever possible that brought racial and class perspectives to bear. I was not able to interview any youth from the choruses, though I did interview a number of directors who have worked with developing youth choruses.

The interview questions included the following, though many of the conversations expanded quite a bit from these.

INTERVIEW QUESTIONS

1. What do you think is the most important thing to tell people about GALA choruses?
2. Tell me about your chorus. (Prompts if needed: Is it all lesbian? All gay men? Mixed? How many singers does it have? What is its history?)
3. How has the group changed over time? Why? Has there been any dissension? What are your feelings about the changes?
4. What are the boundaries of acceptance for the group? Who feels comfortable in your chorus in terms of sexualities or other identities? Who does not? Why?
5. Does it matter what chorus members think politically? What are the boundaries of discourse/acceptance?
6. In what ways does your chorus constitute a community?
7. What relationship does it have to the LGBT community where you live? The larger community?
8. Why is it important for you to sing?
9. Is song more important to you than other music? How and why?
10. What do you think a socially just world would look like?
11. Do you think your singing makes a difference in the world? Individually, as a group, in what ways? Examples?
12. What is your chorus saying about what it means to be LGBT?

Terminology

Queer choral movement works to make social space for otherwise illegible identities to self-name, to be affirmed as such, and to flourish. But as with all such movements, it operates in the midst of the ongoing shifts to find better terminology and better ways to make people legible to each other and to the larger culture. It is an imperfect process, the challenges of which I hope become clearer in this book. But it is a necessary process in which this book comes at a particular place and time. Because choruses range both in degrees of outness and in what they are outing, I have chosen when I speak of the choruses themselves to use a not completely accurate but what I feel is a reasonably balanced alphabet-soup model: LGBTIQA (the *A* is for "allies"—straight people who are willing to be read as queer in public). Some would double the *Q* to cover "queer" and "questioning," but it seems to me that one *Q* can stand for both, just as the *T* stands for "transsexual" and "transgender" and the *G* could arguably stand for both "gay" and "genderqueer." I chose this because it covers the various ways the choruses and their members currently identify.

While I am sensitive to the fact that many members of the choral movement might still find the term *queer* offensive, when I speak of the choral movement as a movement or as a practice, I have chosen to use it for a number of reasons. First of all, it has gained more popular positive usage within the movement, so its sting is not likely to be anywhere near as powerful as it might have been even five years ago. But more so, by harkening back to its original meaning of "different," as well as its potential use as both a noun and a verb, it better resists the sort of static form of identity as a noun that can so easily be assimilated and repurposed by the larger culture (as explained in Chapter 5) to deny full personhood. It keeps open more possibilities for ways of being human. Because I believe that the choral movement is one piece of queer organizing for social justice that enables more creative possibilities for being human, I hope that readers for whom this word still holds some memory of painful times will understand my intention and will be able to find a way to at least let the word be there without harm.

Another usage that may seem strange to the ears of many is my use of *movement* as something in motion rather than the more common usage: "*the* _____ movement." I do this to emphasize at least two aspects of social movements that tend to get lost in "*the* movement" language. One is that there has never been a single version of any social movement. Social movements are more accurately characterized as a conglomeration of many diverse groups of people pressing for similar changes, though often from a wide variety of positions and perspectives that do not necessarily get along. While there may be occasional amalgamation, the seemingly inevitable tendency to homogenize into one single name something that is, in fact, so multifaceted flattens the ability to adequately understand the nature of social change. Another reason is that when we speak of "the civil rights movement," for example, we tend to think of the 1950s and 1960s, but "civil rights movement" continues today. It is just that for the past fifty years the backlash against it has had an impressively loud voice telling the story that this movement is "no longer needed," though we will see in the coming years if the tables might turn on the noisemakers in that shouting match with #BlackLivesMatter.

NOTES

INTRODUCTION

1. In his work *Musicking: The Meanings of Musical Performances* (Hanover: University Press of New England, 1998), Christopher Small coined the term *musicking* to express music making as a social practice that represents a group's idealized relations.

2. I am sensitive to the fact that some members of the choral movement might still find the term *queer* offensive, but I have chosen to use it when I speak of choral movement as a social movement or practice for a number of reasons: (1) it has gained more popular positive usage within this movement, so its sting is not likely to be anywhere near as powerful as it might have been even five years ago; (2) by harkening back to its original meaning of "different," as well as its potential use as both a noun and a verb, it better resists the sort of static form of identity as a noun that can so easily be assimilated and repurposed by the larger culture (as we shall see in chapter 5) to deny people full personhood; and (3) it keeps open more possibilities for ways of being human. Because I believe that choral movement is one piece of queer organizing for social justice that enables more creative possibilities for being human—ones that I will argue need to be based on exploring our capacities for joy together—I hope that those of you for whom this word still holds some memory of painful times, upon understanding my intention, will be able to find a way to at least let the word be there without harm.

3. I use the descriptors *queer* and *straight* here not to essentialize or to imply that all choruses are one or the other. Many straddle these categories in a variety of ways that will become clearer in later chapters. I use the terms as shorthand to denote the identities performed and privileged by the choruses and their umbrella organizations purposely or by default.

4. For those who are interested, a more detailed methodology for this study is offered in the appendix.

5. The Gay and Lesbian Association of Choruses at that time had "International" as part of the name but scaled back in part due to economic pressures and a need for greater accuracy about who they are able to serve, though in recent years, the organization has had an increasingly international aspect to it. "History," *Gala Choruses*, accessed January 2016, http://galachoruses.org/about/history.

6. To hear Angelou perform this poem, see "And Still I Rise," YouTube video, 1:05, posted by "mohitbahi," April 5, 2007, https://www.youtube.com/watch?v=JqOqo5oLSZo.

7. "History," *Gala Choruses*, accessed January 2016, http://www.galachoruses.org/about/history.

8. Names of those I interviewed throughout are pseudonyms unless otherwise noted. See "Methodology" in the appendix for more information.

9. I prefer the use of *movement* as something in motion rather than the more common and more static usage: "*the* _____ movement.*" This shift emphasizes at least two aspects of social movements that tend to get lost: (1) there has never been a single version of any social movement and (2) movement for social justice never ends; it just morphs with the times.

10. I owe a note of gratitude here to Alison Reichle for nursing me through the physical fever as well as being the first sounding board for many years for the more slow-burning intellectual fire that ignited there.

11. For more, see Janos Gereben, "Chorus America and America's Millions of Choral Singers," *San Francisco Classical Voice*, May 23, 2011, accessed July 31, 2016, https://www.sfcv.org/article/chorus-america-and-americas-millions-of-choral -singers.

12. This singer's preferred nongendered pronouns are *ze* (s/he) and *zir* (his/him/her).

13. Numbers here are based on November 2015 listings—a time when choruses were in preparation for the quadrennial festival held in July 2016. The numbers were relatively unchanged in December 2016. Member chorus information is regularly updated at "Membership: Worldwide Map of GLBT Choruses," *Gala Choruses*, accessed December 2016, http://www.galachoruses.org/chorus-map.

14. For a taste of the 2016 festival, see "Events: GALA Festival," *Gala Choruses*, accessed December 2016, http://www.galachoruses.org/events/gala-festival.

15. Rob Rosenthal and Richard Flacks, *Playing for Change: Music and Musicians in the Service of Social Movements* (Boulder, CO: Paradigm, 2011), 25.

16. Ibid.

CHAPTER 1   SINGING AS COUNTERSTORYING PRACTICE

1. The analysis of counterstorying used throughout is primarily based on the work of Hilde Lindemann. For more on different forms and theories of counterstorying practices, see, for example, Dolores Delgado Bernal, Rebeca Burciaga, and Judith Flores Carmona, eds., special issue, "Chicana/Latina Testimonios: Mapping the Methodological, Pedagogical, and Political," *Equity & Excellence in Education* 45, no. 3 (2012): 363–72; and Chela Sandoval, "US Third World Feminism: The Theory and Method of Differential Oppositional Consciousness," in *The Feminist Standpoint Theory Reader: Intellectual and Political Controversies*, ed. Sandra G. Harding, 195–209 (Boulder, CO: Westview Press, 1998).

2. For those not familiar with Western choral singing, there are a number of variations of these voicings (TTBB). For example, a particular piece of music might
call for splitting the soprano voices into two sections and altos into two without tenor or bass. This would be referred to as a piece for SSAA, meaning high
soprano or soprano 1, low soprano or soprano 2, and so on. Choruses sometimes
identify themselves structurally in this manner as well based on the voices they
have in the group: for example, SATB, TB, TTBB.

3. For a social science study and analysis in the U.S. context, see Jane Junn, "Par-
ticipation in Liberal Democracy: The Political Assimilation of Immigrants and
Ethnic Minorities in the United States," *American Behavioral Scientist* 42, no. 9
(July 1999): 1417–38. For a philosophical perspective, see Judith Butler, *Excitable
Speech: A Politics of the Performative* (New York: Routledge, 1997).

4. Thanks to my colleague John Bormanis for the reminder that similar slogan-
eering has repeatedly been used for war. See a list of some ways this language
has been used in Elizabeth Dickinson, "A Bright Shining Slogan: How 'Hearts
and Minds' Came to Be," *FP*, August 22, 2009, accessed January 2016, http://
foreignpolicy.com/2009/08/22/a-bright-shining-slogan/.

5. While it is obviously not the focus of this study, it is important to point
out that music is used for nefarious purposes as well, making our understanding of its workings all the more important. Recent studies on this
include Suzanne G. Cusick, "Afterword to 'You Are in a Place That Is Out of
the World . . .': Music in the Detention Camps of the 'Global War on Terror,'" *Transposition. Musique et Sciences Sociales*, no. 4 (2014); Cusick, "'You
Are in a Place That Is Out of the World . . .': Music in the Detention Camps
of the 'Global War on Terror,'" *Journal of the Society for American Music* 2, no. 1
(2008): 1–26, doi:10.1017/ S1752196308080012; and Bruce Johnson and Martin
Cloonan, *Dark Side of the Tune: Popular Music and Violence*, Ashgate Popular
and Folk Music Series (Burlington, VT: Ashgate, 2008).

6. Hilde Lindemann Nelson, *Damaged Identities, Narrative Repair* (Ithaca: Cornell
University Press, 2001).

7. "Kentucky Clerk Opposed to Gay Marriage Says State Law Negates Appeal,"
Reuters, June 21, 2016, accessed June 29, 2016, http://www.reuters.com/article/
us-kentucky-lgbt-idUSKCN0Z728Q; Curtis M. Wong, "Bakery Owner Vows to
'Stand True to God' after Rejecting Lesbian Couple's Cake," *Huffington Post*,
August 14, 2014, accessed June 29, 2016, http://www.huffingtonpost.com/2014/
08/14/pennsylvania-cake-pros-gay-wedding-_n_5678410.html.

8. Christopher Small, *Musicking: The Meanings of Performing and Listening*, Music/
culture (Hanover: University Press of New England, 1998).

9. Rob Rosenthal and Richard Flacks, *Playing for Change: Music and Musicians in the
Service of Social Movements* (Boulder, CO: Paradigm, 2011), 123.

10. Ibid., 124.

11. Ibid., 125.

12. Joseph E. Stiglitz, *The Price of Inequality: How Today's Divided Society Endangers Our
Future* (New York: W. W. Norton, 2013).

13. Timothy P. Lynch, *Strike Songs of the Depression* (Jackson: University Press of Mississippi, 2001), 6.

14. Philip Foner, *American Labor Songs of the Nineteenth Century*, Musical score (Urbana: University of Illinois Press, 1975). See also Lynch, *Strike Songs*, 5.

15. Kerran Sanger, *"When the Spirit Says Sing!": The Role of Freedom Songs in the Civil Rights Movement* (New York: Garland, 1995), 135.

16. Lynch, *Strike Songs*, 3.

17. Hilde Lindemann, *Holding and Letting Go: The Social Practice of Personal Identities* (New York: Oxford University Press, 2014).

18. A version of the song "Canaan's Happy Shore" can be heard at Alan Lomax, "Oh, Brother Will You Meet Me," Kentucky Recordings, Berea College Special Collections and Archives, accessed January 2016, http://digital.berea.edu/cdm/ref/collection/p16020coll13/id/4.

19. An early version of the song "John Brown's Body" can be heard at "John Brown's Body," YouTube video, 4:28, posted by Gloria Jane, September 29, 2009, https://www.youtube.com/watch?v=bSSn3NddwFQ.

20. The song can be heard at "Solidarity Forever (Pete Seeger)," YouTube video, 2:59, posted by EmberNews, December 2, 2010, https://www.youtube.com/watch?v=pCnEAH5wCzo.

21. Lynch, *Strike Songs*, 125.

22. Ibid., 126.

23. Ibid. The song can be heard at "Pete Seeger, Which Side Are You On," YouTube video, 2:50, posted by commarx, April 12, 2007, https://www.youtube.com/watch?v=5iAIMo2kvog; lyrics may be found at "Songs of the People," accessed January 2016, http://www.zisman.ca/SongsofthePeople/index.html.

24. Lynch, *Strike Songs*, Kindle version, location 1350 of 2280.

25. Bryan K. Garman, *A Race of Singers: Whitman's Working-Class Hero from Guthrie to Springsteen*, Cultural Studies of the United States (Chapel Hill: University of North Carolina Press, 2000), 4.

26. For some explorations of the challenges posed, see Robert Asher and Charles Stephenson, *Labor Divided: Race and Ethnicity in United States Labor Struggles, 1835–1960*, American Labor History (Albany: State University of New York Press, 1990).

27. Sanger, *"When the Spirit Says Sing!,"* 29.

28. While there are countless sources one could use for evidence of how this still is happening, here's just one recent source that documents the persistence of the blindness of white people to the history of slavery: Margaret Biser, "I used to lead tours at a plantation. You won't believe the questions I got about slavery," Vox.com, June 19, 2016, accessed January 2016, http://www.vox.com/2015/6/29/8847385/what-i-learned-from-leading-tours-about-slavery-at-a-plantation.

29. T. V. Reed, *The Art of Protest: Culture and Activism from the Civil Rights Movement to the Streets of Seattle* (Minneapolis: University of Minnesota Press, 2005), 2.

30. Sanger, *"When the Spirit Says Sing!,"* 46–47.

31. Ibid., 9.

CHAPTER 2 CHORAL MUSICKING FOR CHANGE

1. Hilde Lindemann, *Holding and Letting Go: The Social Practice of Personal Identities* (New York: Oxford University Press, 2014).
2. "Link Listing of Musicians, Performers, Song Writers and Vocalists of Labour Music," *XPDNC Music Links*, last updated October 26, 2015, http://www.xpdnc .com/links/music.html.
3. Michael Fried, "Elmer Keeton and His WPA Chorus: Oakland's Musical Civil Rights Pioneers of the New Deal Era," *California History* 75, no. 3 (Fall 1996): 236.
4. Ibid., 248.
5. Ibid., 248, quoting from his interview with historian Lorraine Crouchett.
6. Ibid., 243.
7. "Polar Explorer Ann Bancroft to Narrate 'Oliver Button Is a Sissy,'" Twin Cities Gay Men's Chorus website, accessed December 11, 2016, http://tcgmc.org/ newsroom/polar-explorer-ann-bancroft-to-narrate-oliver-button-is-a-sissy/.
8. "Our Amazing Stories," Twin Cities Gay Men's Chorus website, accessed December 11, 2016, http://tcgmc.org/amazing/.
9. Fried, "Elmer Keeton," 246–47.
10. Monique Wittig, *The Straight Mind and Other Essays* (New York: Beacon Press, 1992).
11. C. Eric Lincoln and Lawrence H. Mamiya, *The Black Church in the African American Experience* (Durham: Duke University Press, 1990), 239–40.
12. Fried, "Elmer Keeton," 239.
13. According to GLSEN's most recent U.S. School Climate Survey, "Schools nationwide are hostile environments for a distressing number of LGBT students. Seventy-four percent were verbally harassed in the past year because of their sexual orientation and 55 percent because of their gender expression. As a result of feeling unsafe or uncomfortable, 30 percent missed at least one day of school in the past month." Gay, Lesbian, and Straight Education Network, "GLSEN Releases New National School Climate Survey," accessed January 2016, http://www.glsen.org/article/glsen -releases-new-national-school-climate-survey#sthash.RDDLNxE2.dpuf.
14. Eliel Cruz, "LGBT People of Faith: Why Are They Staying?," *The Advocate*, September 17, 2015, http://www.advocate.com/religion/2015/9/17/lgbt-people-faith-why -are-they-staying.
15. The claims used against queers include things like "God hates you. You should just kill yourself." For some of the more virulent examples, see the Westboro Baptist Church's God Hates Fags website, http://godhatesfags.com/, accessed January 2016.
16. April 1980 San Francisco Gay Men's Chorus program notes.

CHAPTER 3 PRACTICES OF IDENTITY

1. Phillip Norman, *John Lennon: The Life* (London: Harper Collins, 2009).
2. Hilde Lindemann Nelson, *Damaged Identities, Narrative Repair* (Ithaca: Cornell University Press, 2001), 158. Bracketed word is my addition.

3. Ibid., 158.

4. Ibid., 160.

5. Diana Tietjen Meyers, *Subjection and Subjectivity: Psychoanalytic Feminism and Moral Philosophy*, Thinking Gender (New York: Routledge, 1994), 54.

6. Lindemann, *Damaged Identities*, 18.

7. Hilde Lindemann, *Holding and Letting Go: The Social Practice of Personal Identities* (New York: Oxford University Press, 2014).

8. Lindemann, *Damaged Identities*, 185–86.

9. Some early work includes the research of Havelock Ellis in the late 1800s and the work for greater understanding promoted by the homophile movement of the early twentieth century. See *Sexual Inversion* (Philadelphia: F. A. Davis Company, 1901).

10. For some history and rich analysis of this backlash, see Jean Hardisty, *Mobilizing Resentment: Conservative Resurgence from the John Birch Society to the Promise Keepers* (Boston: Beacon Press, 1999).

11. For particularly useful analysis of these issues, see Janet Jakobsen and Ann Pellegrini, *Love the Sin: Sexual Regulation and the Limits of Religious Tolerance*, Sexual Cultures (New York: New York University Press, 2003).

12. While there are obviously a great many types of what might be called queer community organizing, I have chosen these examples for their scope, range, reach, social justice missions, and longevity.

13. David Carter, "What Made Stonewall Different," *The Gay & Lesbian Review*, July 1, 2009, accessed July 19, 2016, http://www.glreview.org/article/article-509/.

14. Elizabeth A. Armstrong and Suzanna M. Crage, "Movements and Memory: The Making of the Stonewall Myth," *American Sociological Review* 71, no. 5 (2006): 724–51.

15. Carter, "What Made Stonewall Different."

16. Andrew Belonsky, "The Gay Pride Issue," *Queerty*, June 18, 2007, accessed July 19, 2016, http://www.queerty.com/the-gay-pride-issue-20070618/#ixzz2 dxsAykBo.

17. Carl Wittman, "The Gay Manifesto" (New York: Red Butterfly, 1970), 3, available in PDF at *Libcom.org*, accessed July 19, 2016, http://libcom.org/library/gay -manifesto-carl-wittman. Page numbers refer to the pdf version.

18. Alfred Kinsey's substantial studies of human sexuality in the 1940s and 1950s had already documented a broader range of sexual desires and practices that are more fluid during the course of our lives than the identity categories of today suggest. See, for example, *Sexual Behavior in the Human Male* (Bloomington: Indiana University Press, 1998).

19. Wittman, "Gay Manifesto," 3.

20. For a recent discussion of this, see Seán Faye, "The Gay Men Who Hate Women," *Broadly*, November 11, 2015, accessed July 19, 2016, https://broadly.vice.com/en _us/article/the-gay-men-who-hate-women.

21. Wittman, "Gay Manifesto," 4.

22. "About," *Twin Cities Pride*, accessed July 19, 2016, http://www.tcpride.org/about/.

23. For example, as my editor, Kimberley Guinta, was quick to point out, "The NYC Pride 'parade' is still referred to as a march. The Stonewall organization is very clear about that in all their marketing materials. Most people obviously don't refer to it that way, but officially it is still a political march."

24. Belonsky, "Gay Pride Issue."

25. Armstrong and Crage reference the work of Verta Taylor and Nancy Whittier, "Analytical Approaches to Social Movement Culture: The Culture of the Women's Movement," in *Social Movements and Culture*, ed. Hank Johnston and Bert Klandermas (Minneapolis: University of Minnesota Press, 1995), 163–87.

26. Armstrong and Crage, "Movements and Memory," 743–44.

27. Michael Bronski, "Sylvia Rivera: 1951–2002," *Z Magazine*, April 1, 2002, accessed July 19, 2016, https://zcomm.org/zmagazine/sylvia-rivera-1951-2002-by-michael -bronski/.

28. Lindemann, *Damaged Identities*, 181–82.

29. Emanuella Grinberg, "Why Caitlyn Jenner's Transgender Experience Is Far from the Norm," *CNN.com*, July 15, 2015, accessed July 19, 2016, http://www.cnn.com/ 2015/06/03/living/caitlyn-jenner-transgender-reaction-feat/index.html.

30. "Our History: History of the Community Center Movement," *CenterLink*, accessed July 20, 2016, http://www.lgbtcenters.org/centerlink-history.aspx.

31. Ibid.

32. "CenterLink Member LGBT Community Centers around the World," *CenterLink*, accessed July 20, 2016, http://www.lgbtcenters.org/Centers/find-a-center.aspx.

33. CenterLink and the Movement Advancement Project (MAP), *2016 LGBT Community Center Survey Report: Assessing the Capacity and Programs of Lesbian, Gay, Bisexual and Transgender Community Centers* (Fort Lauderdale, FL: CenterLink: The Community of LGBT Centers, June 2016), accessed April 19, 2017, http:// www.lgbtcenters.org/, 1.

34. Ibid., 2.

35. Ibid., 8.

36. "Gay Games History," *Federation of Gay Games*, accessed July 2013, http:// gaygames.com/index.php?id=452.

37. "Economic Impact of Gay Games 9 Exceeds $52 Million," *GG9*, accessed July 21, 2016, http://www.gg9cle.com/media/news/economic-impact-of-gay-games-9 -exceeds-52-million.

38. Gordon Waitt, "The Sydney 2002 Gay Games and Querying Australian National Space," *Environment and Planning D: Society and Space* 23 (2005): 435.

39. Ibid., 435.

40. Ibid., 443.

41. Ibid., 445.

42. See the homepages of the Muslim Alliance for Sexual and Gender Diversity, accessed July 20, 2016, http://www.muslimalliance.org/; Eshel Online, accessed July 20, 2016, http://www.eshelonline.org/; GALVA-108: Gay & Lesbian Vaishnava Association, accessed July 20, 2016, http://www.galva108.org/; DignityUSA, accessed July 20, 2016, https://www.dignityusa.org/; Integrity USA, accessed

July 20, 2016, http://www.integrityusa.org/; AXIOS—Eastern and Orthodox Gay and Lesbian Christians, accessed July 20, 2016, http://www.qrd.org/qrd/www/orgs/axios/; and the Gay Christian Network, accessed July 20, 2016, http://www.gaychristian.net/mission.php.

43. Eliel Cruz, "LGBT People of Faith: Why Are They Staying?," *The Advocate*, September 17, 2015, accessed July 20, 2016, http://www.advocate.com/religion/2015/9/17/lgbt-people-faith-why-are-they-staying; Pew Research Center, "America's Changing Religious Landscape: Christians Decline Sharply as Share of Population; Unaffiliated and Other Faiths Continue to Grow," May 12, 2015, accessed July 16, 2016, http://www.pewforum.org/2015/05/12/americas-changing-religious-landscape/.

44. Melissa Wilcox, "Of Markets and Missions: The Early History of the Universal Fellowship of Metropolitan Community Churches," *Religion and American Culture* 11, no. 1 (Winter 2001): 83. See also Frances FitzGerald, *Cities on a Hill: A Journey through Contemporary American Cultures* (New York: Simon and Schuster, 1986).

45. Ibid., 84.

46. Ibid.

47. Paul F. Bauer, "The Homosexual Subculture at Worship: A Participant Observation Study," *Pastoral Psychology* 25, no. 2 (Winter 1976): 115–27; R. Stephen Warner, "The Metropolitan Community Churches and the Gay Agenda: The Power of Pentecostalism and Essentialism," in *Sex, Lies, and Sanctity: Religion and Deviance in Contemporary North America*, ed. Mary Jo Neitz and Marion S. Goldman (Greenwich, CT: JAI Press, 1995), 81–108.

48. Wilcox, "Of Markets and Missions," 86.

49. Ibid.

50. Ibid., 87–88. In this section, Wilcox references pages 84–85 of Warner's text. She also offers an important note on the history behind the MCCs current "wide range of theological approaches, from evangelical to metaphysical," noting "the *early* UFMCC [w]as *predominantly* (though by no means entirely) evangelical" (105).

51. Ibid., 99.

52. Ibid., 101.

53. Ibid., 88.

54. Melinda Kane, "LGBT Religious Activism: Predicting State Variations in the Number of Metropolitan Community Churches, 1974–2000," *Sociological Forum* 28, no. 1 (March 1, 2013): 137, doi:10.1111/socf.12006.

55. University of Missouri Center on Religion and the Professions, "Missing Voices: A Study of Religious Voices in Mainstream Media Reports about LGBT Equality," *GLAAD*, April 10, 2012, accessed July 16, 2016, http://www.glaad.org/publications/missingvoices.

56. Janet Jakobsen and Ann Pelligrini, *Love the Sin: Sexual Regulation and the Limits of Religious Tolerance*, Sexual Cultures (Boston: Beacon Press, 2004), 151.

57. Ibid., 150.

58. Ibid., 149.

59. Solvej Schou, "Meet the Christian Leaders Who Are Suing for Gay Marriage as a Religious Right," *TakePart*, May 3, 2014, accessed July 21, 2016, http://www.takepart .com/article/2014/05/03/pastors-oppose-north-carolinas-same-sex-marriage-ban.

60. One example of many in the news is the following: "Idaho Bill Would Protect Businesses Refusing Service on Religious Grounds," *The Stream Blog, Aljazeera America*, January 29, 2014, accessed July 21, 2016, http://america.aljazeera .com/watch/shows/the-stream/the-stream-officialblog/2014/1/29/idaho-bill -wouldprotectbusinessesrefusingserviceonreligiousgroun.html.

CHAPTER 4   QUEER CHORAL MUSICKING

1. "1970s: The We Decade," *Chicago Gay History*, accessed July 25, 2016, http:// chicagogayhistory.com/ARTICLE.php?AID=32.

2. "Herstory," *Sister Singers Network*, accessed July 26, 2016, http://www.sistersingers .net/Herstory.shtml.

3. "History," *Gala Choruses*, October 5, 2011, accessed July 26, 2016, http:// galachoruses.org/about/history.

4. "News," *Legato*, accessed July 26, 2016. http://legato-choirs.com/news.

5. "Russian Secret Choir. Berlin, Emmaus-Kirche, 20.06.2014," YouTube video, 17:44, posted by BirdsOfDorian, September 3, 2014, https://www.youtube.com/ watch?v=hasL5dqCroM.

6. "History of Unison," *Unison Festival Unisson 2018*, accessed July 26, 2016, http:// www.unisonfestivalunisson.ca/index.php/the-history-of-the-unison-festival/.

7. "Cromatica 2016: Festival Dei Cori Italiani LGBT," *Cromatica Festival*, accessed July 26, 2016. http://www.cromaticafestival.org/.

8. Christopher Small, *Musicking: The Meanings of Performing and Listening*, Music/culture (Hanover: University Press of New England, 1998).

9. "Chorus Operations Survey Report (2011)," *Chorus America*, accessed July 26, 2016, https://www.chorusamerica.org/management-governance/chorus-operations -survey-report-2011.

10. Sheila Tobias and Shelah Leader, "Vox Populi to Music," *Journal of American Culture* 22, no. 4 (December 1, 1999): 91–101, doi:10.1111/j.1542-734X.1999.2204_91.x.

11. This refers to German love songs that in the choral tradition are generally classical art songs.

12. For example, see Allan Bloom, *The Closing of the American Mind: How Higher Education Has Failed Democracy and Impoverished the Souls of Today's Students* (New York: Simon and Schuster, 2012), in which he blames the "problem" of youth of the 1980s on rock and roll, which he argues "has one appeal only, a barbaric appeal, to sexual desire" (29), as if sexual desire was a bad thing.

13. Adrian J. Villicana, Kevin Delucio, and Monica Biernat, "'Coming Out' among Gay Latino and Gay White Men: Implications of Verbal Disclosure for Well-Being," *Self and Identity* 15, no. 4 (July 3, 2016): 468–87, doi:10.1080/15298868.201 6.1156568., 482.

14. "History," *MUSE*, accessed July 26, 2016. http://musechoir.org/about/history.

15. While there was an early SATB chorus in New York City, Stonewall Chorale, the preponderance of the early choruses in the United States were either SSAA or TTBB.

16. For those not familiar with choral singing in this tradition, there are a number of variations of these voicings (SATB). For example, a particular piece might call for splitting the soprano voices into two sections and altos into two without tenor or bass. This would be referred to as a piece for SSAA, meaning high soprano or soprano 1, low soprano or soprano 2, and so on. Choruses sometimes identify themselves structurally in this manner as well based on the voices they have in the group: for example, SATB, TB, TTBB.

17. Hsien Chew, Pink Singers/Proud Voices, "Arise and Sing (Various Voices)," *Vimeo*, accessed July 26, 2016, https://vimeo.com/134600409.

18. The gendering of and in choruses is one of the issues queer choruses take up. More of them are choosing to refer to themselves and each other as SSAA, TTBB, or SATB rather than relying on gender norms as one way to make their groups more comfortable for trans people.

19. For a range of perspectives, see Eileen M. Hayes, *Songs in Black and Lavender: Race, Sexual Politics, and Women's Music* (Urbana: University of Illinois Press, 2010); Bonnie Morris, *Eden Built by Eves: The Culture of Women's Music Festivals* (Los Angeles: Alyson Books, 1999); and Holly Near (with Derek Richardson), *Fire in the Rain, Singer in the Storm* (New York: William Morrow, 1990).

20. Catherine Roma, "Women's Choral Communities: Singing for Our Lives," *HOT WIRE* 8, no. 1 (1992), 36.

21. Often such groups do not have names because they have no intention of performing beyond the confines of the group. I have participated in a number of these over the years.

22. Russell Hilliard, "A Social and Historical Perspective of the San Francisco Gay Men's Chorus," *Journal of Homosexuality* 54, no. 4 (June 10, 2008): 357–58.

23. Dennis Coleman, "Multiculturalism and Diversity: A Brief History of the Gay and Lesbian Choral Movement," in *The Chorus Handbook: Chorus 101: The How-to Book for Organizing and Operating a Professional or Volunteer Choral Ensemble*, ed. Robert Page, Louise Greenberg, and Fred Leise (Washington, DC: Chorus America, 1999), 105–6.

24. "Tenors and Basses," *Renaissance City Choir—Pittsburgh's LGBTQA Chorus*, accessed July 27, 2016, http://rccpittsburgh.com/about-2/tenors-basses/.

25. "Trans Chorus of Los Angeles," *GMCLA—Gay Men's Chorus of Los Angeles*, accessed July 27, 2016, http://gmcla.org/gmcla3/outreach/tcla/.

26. "GALA—Songs of Courage," YouTube video, 7:42, posted by GALA Choruses, July 13, 2011, https://www.youtube.com/watch?v=8yjKx3SgsdY.

CHAPTER 5   CHORAL TECHNOLOGIES FOR QUEERING

1. Namoli Brennet, "Choose a Box," lyrics performed by Desert Voices live at GALA Festival 2016, Buell Theatre, Denver, Colorado, July 5, 2016.

2. "Anna Crusis Background," *Anna Crusis*, accessed July 15, 2014, http://annacrusis
.com/index.php/about-anna-crusis/background/2-background.

3. This was a theme repeated by my gay male interviewees who survived this
period.

4. "OK, Chorale," *Dallas Voice*, accessed July 28, 2016, http://m.dallasvoice.com/ok
-chorale-2-10169168.html.

5. "'Family' Liner Notes," *Turtle Creek Chorale*, accessed July 15, 2014, http://
turtlecreek.org/index.php?/music/linernotes/family/. Emphasis mine.

6. "About Us," *Turtle Creek Chorale*, accessed July 28, 2016, https://turtlecreekchorale
.com/about-us/.

7. Tri Truong, "TCC to Honor Victims of Orlando Massacre," *Turtle Creek Chorale*,
June 13, 2016, accessed July 27, 2016, https://turtlecreekchorale.com/tcc-news/
tcc-to-honor-victims-of-orlando-massacre/.

8. "About," *Seattle Choruses*, accessed July 28, 2016, http://www.seattlechoruses.org/
about/.

9. "GMCW at We Are One Inaugural Opening Ceremony—HBO," YouTube video,
5:27, posted by dcdanp2, January 27, 2009, https://www.youtube.com/watch?v=
w5SOCgADQhk.

10. I say "nearly" because I have not gone specifically searching for any failed
attempts, but I have asked in meetings, general discussions, and interviews
specifically if anyone knows of this tactic ever going wrong, and no one did.

11. Colloquial use of the word *vendidas* referenced by Chicana lesbian feminists
Cheríe Moraga and Gloria Anzaldúa suggests being sellouts or even traitors.

12. From a personal copy of the recording sent from the chorus (2000).

13. Mercedes Sosa, "Canción Con Todos Lyrics + English Translation," *Lyrics Translate*, accessed July 28, 2016, http://lyricstranslate.com/en/canci%C3%B3n-con
-todos-son-all.html.

14. GMCLA video, *Con Todos*, DVD, 2007.

15. "One Voice: School Engagement," *One Voice: Minnesota's LGBTA Mixed Chorus*, accessed July 28, 2016, http://www.ovmc.org/community-impact/school
-engagement/.

16. "GMCLA's It Gets Better Tour," YouTube video, 6:00, posted by GMCLAvideo,
March 14, 2012, https://www.youtube.com/watch?v=kU8G8yYTFHE.

CHAPTER 6   EMOTIONS, IDENTITIES, AND CHORAL MUSICKING

1. This is a musical variation of an adage whose origins are hazy at best. Though it is
often attributed to Maya Angelou, many earlier variations have been found as well.

2. Langston Hughes, "Let America Be America Again," *Academy of American Poets*,
January 3, 2001, accessed August 3, 2016, https://www.poets.org/poetsorg/poem/
let-america-be-america-again.

3. "GMCW at We Are One Inaugural Opening Ceremony—HBO," YouTube video,
5:27, posted by dcdanp2, January 27, 2009, https://www.youtube.com/watch?v=
w5SOCgADQhk.

4. Studies across fields are exploring the effects of well-documented unconscious bias in a number of areas. For example, see Jeffrey J. Rachlinski, Sheri Lynn Johnson, Andrew J. Wistrich, and Chris Guthrie, "Does Unconscious Racial Bias Affect Trial Judges?," *Notre Dame Law Review* 84, no. 3 (2009), Vanderbilt Public Law Research Paper No. 09-11, available at SSRN, accessed July 28, 2016, http://ssrn.com/abstract=1374497; and Alexander R. Green, et al., "Implicit Bias among Physicians and Its Prediction of Thrombolysis Decisions for Black and White Patients," *Journal of General Internal Medicine* 22, no. 9 (September 2007): 1231–38. doi:10.1007/s11606-007-0258-5.

5. The related field of neurofinance is breaking new ground, challenging a history of assumptions about rational choices in economics. One recent example shows the emotional basis of decision making in risky behavior: Kaisa Hytönen, Guido Baltussen, Martijn J. van den Assem, Vasily Klucharev, Alan G. Sanfey, and Ale Smidts, "Path Dependence in Risky Choice: Affective and Deliberative Processes in Brain and Behavior," *Journal of Economic Behavior & Organization*, Empirical Behavioral Finance, 107, part B (November 2014): 566–81, doi:10.1016/j.jebo.2014.01.016.

6. See, for example, Lisa Sayegh, William P. Anthony, and Pamela L. Perrewé, "Managerial Decision-Making under Crisis: The Role of Emotion in an Intuitive Decision Process," *Human Resource Management Review* 14, no. 2 (June 2004): 179–99, doi:10.1016/j.hrmr.2004.05.002.

7. The work of neuroscientists such as Andrew Newburg and David Eagleman have helped make such research more accessible to those not conversant in the field.

8. Jeff Goodwin, James M. Jasper, and Francesca Polletta, *Passionate Politics: Emotions and Social Movements* (Chicago: University of Chicago Press, 2001), 9. Their emphasis.

9. Ibid., 18–19.

10. Sara Warner, *Acts of Gaiety: LGBT Performance and the Politics of Pleasure* (Ann Arbor: University of Michigan Press, 2012).

11. Benjamin Heim Shepard, *Queer Political Performance and Protest: Play, Pleasure and Social Movement* (New York: Routledge, 2010), 21.

12. Ibid., 17.

13. "Home," *ACT UP New York*, accessed July 31, 2016. http://actupny.com/actions/.

14. "25 Yr Chronology," *ACT UP New York*, accessed July 31, 2016, http://www.actupny.com/actions/index.php/the-community.

15. Hilde Lindemann, *Holding and Letting Go: The Social Practice of Personal Identities* (New York: Oxford University Press, 2014), 121.

16. Ibid.

17. Ibid.

18. Ibid., 198.

19. Ibid., 197.

20. Ibid.

21. Ibid., 6–7.

22. Ibid., 7.

23. Ibid., 142.

24. Ibid., 101.

25. Ibid., 102.

26. "Eric Whitacre's Virtual Choir—'Lux Aurumque,'" YouTube video, 6:20, posted by Eric Whitacre's Virtual Choir, March 21, 2010, https://www.youtube.com/watch?v=D7o7BrlbaDs.

27. Janos Gereben, "Chorus America and America's Millions of Choral Singers," *San Francisco Classical Voice*, May 23, 2011, accessed July 31, 2016, https://www.sfcv.org/article/chorus-america-and-americas-millions-of-choral-singers.

28. Lindemann, *Holding and Letting Go*, xiii.

29. Ibid., 65–77.

30. For example, see Yohko M. Shimada, "Infant Vocalization When Alone: Possibility of Early Sound Playing," *International Journal of Behavioral Development* 36, no. 6 (November 1, 2012): 407–12, doi:10.1177/0165025411431408.

31. Small, *Musicking: The Meanings of Performing and Listening*, Music/culture (Hanover: University Press of New England, 1998), 40.

32. Ibid., 39.

33. Ibid.

34. Ibid., 40.

35. Robert Putnam, *Bowling Alone: The Collapse and Revival of American Community* (New York: Simon and Schuster, 2000).

36. Michael L. Cobb, *Single: Arguments for the Uncoupled* (New York: New York University Press, 2012).

37. Ibid.

38. Small, *Musicking*, 30.

39. Ibid.

40. Ibid., 51, emphasis his.

41. Mary Douglas, *Purity and Danger: An Analysis of Concepts of Pollution and Taboo* (London: Routledge, 2015).

42. William Greider, "Bloom and Doom: 'The Closing of the American Mind,'" *Rolling Stone*, October 8, 1987, accessed August 1, 2016, http://www.rollingstone.com/culture/news/bloom-and-doom-19871008.

43. Liz Garnett, "Choral Singing as Bodily Regime: Zborsko Pjevanje Kao Tjelesni Režim on JSTOR," *International Review of the Aesthetics and Sociology of Music* 36, no. 2 (2005): 261.

44. Ibid., 261.

45. "Susan McClary's, *Feminine Endings: Music, Gender, and Sexuality* (1991) laid the groundwork for *Queering the Pitch: The New Gay and Lesbian Musicology* (1994), which created a new sub-field, as well as predictable backlash." See also Susan McClary, *Feminine Endings: Music, Gender, and Sexuality* (Minneapolis: University of Minnesota Press, 1991); Philip Brett, Elizabeth Wood, and Gary C Thomas, *Queering the Pitch: The New Gay and Lesbian Musicology* (New York: Routledge, 1994); and Julia Balén, "Erotics, Agency, and Social Movement: Communities of Sexuality and Musicality in LGBT Choruses," in *The Queer Community: Continuing*

the Struggle for Social Justice, ed. Richard Greggory Johnson, Beth Mintz, and Glen Elder (San Diego, CA: Birkdale, 2009).

46. Judith Ann Peraino, "Listening to the Sirens: Music as Queer Ethical Practice," *GLQ: A Journal of Lesbian and Gay Studies* 9, no. 4 (2003): 434.

47. Ibid., 434.

48. Ibid., 436.

49. Ibid., 436 (emphasis hers).

50. Fees as of December 2015 for community choruses average around $150 a year, with a range from $50 to more than $500, as compared to about half that for community orchestras or bands based on a sampling of two hundred of a spectrum of community choral and orchestral websites from across the United States.

51. "About Us," *Lakeshore Community Chorus*, accessed August 1, 2016, http://www.lakeshorecommunitychorus.org/about-us.html.

52. A survey of a sample of one hundred choral mission statements shows remarkable similarity in the inclusion of some variation on the theme of these elements.

53. Christianity has always had a fraught relationship to pleasure. One need only look at the works of Augustine for a detailed articulation of the dangers in the pleasure of music—specifically song. But one can also peruse any number of current Christian singers' sites for discussion of the sinfulness of ego in evangelical singing. For example, see Vaughan Roberts, "The Place of Music and Singing in Church," 2005, *The Theologian*, accessed August 1, 2016, http://www.theologian.org.uk/pastoralia/music.html.

54. See, for example, R. J. Beck, T. C. Cesario, A. Yousefi, and H. Enamoto, "Choral Singing, Performance Perception, and Immune System Changes in Salivary Immunoglobulin A and Cortisol," *Music Perception: An Interdisciplinary Journal* 18, no. 1 (October 1, 2000): 87–106, doi:10.2307/40285902; Genevieve A. Dingle, Christopher Brander, Julie Ballantyne, and Felicity A. Baker, "'To Be Heard': The Social and Mental Health Benefits of Choir Singing for Disadvantaged Adults," *Psychology of Music*, February 8, 2012, doi:10.1177/0305735611430081; and Rosie Stacy, Katie Brittain, and Sandra Kerr, "Singing for Health: An Exploration of the Issues," *Health Education* 102, no. 4 (August 1, 2002): 156–62, doi:10.1108/09654280210434228.

55. Mona Lisa Chanda and Daniel J. Levitin, "The Neurochemistry of Music," *Trends in Cognitive Sciences* 17, no. 4 (April 2013): 179–93, doi:10.1016/j.tics.2013.02.007.

56. Bruce Johnson and Martin Cloonan, *Dark Side of the Tune: Popular Music and Violence*, Ashgate Popular and Folk Music Series (Burlington, VT: Ashgate, 2008), http://summit.csuci.edu:2048/login?url=http://site.ebrary.com/lib/csuci/Doc?id=10325925, 4.

CHAPTER 7   COMMUNAL EROTICS

1. Hilde Lindemann Nelson, *Damaged Identities, Narrative Repair* (Ithaca: Cornell University Press, 2001), 106.

2. For more on sex as a social good, see Jakobsen and Pellegrini, *Love the Sin*.

3. For example, see William Greider, "Bloom and Doom: 'The Closing of the American Mind,'" *Rolling Stone*, October 8, 1987, accessed August 1, 2016, http://www.rollingstone.com/culture/news/bloom-and-doom-19871008.

4. Audre Lorde, *Sister Outsider: Essays and Speeches* (Trumansburg, NY: Crossing Press, 1984), 54.

5. Ibid., 53–59.

6. Ibid., 53.

7. Ibid., 56–57.

8. Ibid., 57.

9. Ibid., 58.

10. Ibid., 56.

11. Rob Rosenthal and Richard Flacks, *Playing for Change: Music and Musicians in the Service of Social Movements* (Boulder, CO: Paradigm, 2011), 11–12.

12. Ibid., 12.

13. Ibid., 123.

14. It's important to note that Rosenthal and Flacks include a range of social movements in their study, from civil rights to white supremacy, so they have focused on elements that are true for all of them. Also important, Lynch and Sanger, in their studies of the use of music in labor and civil rights movements, respectively, while not focused on general functions of musicking in social movement, each discuss identity development roles that musicking has played in each of these movements.

15. This is not to pretend that the form can't be used for less noble ends, though it is perhaps telling that at a variety of times and places (early Christian music, for example), only unison sound was allowed.

16. I borrow here from Roland Barthes's lovely development of the embodied particularities of our voices: Roland Barthes *Image, Music, Text*, trans. Stephen Heath, (New York: Hill and Wang, 1977).

17. Christopher Small, *Musicking: The Meanings of Performing and Listening*, Music/culture (Hanover: University Press of New England, 1998), 183.

18. Peraino, "Listening to the Sirens: Music as Queer Ethical Practice," *GLQ: A Journal of Lesbian and Gay Studies* 9, no. 4 (2003): 457.

APPENDIX

1. Rosenthal and Flacks, *Playing for Change: Music and Musicians in the Service of Social Movements* (Boulder, CO: Paradigm, 2011), 25.

2. Ibid.

3. Ibid., 8.

BIBLIOGRAPHY

"About." *Seattle Choruses*. Accessed July 28, 2016. http://www.seattlechoruses.org/about/.

"About." *Twin Cities Pride*. Accessed July 19, 2016. http://www.tcpride.org/about/.

"About Us." *Lakeshore Community Chorus*. Accessed August 1, 2016. http://www.lakeshorecommunitychorus.org/about-us.html.

"About Us." *Turtle Creek Chorale*. Accessed July 28, 2016. https://turtlecreekchorale.com/about-us/.

"Anna Crusis Background." *Anna Crusis*. Accessed July 15, 2014. http://annacrusis.com/index.php/about-anna-crusis/background/2-background.

"Arise and Sing (Various Voices)." *Vimeo*. Accessed July 26, 2016. https://vimeo.com/134600409.

Armstrong, Elizabeth A., and Suzanna M. Crage. "Movements and Memory: The Making of the Stonewall Myth." *American Sociological Review* 71, no. 5 (2006): 724–51.

Asher, Robert, and Charles Stephenson. *Labor Divided: Race and Ethnicity in United States Labor Struggles, 1835–1960*. American Labor History. Albany: State University of New York Press, 1990.

"AXIOS—Eastern and Orthodox Gay and Lesbian Christians." *Queer Resources Directory*. Accessed July 20, 2016. http://www.qrd.org/qrd/www/orgs/axios/.

Balén, Julia. "Erotics, Agency, and Social Movement: Communities of Sexuality and Musicality in LGBT Choruses." In *The Queer Community: Continuing the Struggle for Social Justice*, edited by Richard Greggory Johnson, Beth Mintz, and Glen Elder. San Diego, CA: Birkdale, 2009.

Barthes, Roland. *Image, Music, Text*. Translated by Stephen Heath. New York: Hill and Wang, 1977.

Bauer, Paul F. "The Homosexual Subculture at Worship: A Participant Observation Study." *Pastoral Psychology* 25, no. 2 (Winter 1976): 115–27.

Beck, R. J., T. C. Cesario, A. Yousefi, and H. Enamoto. "Choral Singing, Performance Perception, and Immune System Changes in Salivary Immunoglobulin A and Cortisol." *Music Perception: An Interdisciplinary Journal* 18, no. 1 (October 1, 2000): 87–106. doi:10.2307/40285902.

Bell, Cindy L. "Update on Community Choirs and Singing in the United States." *International Journal of Research in Choral Singing* 2, no. 1 (2004): 39–52.

Belonsky, Andrew. "The Gay Pride Issue." *Queerty*, June 18, 2007. Accessed July 19, 2016. http://www.queerty.com/the-gay-pride-issue-20070618/#ixzz2dxsAykBo.

Bernal, Dolores Delgado, Rebeca Burciaga, and Judith Flores Carmona, eds. Special issue, "Chicana/Latina Testimonios: Mapping the Methodological, Pedagogical, and Political." *Equity & Excellence in Education* 45, no. 3 (2012): 363–72.

Bloom, Allan. *The Closing of the American Mind: How Higher Education Has Failed Democracy and Impoverished the Souls of Today's Students*. New York: Simon and Schuster, 2012.

Brett, Philip, Elizabeth Wood, and Gary C. Thomas. *Queering the Pitch: The New Gay and Lesbian Musicology*. New York: Routledge, 1994.

Bronski, Michael. "Sylvia Rivera: 1951–2002." *Z Magazine*, April 1, 2002. Accessed July 19, 2016. https://zcomm.org/zmagazine/sylvia-rivera-1951-2002-by-michael -bronski/.

Butler, Judith. *Excitable Speech: A Politics of the Performative*. New York: Routledge, 1997.

Carter, David. "What Made Stonewall Different." *The Gay & Lesbian Review*, July 1, 2009. Accessed July 19, 2016. http://www.glreview.org/article/article-509/.

CenterLink and the Movement Advancement Project (MAP). *2016 LGBT Community Center Survey Report: Assessing the Capacity and Programs of Lesbian, Gay, Bisexual and Transgender Community Centers*. Fort Lauderdale, FL: CenterLink: The Community of LGBT Centers, June 2016. Accessed April 19, 2017. http://www.lgbtmap .org/2016-lgbt-community-center-survey-report.

"CenterLink Member LGBT Community Centers around the World." *CenterLink*. Accessed July 20, 2016. http://www.lgbtcenters.org/Centers/find-a-center.aspx.

Chanda, Mona Lisa, and Daniel J. Levitin. "The Neurochemistry of Music." *Trends in Cognitive Sciences* 17, no. 4 (April 2013): 179–93. doi:10.1016/j.tics.2013.02.007.

"Chorus Operations Survey Report (2011)." *Chorus America*. Accessed July 27, 2016. https://www.chorusamerica.org/management-governance/chorus-operations -survey-report-2011.

Cobb, Michael L. *Single: Arguments for the Uncoupled*. New York: New York University Press, 2012. http://public.eblib.com/choice/publicfullrecord.aspx?p=866102.

Coleman, Dennis. "Multiculturalism and Diversity: A Brief History of the Gay and Lesbian Choral Movement." In *The Chorus Handbook: Chorus 101: The How-to Book for Organizing and Operating a Professional or Volunteer Choral Ensemble*, edited by Robert Page, Louise Greenberg, and Fred Leise, 105–6. Washington, DC: Chorus America, 1999.

"Cromatica 2016: Festival Dei Cori Italiani LGBT." *Cromatica Festival*. Accessed July 27, 2016. http://www.cromaticafestival.org/.

Cruz, Eliel. "LGBT People of Faith: Why Are They Staying?," *Advocate.com*, September 17, 2015. Accessed July 20, 2016. http://www.advocate.com/religion/2015/9/ 17/lgbt-people-faith-why-are-they-staying.

Cusick, Suzanne G. "Afterword to 'You Are in a Place That Is Out of the World . . .': Music in the Detention Camps of the 'Global War on Terror.'" *Transposition. Musique et Sciences Sociales*, no. 4 (July 15, 2014). doi:10.4000/transposition.493.

———. "'You Are in a Place That Is Out of the World . . .': Music in the Detention Camps of the 'Global War on Terror.'" *Journal of the Society for American Music* 2, no. 1 (2008): 1–26. doi:10.1017/S1752196308080012.

Dickinson, Elizabeth. "A Bright Shining Slogan: How 'Hearts and Minds' Came to Be." *FP*. August 22, 2009. Accessed June 28, 2016. http://foreignpolicy.com/2009/08/22/a-bright-shining-slogan/.

"DignityUSA." *DignityUSA*. Accessed July 20, 2016. https://www.dignityusa.org/.

Dingle, Genevieve A., Christopher Brander, Julie Ballantyne, and Felicity A. Baker. "'To Be Heard': The Social and Mental Health Benefits of Choir Singing for Disadvantaged Adults." *Psychology of Music*, February 8, 2012. doi:10.1177/0305735611430081.

Douglas, Mary. *Purity and Danger: An Analysis of Concepts of Pollution and Taboo*. London: Routledge, 2015.

"Economic Impact of Gay Games 9 Exceeds $52 Million." *GG9*. Accessed July 21, 2016, http://www.gg9cle.com/media/news/economic-impact-of-gay-games-9-exceeds-52-million.

Ellis, Havelock. *Sexual Inversion*. Philadelphia: F. A. Davis, 1901.

"Eric Whitacre's Virtual Choir—'Lux Aurumque.'" YouTube video, 6:20. Posted by Eric Whitacre's Virtual Choir. March 21, 2010. https://www.youtube.com/watch?v=D7o7BrlbaDs.

"Eshel Online: Creating Inclusive Orthodox Communities for LGBTQ+ Jews and Their Families." Accessed July 20, 2016. http://www.eshelonline.org/.

"'Family' Liner Notes." *Turtle Creek Chorale*. Accessed July 15, 2014. http://turtlecreek.org/index.php?/music/linernotes/family/.

Faye, Seán. "The Gay Men Who Hate Women." *Broadly*, November 11, 2015. Accessed July 19, 2016. https://broadly.vice.com/en_us/article/the-gay-men-who-hate-women.

FitzGerald, Frances. *Cities on a Hill: A Journey through Contemporary American Cultures*. New York: Simon and Schuster, 1986.

Foner, Philip Sheldon. *American Labor Songs of the Nineteenth Century*. Musical score. Urbana: University of Illinois Press, 1975.

Fried, Michael. "Elmer Keeton and His WPA Chorus: Oakland's Musical Civil Rights Pioneers of the New Deal Era." *California History* 75, no. 3 (Fall 1996): 236.

"GALA—Songs of Courage." Clips from video commissioned in 2008. YouTube video, 7:42. Posted by GALA Choruses. July 13, 2011. https://www.youtube.com/watch?v=8yjKx3SgsdY.

"GALVA-108: Gay & Lesbian Vaishnava Association." *GALVA-108: Gay & Lesbian Vaishnava Association*. Accessed July 20, 2016. http://www.galva108.org/.

Garman, Bryan K. *A Race of Singers: Whitman's Working-Class Hero from Guthrie to Springsteen*. Cultural Studies of the United States. Chapel Hill: University of North Carolina Press, 2000.

Garnett, Liz. "Choral Singing as Bodily Regime / Zborsko Pjevanje Kao Tjelesni Režim." *International Review of the Aesthetics and Sociology of Music* 36, no. 2 (2005): 249–69. http://www.jstor.org/stable/30032171.

Gay, Lesbian, and Straight Education Network. "GLSEN Releases New National School Climate Survey." *GLSEN*. Accessed January 2016. http://www.glsen.org/article/ glsen-releases-new-national-school-climate-survey#sthash.RDDLNxE2.dpuf.

"Gay Games History." *Federation of Gay Games*. Accessed July 2013. http://gaygames .com/index.php?id=452.

Gereben, Janos. "Chorus America and America's Millions of Choral Singers." *San Francisco Classical Voice*, May 23, 2011. Accessed July 31, 2016. https://www.sfcv .org/article/chorus-america-and-americas-millions-of-choral-singers.

"GMCLA's It Gets Better Tour." YouTube video, 6:00. Posted by GMCLAvideo. March 14, 2012. https://www.youtube.com/watch?v=kU8G8yYTFHE.

"GMCW at We Are One Inaugural Opening Ceremony—HBO." YouTube video, 5:27. Posted by dcdanp2. January 27, 2009. https://www.youtube.com/watch?v= w5SOCgADQhk.

Goodwin, Jeff, James M. Jasper, and Francesca Polletta. *Passionate Politics: Emotions and Social Movements*. Chicago: University of Chicago Press, 2001.

Green, Alexander R., Dana R. Carney, Daniel J. Pallin, Long H. Ngo, Kristal L. Raymond, Lisa I. Iezzoni, and Mahzarin R. Banaji. "Implicit Bias among Physicians and Its Prediction of Thrombolysis Decisions for Black and White Patients." *Journal of General Internal Medicine* 22, no. 9 (September 2007): 1231–38. doi:10.1007/ s11606-007-0258-5.

Greider, William. "Bloom and Doom: 'The Closing of the American Mind.'" *Rolling Stone*, October 8, 1987. Accessed August 1, 2016. http://www.rollingstone.com/ culture/news/bloom-and-doom-19871008.

Grinberg, Emanuella. "Why Caitlyn Jenner's Transgender Experience Is Far from the Norm." *CNN.com*, July 12, 2015. Accessed July 19, 2016. http://www.cnn.com/ 2015/06/03/living/caitlyn-jenner-transgender-reaction-feat/.

Hardisty, Jean V. *Mobilizing Resentment: Conservative Resurgence from the John Birch Society to the Promise Keepers*. Boston: Beacon Press, 1999.

Hayes, Eileen M. *Songs in Black and Lavender: Race, Sexual Politics, and Women's Music*. Urbana: University of Illinois Press, 2010.

"Herstory." *Sister Singers Network*. Accessed July 26, 2016. http://www.sistersingers .net/Herstory.shtml.

Hilliard, Russell E. "A Social and Historical Perspective of the San Francisco Gay Men's Chorus." *Journal of Homosexuality* 54, no. 4 (June 10, 2008): 345–61. doi:10.1080/00918360801991208.

"History." *Gala Choruses*, October 5, 2011. Accessed January 2016. http://www .galachoruses.org/about/history.

"History." *MUSE*. Accessed July 27, 2016. http://musechoir.org/about/history.

"History of Unison." *Unison Festival Unisson 2018*. Accessed July 27, 2016. http://www .unisonfestivalunisson.ca/index.php/the-history-of-the-unison-festival/.

"Home." *ACT UP New York*. Accessed July 31, 2016. http://actupny.com/actions/.

Hughes, Langston. "Let America Be America Again." *Academy of American Poets*, January 3, 2001. Accessed August 3, 2016. https://www.poets.org/poetsorg/poem/let -america-be-america-again.

Hytönen, Kaisa, Guido Baltussen, Martijn J. van den Assem, Vasily Klucharev, Alan G. Sanfey, and Ale Smidts. "Path Dependence in Risky Choice: Affective and Deliberative Processes in Brain and Behavior." *Journal of Economic Behavior & Organization*, Empirical Behavioral Finance, 107, part B (November 2014): 566–81. doi:10.1016/j.jebo.2014.01.016.

"Idaho Bill Would Protect Businesses Refusing Service on Religious Grounds." *The Stream Blog, Aljazeera America.* January 29, 2014. http://america.aljazeera .com/watch/shows/the-stream/the-stream-officialblog/2014/1/29/idaho-bill -wouldprotectbusinessesrefusingserviceonreligiousgroun.html.

"Integrity USA." *Integrity USA.* Accessed July 20, 2016. http://www.integrityusa.org/.

Jakobsen, Janet R., and Ann Pellegrini. *Love the Sin: Sexual Regulation and the Limits of Religious Tolerance.* Sexual Cultures. New York: New York University Press, 2003.

Johnson, Bruce, and Martin Cloonan. *Dark Side of the Tune: Popular Music and Violence.* Ashgate Popular and Folk Music Series. Burlington, VT: Ashgate, 2008.

Junn, Jane. "Participation in Liberal Democracy: The Political Assimilation of Immigrants and Ethnic Minorities in the United States." *American Behavioral Scientist* 42, no. 9 (July 1999): 1417–38.

Kane, Melinda D. "LGBT Religious Activism: Predicting State Variations in the Number of Metropolitan Community Churches, 1974–2000." *Sociological Forum* 28, no. 1 (March 1, 2013): 135–58. doi:10.1111/socf.12006.

"Kentucky Clerk Opposed to Gay Marriage Says State Law Negates Appeal." Reuters. Accessed June 30, 2016. http://www.reuters.com/article/us-kentucky-lgbt -idUSKCN0Z728Q.

Kinsey, Alfred. *Sexual Behavior in the Human Male.* Bloomington: Indiana University Press, 1998.

Lincoln, C. Eric, and Lawrence H. Mamiya. *The Black Church in the African American Experience.* Durham: Duke University Press, 1990.

Lindemann, Hilde. *Holding and Letting Go: The Social Practice of Personal Identities.* New York: Oxford University Press, 2014.

Lindemann Nelson, Hilde. *Damaged Identities, Narrative Repair.* Ithaca: Cornell University Press, 2001.

"Link Listing of Musicians, Performers, Song Writers and Vocalists of Labour Music." *XPDNC Music Links.* Last updated October 26, 2015. http://www.xpdnc.com/ links/music.html.

Lorde, Audre. *Sister Outsider: Essays and Speeches.* Trumansburg, NY: Crossing Press, 1984.

Lynch, Timothy P. *Strike Songs of the Depression.* Jackson: University Press of Mississippi, 2001.

"Mallorca LGTB Chorus Festival." *Mallorca LGTB Chorus Festival.* Accessed July 27, 2016. http://www.mallorcalgtbchorusfestival.com/.

McClary, Susan. *Feminine Endings: Music, Gender, and Sexuality.* Minneapolis: University of Minnesota Press, 1991.

Meyers, Diana T. *Subjection and Subjectivity: Psychoanalytic Feminism and Moral Philosophy.* Thinking Gender. New York: Routledge, 1994.

Morris, Bonnie. *Eden Built by Eves: The Culture of Women's Music Festivals*. Los Angeles: Alyson Books, 1999.

"Muslim Alliance for Sexual and Gender Diversity." *Muslim Alliance*. Accessed July 20, 2016. http://www.muslimalliance.org/.

Near, Holly (with Derek Richardson). *Fire in the Rain, Singer in the Storm*. New York: William Morrow, 1990.

"News." *Legato*. Accessed July 26, 2016. http://legato-choirs.com/news.

"1970s: The We Decade." *Chicago Gay History*. Accessed July 25, 2016. http://chicagogayhistory.com/ARTICLE.php?AID=32.

Norman, Philip. *John Lennon: The Life*. London: Harper Collins, 2009.

"OK, Chorale." *Dallas Voice*. Accessed July 28, 2016. http://m.dallasvoice.com/ok-chorale-2-10169168.html.

"One Voice: School Engagement." *One Voice: Minnesota's LGBTA Mixed Chorus*. Accessed July 28, 2016. http://www.ovmc.org/community-impact/school-engagement/.

"Our Amazing Stories," *Twin Cities Gay Men's Chorus*, accessed December 11, 2016, http://tcgmc.org/amazing/.

"Our History: History of the Community Center Movement." *CenterLink*. Accessed July 20, 2016. http://www.lgbtcenters.org/centerlink-history.aspx.

"Our Mission." *Gay Christian Network*. Accessed July 20, 2016. http://www.gaychristian.net/mission.php.

Peraino, Judith Ann. "Listening to the Sirens: Music as Queer Ethical Practice." *GLQ: A Journal of Lesbian and Gay Studies* 9, no. 4 (2003): 433–70.

Pew Research Center. "America's Changing Religious Landscape: Christians Decline Sharply as Share of Population; Unaffiliated and Other Faiths Continue to Grow," May 12, 2015. Accessed July 16, 2016. http://www.pewforum.org/2015/05/12/americas-changing-religious-landscape/.

"Polar Explorer Ann Bancroft to Narrate 'Oliver Button Is a Sissy.'" *Twin Cities Gay Men's Chorus*. Accessed December 11, 2016. http://tcgmc.org/newsroom/polar-explorer-ann-bancroft-to-narrate-oliver-button-is-a-sissy/.

Putnam, Robert. *Bowling Alone: The Collapse and Revival of American Community*. New York: Simon and Schuster, 2000.

Rachlinski, Jeffrey J., Sheri Lynn Johnson, Andrew J. Wistrich, and Chris Guthrie. "Does Unconscious Racial Bias Affect Trial Judges?" *Notre Dame Law Review* 84, no. 3 (2009). Vanderbilt Public Law Research Paper No. 09-11. Available at SSRN. Accessed July 28, 2016. http://ssrn.com/abstract=1374497.

Reed, T. V. *The Art of Protest: Culture and Activism from the Civil Rights Movement to the Streets of Seattle*. Minneapolis: University of Minnesota Press, 2005.

Roberts, Vaughan. "The Place of Music and Singing in Church." *The Theologian*, 2005. Accessed August 1, 2016. http://www.theologian.org.uk/pastoralia/music.html.

Roma, Catherine. "Women's Choral Communities: Singing for Our Lives." *HOT WIRE* 8, no. 1 (1992): 36–52.

Rosenthal, Rob, and Richard Flacks. *Playing for Change: Music and Musicians in the Service of Social Movements*. Boulder, CO: Paradigm, 2011.

"Russian Secret Choir. Berlin, Emmaus-Kirche, 20.06.2014." YouTube video, 17:44. Posted by BirdsOfDorian. September 3, 2014. https://www.youtube.com/watch ?v=hasL5dqCroM.

Sandoval, Chela. "US Third World Feminism: The Theory and Method of Differential Oppositional Consciousness." In *The Feminist Standpoint Theory Reader: Intellectual and Political Controversies*, edited by Sandra G. Harding, 195–209. Boulder: Westview Press, 1998.

Sanger, Kerran L. *"When the Spirit Says Sing!": The Role of Freedom Songs in the Civil Rights Movement*. New York: Garland, 1995.

Sayegh, Lisa, William P. Anthony, and Pamela L. Perrewé. "Managerial Decision-Making under Crisis: The Role of Emotion in an Intuitive Decision Process." *Human Resource Management Review* 14, no. 2 (June 2004): 179–99. doi:10.1016/j.hrmr.2004.05.002.

Schou, Solvej. "Meet the Christian Leaders Who Are Suing for Gay Marriage as a Religious Right." *TakePart*, May 3, 2014. Accessed July 21, 2016. http://www.takepart .com/article/2014/05/03/pastors-oppose-north-carolinas-same-sex-marriage -ban.

Shepard, Benjamin Heim. *Queer Political Performance and Protest: Play, Pleasure and Social Movement*. New York: Routledge, 2010.

Shimada, Yohko M. "Infant Vocalization When Alone: Possibility of Early Sound Playing." *International Journal of Behavioral Development* 36, no. 6 (November 1, 2012): 407–12. doi:10.1177/0165025411431408.

Small, Christopher. *Musicking: The Meanings of Performing and Listening*. Music/culture. Hanover: University Press of New England, 1998.

Sosa, Mercedes. "Canción Con Todos Lyrics + English Translation." *Lyrics Translate*. Accessed July 28, 2016. http://lyricstranslate.com/en/canci%C3%B3n-con-todos -son-all.html.

Stacy, Rosie, Katie Brittain, and Sandra Kerr. "Singing for Health: An Exploration of the Issues." *Health Education* 102, no. 4 (August 1, 2002): 156–62. doi:10.1108/09654280210434228.

Stiglitz, Joseph E. *The Price of Inequality: How Today's Divided Society Endangers Our Future*. New York: W. W. Norton, 2013.

Strachan, Jill. "The Voice Empowered: Harmonic Convergence of Music and Politics in the GLBT Choral Movement." In *Chorus and Community*, edited by Karen Ahlquist. Urbana: University of Illinois Press, 2006.

Taylor, Verta, and Nancy Whittier. "Analytical Approaches to Social Movement Culture: The Culture of the Women's Movement." In *Social Movements and Culture*, edited by Hank Johnston and Bert Klandermas, 163–87. Minneapolis, MN: University of Minnesota Press, 1995.

"Tenors and Basses." *Renaissance City Choir—Pittsburgh's LGBTQA Chorus*. Accessed July 27, 2016. http://rccpittsburgh.com/about-2/tenors-basses/.

Tobias, Sheila, and Shelah Leader. "Vox Populi to Music." *Journal of American Culture* 22, no. 4 (December 1, 1999): 91–101. doi:10.1111/j.1542-734X.1999.2204_91.x.

"Trans Chorus of Los Angeles." *GMCLA—Gay Men's Chorus of Los Angeles*. Accessed July 27, 2016. http://gmcla.org/gmcla3/outreach/tcla/.

Truong, Tri. "TCC to Honor Victims of Orlando Massacre." *Turtle Creek Chorale*, June 13, 2016. Accessed July 27, 2016. https://turtlecreekchorale.com/tcc-news/tcc-to-honor-victims-of-orlando-massacre/.

"25 Yr Chronology." *ACT UP New York*. Accessed July 31, 2016. http://www.actupny.com/actions/index.php/the-community.

University of Missouri Center on Religion and the Professions. "Missing Voices: A Study of Religious Voices in Mainstream Media Reports about LGBT Equality." *GLAAD*, April 10, 2012. Accessed July 16, 2016. http://www.glaad.org/publications/missingvoices.

Villicana, Adrian J., Kevin Delucio, and Monica Biernat. "'Coming Out' among Gay Latino and Gay White Men: Implications of Verbal Disclosure for Well-Being." *Self and Identity* 15, no. 4 (July 3, 2016): 468–87. doi:10.1080/15298868.2016.1156568.

Waitt, Gordon. "Gay Games: Performing 'Community' out from the Closet of the Locker Room." *Social and Cultural Geography* 4, no. 2 (June 2003): 167–82.

———. "The Sydney 2002 Gay Games and Querying Australian National Space." *Environment and Planning D: Society and Space* 23 (2005): 435–52.

Warner, R. Stephen. "The Metropolitan Community Churches and the Gay Agenda: The Power of Pentecostalism and Essentialism." In *Sex, Lies, and Sanctity: Religion and Deviance in Contemporary North America*, edited by Mary Jo Neitz and Marion S. Goldman, 81–108. Greenwich, CT: JAI Press, 1995.

Warner, Sara. *Acts of Gaiety: LGBT Performance and the Politics of Pleasure*. Ann Arbor: University of Michigan Press, 2012.

Wilcox, Melissa M. "Of Markets and Missions: The Early History of the Universal Fellowship of Metropolitan Community Churches." *Religion and American Culture* 11, no. 1 (Winter 2001): 83.

Wittig, Monique. *The Straight Mind and Other Essays*. New York: Beacon Press, 1992.

Wittman, Carl. "The Gay Manifesto." *Libcom.org*. Accessed July 19, 2016. http://libcom.org/library/gay-manifesto-carl-wittman.

Wong, Curtis M. "Bakery Owner Vows to 'Stand True to God' after Rejecting Lesbian Couple's Cake." *Huffington Post*, August 14, 2016. Accessed June 29, 2016. http://www.huffingtonpost.com/2014/08/14/pennsylvania-cake-pros-gay-wedding-_n_5678410.html.

INDEX

Page numbers followed by *f* refer to figures.

ABOUT THE AUTHOR

JULIA "JULES" BALÉN, professor at California State University Channel Islands, helped develop and teaches in freedom and justice studies, philosophy, Chicanx studies, and English. With a PhD in comparative cultural and literary studies, Balén focuses on issues of embodiment and power relations across social differences and their intersections in ways that integrate theory and practice. Balén's publications include "Erotics, Agency, and Social Movement: Communities of Sexuality and Musicality in LGBT Choruses," in *The Queer Community: Continuing the Struggle for Social Justice*, ed. Richard G. Johnson III (2009), and "Practicing What We Teach," in *Women's Studies for the Future: Foundations, Interrogations, Politics*, ed. Elizabeth Lapovsky Kennedy and Agatha Beins (New Brunswick: Rutgers University Press, 2005).